Asynchronous Programming in Rust

Learn asynchronous programming by building working examples of futures, green threads, and runtimes

Carl Fredrik Samson

Asynchronous Programming in Rust

Copyright © 2024 Packt Publishing

All rights reserved. No part of this book may be reproduced, stored in a retrieval system, or transmitted in any form or by any means, without the prior written permission of the publisher, except in the case of brief quotations embedded in critical articles or reviews.

Every effort has been made in the preparation of this book to ensure the accuracy of the information presented. However, the information contained in this book is sold without warranty, either express or implied. Neither the author, nor Packt Publishing or its dealers and distributors, will be held liable for any damages caused or alleged to have been caused directly or indirectly by this book.

Packt Publishing has endeavored to provide trademark information about all of the companies and products mentioned in this book by the appropriate use of capitals. However, Packt Publishing cannot guarantee the accuracy of this information.

Publishing Product Manager: Samriddhi Murarka

Group Product Manager: Kunal Sawant

Senior Editor: Kinnari Chohan

Technical Editor: Rajdeep Chakraborty

Copy Editor: Safis Editing

Project Coordinator: Manisha Singh

Indexer: Rekha Nair

Production Designer: Joshua Misquitta

Marketing DevRel Coordinator: Sonia Chauhan

First published: February 2024

Production reference: 2020224

Published by Packt Publishing Ltd.
Livery Place
35 Livery Street
Birmingham
B3 2PB, UK.

ISBN 978-1-80512-813-7

www.packtpub.com

To my family—my brother, my parents, and especially my beloved wife and fantastic children that make every day an absolute joy.

– Carl Fredrik Samson

Contributors

About the author

Carl Fredrik Samson is a popular technology writer and has been active in the Rust community since 2018. He has an MSc in Business Administration where he specialized in strategy and finance. When not writing, he's a father of two children and a CEO of a company with 300 employees. He's been interested in different kinds of technologies his whole life and his programming experience ranges from programming against old IBM mainframes to modern cloud computing, using everything from assembly to Visual Basic for Applications. He has contributed to several open source projects including the official documentation for asynchronous Rust.

I want to thank the Rust community for being so constructive, positive and welcoming. This book would not have happened had it not been for all the positive and insightful interaction with the community. A special thanks goes to the implementors of all the libraries that underpins the async ecosystem today like mio, Tokio, and async-std.

I also want to thank my editor, Kinnari, who has been extraordinarily patient and helpful during the process of writing this book.

About the reviewer

Evgeni Pirianov is an experienced Senior Software Engineer with a deep expertise in Backend Technologies, Web3 an Blockchain. Evgeni has graduated with a degree in Engineering from Imperial College, London and has worked for a few years developing non-linear solvers in C++ . Ever since, he has been at the forefront of architecturing, designing, and implementing decentralized applications in the fields of Defi and Metaverse. Evgeni's passion for Rust is unsurpassed and he is a true believer of its bright future and wide range of applications.

Yage Hu is a software engineer specializing in systems programming and computer architecture. He has cut code in companies such as Uber, Amazon, and Meta and is currently conducting systems research with WebAssembly and Rust. Yage and his wife have just welcomed their first child, Maxine.

Table of Contents

Preface — xiii

Part 1: Asynchronous Programming Fundamentals

1

Concurrency and Asynchronous Programming: a Detailed Overview — 3

Technical requirements	4
An evolutionary journey of multitasking	4
Non-preemptive multitasking	4
Preemptive multitasking	5
Hyper-threading	5
Multicore processors	6
Do you really write synchronous code?	6
Concurrency versus parallelism	7
The mental model I use	8
Let's draw some parallels to process economics	9
Concurrency and its relation to I/O	11
What about threads provided by the operating system?	12
Choosing the right reference frame	12
Asynchronous versus concurrent	12

The role of the operating system	13
Concurrency from the operating system's perspective	13
Teaming up with the operating system	14
Communicating with the operating system	14
The CPU and the operating system	15
Down the rabbit hole	16
How does the CPU prevent us from accessing memory we're not supposed to access?	17
But can't we just change the page table in the CPU?	18
Interrupts, firmware, and I/O	19
A simplified overview	19
Interrupts	22
Firmware	22
Summary	23

2

How Programming Languages Model Asynchronous Program Flow   25

Definitions	26	Fibers and green threads	33
Threads	27	Each stack has a fixed space	34
Threads provided by the operating system	**29**	Context switching	35
		Scheduling	35
		FFI	36
Creating new threads takes time	29	**Callback based approaches**	**37**
Each thread has its own stack	29	**Coroutines: promises and futures**	**38**
Context switching	30	Coroutines and async/await	39
Scheduling	30		
The advantage of decoupling asynchronous operations from OS threads	31	**Summary**	**41**
Example	31		

3

Understanding OS-Backed Event Queues, System Calls, and Cross-Platform Abstractions   43

Technical requirements	44	epoll, kqueue, and IOCP	49
Running the Linux examples	45	**Cross-platform event queues**	**50**
Why use an OS-backed event queue?	**45**	**System calls, FFI, and cross-platform abstractions**	**51**
Blocking I/O	46		
Non-blocking I/O	46	The lowest level of abstraction	51
Event queuing via epoll/kqueue and IOCP	47	The next level of abstraction	55
Readiness-based event queues	**47**	The highest level of abstraction	61
Completion-based event queues	**48**	**Summary**	**61**

Part 2: Event Queues and Green Threads

4

Create Your Own Event Queue 65

Technical requirements	65	Level-triggered versus edge-triggered events	78
Design and introduction to epoll	66	The Poll module	81
Is all I/O blocking?	72	The main program	84
The ffi module	73	Summary	93
Bitflags and bitmasks	76		

5

Creating Our Own Fibers 95

Technical requirements	96	Running our example	107
How to use the repository alongside the book	96	The stack	109
Background information	97	What does the stack look like?	109
Instruction sets, hardware architectures, and ABIs	97	Stack sizes	111
The System V ABI for x86-64	99	Implementing our own fibers	112
A quick introduction to Assembly language	102	Implementing the runtime	115
An example we can build upon	103	Guard, skip, and switch functions	121
Setting up our project	103	Finishing thoughts	125
An introduction to Rust inline assembly macro	105	Summary	126

Part 3: Futures and async/await in Rust

6

Futures in Rust 129

What is a future?	130	Non-leaf futures	130
Leaf futures	130	A mental model of an async runtime	131

| What the Rust language and standard library take care of | 133 | I/O vs CPU-intensive tasks | 134 |
| Summary | | | 135 |

7

Coroutines and async/await — 137

Technical requirements	137	async/await	154
Introduction to stackless coroutines	138	coroutine/wait	155
		corofy—the coroutine preprocessor	155
An example of hand-written coroutines	139	b-async-await—an example of a coroutine/wait transformation	156
Futures module	141	c-async-await—concurrent futures	160
HTTP module	142		
Do all futures have to be lazy?	146	Final thoughts	165
Creating coroutines	147	Summary	166

8

Runtimes, Wakers, and the Reactor-Executor Pattern — 167

Technical requirements	168	Changing the Future definition	191
Introduction to runtimes and why we need them	169	Step 2 – Implementing a proper Executor	192
Reactors and executors	170	Step 3 – Implementing a proper Reactor	199
Improving our base example	171		
Design	173	Experimenting with our new runtime	208
Changing the current implementation	177	An example using concurrency	208
Creating a proper runtime	184	Running multiple futures concurrently and in parallel	209
Step 1 – Improving our runtime design by adding a Reactor and a Waker	187	Summary	211
Creating a Waker	188		

9

Coroutines, Self-Referential Structs, and Pinning — 213

Technical requirements	214	Pinning in theory	234
Improving our example		Definitions	234
1 – variables	214	Pinning to the heap	235
Setting up the base example	215	Pinning to the stack	237
Improving our base example	217	Pin projections and structural pinning	240
Improving our example 2 – references	222	Improving our example 4 – pinning to the rescue	241
Improving our example 3 – this is… not… good…	227	future.rs	242
		http.rs	242
Discovering self-referential structs	229	Main.rs	244
What is a move?	231	executor.rs	246
Pinning in Rust	233	Summary	248

10

Creating Your Own Runtime — 251

Technical requirements	251	Explicit versus implicit reactor instantiation	265
Setting up our example	253	Ergonomics versus efficiency and flexibility	266
main.rs	253		
future.rs	254		
http.rs	254	Common traits that everyone agrees about	267
executor.rs	256		
reactor.rs	259	Async drop	268
Experimenting with our runtime	261	The future of asynchronous Rust	269
Challenges with asynchronous Rust	265	Summary	269
		Epilogue	272

Index — 275

Other Books You May Enjoy — 282

Preface

The content in this book was initially written as a series of shorter books for programmers wanting to learn asynchronous programming from the ground up using Rust. I found the existing material I came upon at the time to be in equal parts frustrating, enlightening, and confusing, so I wanted to do something about that.

Those shorter books became popular, so when I got the chance to write everything a second time, improve the parts that I was happy with, and completely rewrite everything else and put it in a single, coherent book, I just had to do it. The result is right in front of you.

People start programming for a variety of different reasons. Scientists start programming to model problems and perform calculations. Business experts create programs that solve specific problems that help their businesses. Some people start programming as a hobby or in their spare time. Common to these programmers is that they learn programming from the top down.

Most of the time, this is perfectly fine, but on the topic of asynchronous programming in general, and Rust in particular, there is a clear advantage to learning about the topic from first principles, and this book aims to provide a means to do just that.

Asynchronous programming is a way to write programs where you divide your program into tasks that can be stopped and resumed at specific points. This, in turn, allows a language runtime, or a library, to drive and schedule these tasks so their progress interleaves.

Asynchronous programming will, by its very nature, affect the entire program flow, and it's very invasive. It rewrites, reorders, and schedules the program you write in a way that's not always obvious to you as a programmer.

Most programming languages try to make asynchronous programming so easy that you don't really have to understand how it works just to be productive in it.

You can get quite productive writing asynchronous Rust without really knowing how it works as well, but Rust is more explicit and surfaces more complexity to the programmer than most other languages. You will have a much easier time handling this complexity if you get a deep understanding of asynchronous programming in general and what really happens when you write asynchronous Rust.

Another huge upside is that learning from first principles results in knowledge that is applicable way beyond Rust, and it will, in turn, make it easier to pick up asynchronous programming in other languages as well. I would even go so far as to say that most of this knowledge will be useful even in your day-to-day programming. At least, that's how it's been for me.

I want this book to feel like you're joining me on a journey, where we build our knowledge topic by topic and learn by creating examples and experiments along the way. I don't want this book to feel like a lecturer simply telling you how everything works.

This book is created for people who are curious by nature, the kind of programmers who want to understand the systems they use, and who like creating small and big experiments as a way to explore and learn.

Who this book is for

This book is for developers with some prior programming experience who want to learn asynchronous programming from the ground up so they can be proficient in async Rust and be able to participate in technical discussions on the subject. The book is perfect for those who like writing working examples they can pick apart, expand, and experiment with.

There are two kinds of personas that I feel this book is especially relevant to:

- Developers coming from higher-level languages with a garbage collector, interpreter, or runtime, such as C#, Java, JavaScript, Python, Ruby, Swift, or Go. Programmers who have extensive experience with asynchronous programming in any of these languages but want to learn it from the ground up and programmers with no experience with asynchronous programming should both find this book equally useful.

- Developers with experience in languages such as C or C++ that have limited experience with asynchronous programming.

What this book covers

Chapter 1, *Concurrency and Asynchronous Programming: A Detailed Overview*, provides a short history leading up to the type of asynchronous programming we use today. We give several important definitions and provide a mental model that explains what kind of problems asynchronous programming really solves, and how concurrency differs from parallelism. We also cover the importance of choosing the correct reference frame when discussing asynchronous program flow, and we go through several important and fundamental concepts about CPUs, operating systems, hardware, interrupts, and I/O.

Chapter 2, *How Programming Languages Model Asynchronous Program Flow*, narrows the scope from the previous chapter and focuses on the different ways programming languages deal with asynchronous programming. It starts by giving several important definitions before explaining stackful and stackless coroutines, OS threads, green threads, fibers, callbacks, promises, futures, and async/await.

Chapter 3, *Understanding OS-Backed Event Queues, System Calls, and Cross-Platform Abstractions*, explains what epoll, kqueue, and IOCP are and how they differ. It prepares us for the next chapters by giving an introduction to syscalls, FFI, and cross-platform abstractions.

Chapter 4, *Create Your Own Event Queue*, is the chapter where you create your own event queue that mimics the API of *mio* (the popular Rust library that underpins much of the current async ecosystem). The example will center around epoll and go into quite a bit of detail on how it works.

Chapter 5, *Creating Our Own Fibers*, walks through an example where we create our own kind of stackful coroutines called fibers. They're the same kind of green threads that Go uses and show one of the most widespread and popular alternatives to the type of abstraction Rust uses with futures and async/await today. Rust used this kind of abstraction in its early days before it reached 1.0, so it's also a part of Rust's history. This chapter will also cover quite a few general programming concepts, such as stacks, assembly, **Application Binary Interfaces (ABIs)**, and **instruction set architecture (ISAs)**, that are useful beyond the context of asynchronous programming as well.

Chapter 6, *Futures in Rust*, gives a short introduction and overview of futures, runtimes, and asynchronous programming in Rust.

Chapter 7, *Coroutines and async/await*, is a chapter where you write your own coroutines that are simplified versions of the ones created by async/await in Rust today. We'll write a few of them by hand and introduce a new syntax that allows us to programmatically rewrite what look like regular functions into the coroutines we wrote by hand.

Chapter 8, *Runtimes, Wakers, and the Reactor-Executor Pattern*, introduces runtimes and runtime design. By iterating on the example we created in *Chapter 7*, we'll create a runtime for our coroutines that we'll gradually improve. We'll also do some experiments with our runtime once it's done to better understand how it works.

Chapter 9, *Coroutines, Self-Referential Structs, and Pinning*, is the chapter where we introduce self-referential structs and pinning in Rust. By improving our coroutines further, we'll experience first-hand why we need something such as Pin, and how it helps us solve the problems we encounter.

Chapter 10, *Create Your Own Runtime*, is the chapter where we finally put all the pieces together. We'll improve the same example from the previous chapters further so we can run Rust futures, which will allow us to use the full power of async/await and asynchronous Rust. We'll also do a few experiments that show some of the difficulties with asynchronous Rust and how we can best solve them.

To get the most out of this book

You should have some prior programming experience and, preferably, some knowledge about Rust. Reading the free, and excellent, introductory book *The Rust Programming Language* (https://doc.rust-lang.org/book/) should give you more than enough knowledge about Rust to follow along since any advanced topics will be explained step by step.

The ideal way to read this book is to have the book and a code editor open side by side. You should also have the accompanying repository available so you can refer to that if you encounter any issues.

Software/hardware covered in the book	Operating system requirements
Rust (version 1.51 or later)	Windows, macOS, or Linux

You need Rust installed. If you haven't already, follow the instructions here: https://www.rust-lang.org/tools/install.

Some examples will require you to use **Windows Subsystem for Linux** (**WSL**) on Windows. If you're following along on a Windows machine, I recommend that you enable WSL (https://learn.microsoft.com/en-us/windows/wsl/install) now and install Rust by following the instructions for installing Rust on WSL here: https://www.rust-lang.org/tools/install.

If you are using the digital version of this book, we advise you to type the code yourself or access the code from the book's GitHub repository (a link is available in the next section). Doing so will help you avoid any potential errors related to the copying and pasting of code.

The accompanying repository is organized in the following fashion:

- Code that belongs to a specific chapter is in that chapter's folder (e.g., ch01).
- Each example is organized as a separate crate.
- The letters in front of the example names indicate in what order the different examples are presented in the book. For example, the a-runtime example comes before the b-reactor-executor example. This way, they will be ordered chronologically (at least by default on most systems).
- Some examples have a version postfixed with -bonus. These versions will be mentioned in the book text and often contain a specific variant of the example that might be interesting to check out but is not important to the topic at hand.

Download the example code files

You can download the example code files for this book from GitHub at https://github.com/PacktPublishing/Asynchronous-Programming-in-Rust. If there's an update to the code, it will be updated in the GitHub repository.

We also have other code bundles from our rich catalog of books and videos available at https://github.com/PacktPublishing/. Check them out!

Conventions used

There are a number of text conventions used throughout this book.

`Code in text`: Indicates code words in text, database table names, folder names, filenames, file extensions, pathnames, dummy URLs, user input, and Twitter handles. Here is an example: "So, now we have created our own async runtime that uses Rust's `Futures`, `Waker`, `Context`, and `async/await`."

A block of code is set as follows:

```
pub trait Future {
    type Output;
    fn poll(&mut self) -> PollState<Self::Output>;
}
```

When we wish to draw your attention to a particular part of a code block, the relevant lines or items are set in bold:

```
struct Coroutine0 {
    stack: Stack0,
    state: State0,
}
```

Any command-line input or output is written as follows:

```
$ cargo run
```

> **Tips or important notes**
> Appear like this.

Get in touch

Feedback from our readers is always welcome.

General feedback: If you have questions about any aspect of this book, email us at customercare@packtpub.com and mention the book title in the subject of your message.

Errata: Although we have taken every care to ensure the accuracy of our content, mistakes do happen. If you have found a mistake in this book, we would be grateful if you would report this to us. Please visit www.packtpub.com/support/errata and fill in the form.

Piracy: If you come across any illegal copies of our works in any form on the internet, we would be grateful if you would provide us with the location address or website name. Please contact us at copyright@packt.com with a link to the material.

If you are interested in becoming an author: If there is a topic that you have expertise in and you are interested in either writing or contributing to a book, please visit authors.packtpub.com.

Share your thoughts

Once you've read *Asynchronous Programming in Rust*, we'd love to hear your thoughts! Scan the QR code below to go straight to the Amazon review page for this book and share your feedback.

https://packt.link/r/1805128132

Your review is important to us and the tech community and will help us make sure we're delivering excellent quality content.

Download a free PDF copy of this book

Thanks for purchasing this book!

Do you like to read on the go but are unable to carry your print books everywhere?

Is your eBook purchase not compatible with the device of your choice?

Don't worry, now with every Packt book you get a DRM-free PDF version of that book at no cost.

Read anywhere, any place, on any device. Search, copy, and paste code from your favorite technical books directly into your application.

The perks don't stop there, you can get exclusive access to discounts, newsletters, and great free content in your inbox daily

Follow these simple steps to get the benefits:

1. Scan the QR code or visit the link below

`https://packt.link/free-ebook/9781805128137`

2. Submit your proof of purchase
3. That's it! We'll send your free PDF and other benefits to your email directly

Part 1: Asynchronous Programming Fundamentals

In this part, you'll receive a thorough introduction to concurrency and asynchronous programming. We'll also explore various techniques that programming languages employ to model asynchrony, examining the most popular ones and covering some of the pros and cons associated with each. Finally, we'll explain the concept of OS-backed event queues, such as epoll, kqueue, and IOCP, detailing how system calls are used to interact with the operating system and addressing the challenges encountered in creating cross-platform abstractions like mio. This section comprises the following chapters:

- *Chapter 1, Concurrency and Asynchronous Programming: A Detailed Overview*
- *Chapter 2, How Programming Languages Model Asynchronous Program Flow*
- *Chapter 3, Understanding OS-Backed Event Queues, System Calls and Cross Platform Abstractions*

1
Concurrency and Asynchronous Programming: a Detailed Overview

Asynchronous programming is one of those topics many programmers find confusing. You come to the point when you think you've got it, only to later realize that the rabbit hole is much deeper than you thought. If you participate in discussions, listen to enough talks, and read about the topic on the internet, you'll probably also come across statements that seem to contradict each other. At least, this describes how I felt when I first was introduced to the subject.

The cause of this confusion is often a lack of context, or authors assuming a specific context without explicitly stating so, combined with terms surrounding concurrency and asynchronous programming that are rather poorly defined.

In this chapter, we'll be covering a lot of ground, and we'll divide the content into the following main topics:

- Async history
- Concurrency and parallelism
- The operating system and the CPU
- Interrupts, firmware, and I/O

This chapter is general in nature. It doesn't specifically focus on **Rust**, or any specific programming language for that matter, but it's the kind of background information we need to go through so we know that everyone is on the same page going forward. The upside is that this will be useful no matter what programming language you use. In my eyes, that fact also makes this one of the most interesting chapters in this book.

There's not a lot of code in this chapter, so we're off to a soft start. It's a good time to make a cup of tea, relax, and get comfortable, as we're about start this journey together.

Technical requirements

All examples will be written in Rust, and you have two alternatives for running the examples:

- Write and run the examples we'll write on the Rust playground
- Install Rust on your machine and run the examples locally (recommended)

The ideal way to read this chapter is to clone the accompanying repository (https://github.com/PacktPublishing/Asynchronous-Programming-in-Rust/tree/main/ch01/a-assembly-dereference) and open the ch01 folder and keep it open while you read the book. There, you'll find all the examples we write in this chapter and even some extra information that you might find interesting as well. You can of course also go back to the repository later if you don't have that accessible right now.

An evolutionary journey of multitasking

In the beginning, computers had one CPU that executed a set of instructions written by a programmer one by one. No **operating system** (**OS**), no scheduling, no threads, no multitasking. This was how computers worked for a long time. We're talking back when a program was assembled in a deck of punched cards, and you got in big trouble if you were so unfortunate that you dropped the deck onto the floor.

There were operating systems being researched very early and when personal computing started to grow in the 80s, operating systems such as DOS were the standard on most consumer PCs.

These operating systems usually yielded control of the entire CPU to the program currently executing, and it was up to the programmer to make things work and implement any kind of multitasking for their program. This worked fine, but as interactive UIs using a mouse and windowed operating systems became the norm, this model simply couldn't work anymore.

Non-preemptive multitasking

Non-preemptive multitasking was the first method used to be able to keep a UI interactive (and running background processes).

This kind of multitasking put the responsibility of letting the OS run other tasks, such as responding to input from the mouse or running a background task, in the hands of the programmer.

Typically, the programmer *yielded* control to the OS.

Besides offloading a huge responsibility to every programmer writing a program for your platform, this method was naturally error-prone. A small mistake in a program's code could halt or crash the entire system.

> **Note**
> Another popular term for what we call non-preemptive multitasking is **cooperative multitasking**. Windows 3.1 used cooperative multitasking and required programmers to yield control to the OS by using specific system calls. One badly-behaving application could thereby halt the entire system.

Preemptive multitasking

While non-preemptive multitasking sounded like a good idea, it turned out to create serious problems as well. Letting every program and programmer out there be responsible for having a responsive UI in an operating system can ultimately lead to a bad user experience, since every bug out there could halt the entire system.

The solution was to place the responsibility of scheduling the CPU resources between the programs that requested it (including the OS itself) in the hands of the OS. The OS can stop the execution of a process, do something else, and switch back.

On such a system, if you write and run a program with a graphical user interface on a single-core machine, the OS will stop your program to update the mouse position before it switches back to your program to continue. This happens so frequently that we don't usually observe any difference whether the CPU has a lot of work or is idle.

The OS is responsible for scheduling tasks and does this by switching contexts on the CPU. This process can happen many times each second, not only to keep the UI responsive but also to give some time to other background tasks and IO events.

This is now the prevailing way to design an operating system.

> **Note**
> Later in this book, we'll write our own green threads and cover a lot of basic knowledge about context switching, threads, stacks, and scheduling that will give you more insight into this topic, so stay tuned.

Hyper-threading

As CPUs evolved and added more functionality such as several **arithmetic logic units** (**ALUs**) and additional logic units, the CPU manufacturers realized that the entire CPU wasn't fully utilized. For example, when an operation only required some parts of the CPU, an instruction could be run on the ALU simultaneously. This became the start of **hyper-threading**.

Your computer today, for example, may have 6 cores and 12 logical cores.. This is exactly where hyper-threading comes in. It "simulates" two cores on the same core by using unused parts of the CPU to drive progress on thread *2* and simultaneously running the code on thread *1*. It does this by using a number of smart tricks (such as the one with the ALU).

Now, using hyper-threading, we could actually offload some work on one thread while keeping the UI interactive by responding to events in the second thread even though we only had one CPU core, thereby utilizing our hardware better.

> **You might wonder about the performance of hyper-threading**
> It turns out that hyper-threading has been continuously improved since the 90s. Since you're not actually running two CPUs, there will be some operations that need to wait for each other to finish. The performance gain of hyper-threading compared to multitasking in a single core seems to be somewhere close to 30% but it largely depends on the workload.

Multicore processors

As most know, the clock frequency of processors has been flat for a long time. Processors get faster by improving **caches**, **branch prediction**, and **speculative execution**, and by working on the **processing pipelines** of the processors, but the gains seem to be diminishing.

On the other hand, new processors are so small that they allow us to have many on the same chip. Now, most CPUs have many cores and most often, each core will also have the ability to perform hyper-threading.

Do you really write synchronous code?

Like many things, this depends on your perspective. From the perspective of your process and the code you write, everything will normally happen in the order you write it.

From the operating system's perspective, it might or might not interrupt your code, pause it, and run some other code in the meantime before resuming your process.

From the perspective of the CPU, it will mostly execute instructions one at a time.* It doesn't care who wrote the code, though, so when a **hardware interrupt** happens, it will immediately stop and give control to an interrupt handler. This is how the CPU handles concurrency.

> **Note**
>
> *However, modern CPUs can also do a lot of things in parallel. Most CPUs are pipelined, meaning that the next instruction is loaded while the current one is executing. It might have a branch predictor that tries to figure out what instructions to load next.
>
> The processor can also reorder instructions by using **out-of-order execution** if it believes it makes things faster this way without 'asking' or 'telling' the programmer or the OS, so you might not have any guarantee that A happens before B.
>
> The CPU offloads some work to separate 'coprocessors' such as the FPU for floating-point calculations, leaving the main CPU ready to do other tasks et cetera.
>
> As a high-level overview, it's OK to model the CPU as operating in a synchronous manner, but for now, let's just make a mental note that this is a model with some caveats that become especially important when talking about parallelism, synchronization primitives (such as mutexes and atomics), and the security of computers and operating systems.

Concurrency versus parallelism

Right off the bat, we'll dive into this subject by defining what **concurrency** is. Since it is quite easy to confuse *concurrent* with *parallel*, we will try to make a clear distinction between the two from the get-go.

> **Important**
>
> Concurrency is about *dealing* with a lot of things at the same time.
>
> Parallelism is about *doing* a lot of things at the same time.

We call the concept of progressing multiple tasks at the same time *multitasking*. There are two ways to multitask. One is by *progressing* tasks concurrently, but not at the same time. Another is to progress tasks at the exact same time in parallel. *Figure 1.1* depicts the difference between the two scenarios:

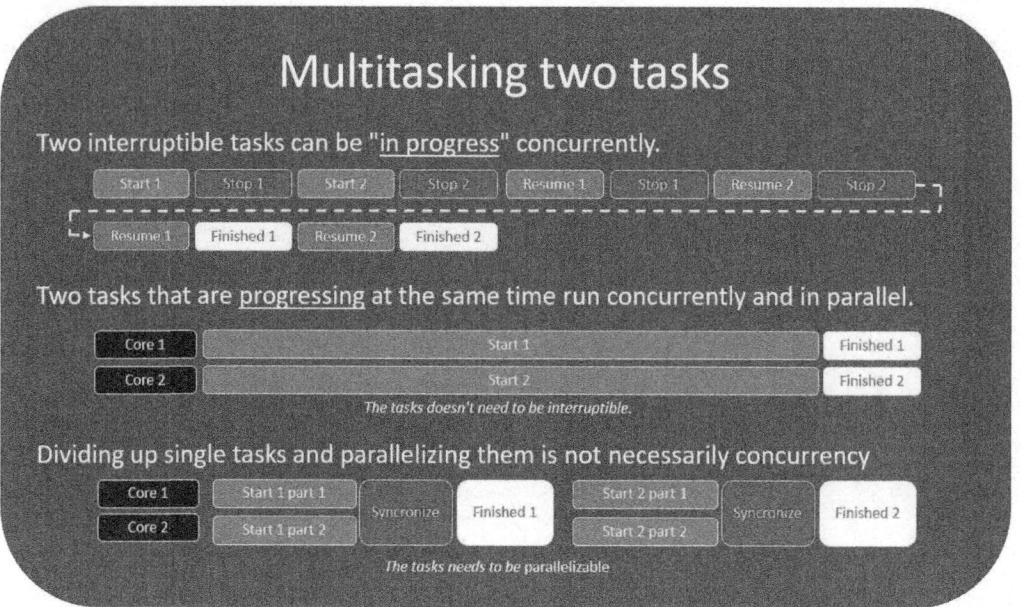

Figure 1.1 – Multitasking two tasks

First, we need to agree on some definitions:

- **Resource**: This is something we need to be able to progress a task. Our resources are limited. This could be CPU time or memory.
- **Task**: This is a set of operations that requires some kind of resource to progress. A task must consist of several sub-operations.
- **Parallel**: This is something happening independently at the *exact* same time.
- **Concurrent**: These are tasks that are *in progress* at the same time, but not necessarily progressing simultaneously.

This is an important distinction. If two tasks are running concurrently, but are not running in parallel, they must be able to stop and resume their progress. We say that a task is *interruptible* if it allows for this kind of concurrency.

The mental model I use

I firmly believe the main reason we find parallel and concurrent programming hard to differentiate stems from how we model events in our everyday life. We tend to define these terms loosely, so our intuition is often wrong.

> **Note**
> It doesn't help that *concurrent* is defined in the dictionary as *operating or occurring at the same time*, which doesn't really help us much when trying to describe how it differs from *parallel*.

For me, this first clicked when I started to understand why we want to make a distinction between parallel and concurrent in the first place!

The *why* has everything to do with resource utilization and efficiency.

Efficiency is the (often measurable) ability to avoid wasting materials, energy, effort, money, and time in doing something or in producing a desired result.

Parallelism is increasing the resources we use to solve a task. It has nothing to do with *efficiency*.

Concurrency has everything to do with efficiency and resource utilization. Concurrency can never make *one single task go faster*. It can only help us utilize our resources better and thereby *finish a set of tasks faster*.

Let's draw some parallels to process economics

In businesses that manufacture goods, we often talk about **LEAN** processes. This is pretty easy to compare with why programmers care so much about what we can achieve if we handle tasks concurrently.

Let's pretend we're running a bar. We only serve Guinness beer and nothing else, but we serve our Guinness to perfection. Yes, I know, it's a little niche, but bear with me.

You are the manager of this bar, and your goal is to run it as efficiently as possible. Now, you can think of each bartender as a *CPU core*, and each order as a *task*. To manage this bar, you need to know the steps to serve a perfect Guinness:

- Pour the Guinness draught into a glass tilted at 45 degrees until it's 3-quarters full (15 seconds).
- Allow the surge to settle for 100 seconds.
- Fill the glass completely to the top (5 seconds).
- Serve.

Since there is only one thing to order in the bar, customers only need to signal using their fingers how many they want to order, so we assume taking new orders is instantaneous. To keep things simple, the same goes for payment. In choosing how to run this bar, you have a few alternatives.

Alternative 1 – Fully synchronous task execution with one bartender

You start out with only one bartender (CPU). The bartender takes one order, finishes it, and progresses to the next. The line is out the door and going two blocks down the street – great! One month later, you're almost out of business and you wonder why.

Well, even though your bartender is very fast at taking new orders, they can only serve 30 customers an hour. Remember, they're waiting for 100 seconds while the beer settles and they're practically just standing there, and they only use 20 seconds to actually fill the glass. Only after one order is completely finished can they progress to the next customer and take their order.

The result is bad revenue, angry customers, and high costs. That's not going to work.

Alternative 2 – Parallel and synchronous task execution

So, you hire 12 bartenders, and you calculate that you can serve about 360 customers an hour. The line is barely going out the door now, and revenue is looking great.

One month goes by and again, you're almost out of business. How can that be?

It turns out that having 12 bartenders is pretty expensive. Even though revenue is high, the costs are even higher. Throwing more resources at the problem doesn't really make the bar more efficient.

Alternative 3 – Asynchronous task execution with one bartender

So, we're back to square one. Let's think this through and find a smarter way of working instead of throwing more resources at the problem.

You ask your bartender whether they can start taking new orders while the beer settles so that they're never just standing and waiting while there are customers to serve. The opening night comes and...

Wow! On a busy night where the bartender works non-stop for a few hours, you calculate that they now only use just over 20 seconds on an order. You've basically eliminated all the waiting. Your theoretical throughput is now 240 beers per hour. If you add one more bartender, you'll have higher throughput than you did while having 12 bartenders.

However, you realize that you didn't actually accomplish 240 beers an hour, since orders come somewhat erratically and not evenly spaced over time. Sometimes, the bartender is busy with a new order, preventing them from topping up and serving beers that are finished almost immediately. In real life, the throughput is only 180 beers an hour.

Still, two bartenders could serve 360 beers an hour this way, the same amount that you served while employing 12 bartenders.

This is good, but you ask yourself whether you can do even better.

Alternative 4 – Parallel and asynchronous task execution with two bartenders

What if you hire two bartenders, and ask them to do just what we described in Alternative 3, but with one change: you allow them to steal each other's tasks, so *bartender 1* can start pouring and set the beer down to settle, and *bartender 2* can top it up and serve it if *bartender 1* is busy pouring a new order at that time? This way, it is only rarely that both bartenders are busy at the same time as one of the beers-in-progress becomes ready to get topped up and served. Almost all orders are finished and served in the shortest amount of time possible, letting customers leave the bar with their beer faster and giving space to customers who want to make a new order.

Now, this way, you can increase throughput even further. You still won't reach the theoretical maximum, but you'll get very close. On the opening night, you realize that the bartenders now process 230 orders an hour each, giving a total throughput of 460 beers an hour.

Revenue looks good, customers are happy, costs are kept at a minimum, and you're one happy manager of the weirdest bar on earth (an extremely efficient bar, though).

> **The key takeaway**
> Concurrency is about working smarter. Parallelism is a way of throwing more resources at the problem.

Concurrency and its relation to I/O

As you might understand from what I've written so far, writing async code mostly makes sense when you need to be smart to make optimal use of your resources.

Now, if you write a program that is working hard to solve a problem, there is often no help in concurrency. This is where parallelism comes into play, since it gives you a way to throw more resources at the problem if you can split it into parts that you can work on in parallel.

Consider the following two different use cases for concurrency:

- When performing I/O and you need to wait for some external event to occur
- When you need to divide your attention and prevent one task from waiting too long

The first is the classic I/O example: you have to wait for a network call, a database query, or something else to happen before you can progress a task. However, you have many tasks to do so instead of waiting, you continue to work elsewhere and either check in regularly to see whether the task is ready to progress, or make sure you are notified when that task is ready to progress.

The second is an example that is often the case when having a UI. Let's pretend you only have one core. How do you prevent the whole UI from becoming unresponsive while performing other CPU-intensive tasks?

Well, you can stop whatever task you're doing every 16 ms, run the *update UI* task, and then resume whatever you were doing afterward. This way, you will have to stop/resume your task 60 times a second, but you will also have a fully responsive UI that has a roughly 60 Hz refresh rate.

What about threads provided by the operating system?

We'll cover threads a bit more when we talk about strategies for handling I/O later in this book, but I'll mention them here as well. One challenge when using OS threads to understand concurrency is that they appear to be mapped to cores. That's not necessarily a correct mental model to use, even though most operating systems will try to map one thread to one core up to the number of threads equal to the number of cores.

Once we create more threads than there are cores, the OS will switch between our threads and progress each of them concurrently using its scheduler to give each thread some time to run. You also must consider the fact that your program is not the only one running on the system. Other programs might spawn several threads as well, which means there will be many more threads than there are cores on the CPU.

Therefore, threads can be a means to perform tasks in parallel, but they can also be a means to achieve concurrency.

This brings me to the last part about concurrency. It needs to be defined in some sort of reference frame.

Choosing the right reference frame

When you write code that is perfectly synchronous from your perspective, stop for a second and consider how that looks from the operating system perspective.

The operating system might not run your code from start to end at all. It might stop and resume your process many times. The CPU might get interrupted and handle some inputs while you think it's only focused on your task.

So, synchronous execution is only an illusion. But from the perspective of you as a programmer, it's not, and that is the important takeaway:

When we talk about concurrency without providing any other context, we are using you as a programmer and your code (your process) as the reference frame. If you start pondering concurrency without keeping this in the back of your head, it will get confusing very fast.

The reason I'm spending so much time on this is that once you realize the importance of having the same definitions and the same reference frame, you'll start to see that some of the things you hear and learn that might seem contradictory really are not. You'll just have to consider the reference frame first.

Asynchronous versus concurrent

So, you might wonder why we're spending all this time talking about multitasking, concurrency, and parallelism, when the book is about asynchronous programming.

The main reason for this is that all these concepts are closely related to each other, and can even have the same (or overlapping) meanings, depending on the context they're used in.

In an effort to make the definitions as distinct as possible, we'll define these terms more narrowly than you'd normally see. However, just be aware that we can't please everyone and we do this for our own sake of making the subject easier to understand. On the other hand, if you fancy heated internet debates, this is a good place to start. Just claim someone else's definition of concurrent is 100 % wrong or that yours is 100 % correct, and off you go.

For the sake of this book, we'll stick to this definition: asynchronous programming is the way a programming language or library abstracts over concurrent operations, and how we as users of a language or library use that abstraction to execute tasks concurrently.

The operating system already has an existing abstraction that covers this, called **threads**. Using OS threads to handle asynchrony is often referred to **as multithreaded programming**. To avoid confusion, we'll not refer to using OS threads directly as asynchronous programming, even though it solves the same problem.

Given that asynchronous programming is now scoped to be about abstractions over concurrent or parallel operations in a language or library, it's also easier to understand that it's just as relevant on embedded systems without an operating system as it is for programs that target a complex system with an advanced operating system. The definition itself does not imply any specific implementation even though we'll look at a few popular ones throughout this book.

If this still sounds complicated, I understand. Just sitting and reflecting on concurrency is difficult, but if we try to keep these thoughts in the back of our heads when we work with async code I promise it will get less and less confusing.

The role of the operating system

The operating system (OS) stands in the center of everything we do as programmers (well, unless you're writing an operating system or working in the embedded realm), so there is no way for us to discuss any kind of fundamentals in programming without talking about operating systems in a bit of detail.

Concurrency from the operating system's perspective

This ties into what I talked about earlier when I said that concurrency needs to be talked about within a reference frame, and I explained that the OS might stop and start your process at any time.

What we call synchronous code is, in most cases, code that appears synchronous to us as programmers. Neither the OS nor the CPU lives in a fully synchronous world.

Operating systems use preemptive multitasking and as long as the operating system you're running is preemptively scheduling processes, you won't have a guarantee that your code runs instruction by instruction without interruption.

The operating system will make sure that all important processes get some time from the CPU to make progress.

> **Note**
> This is not as simple when we're talking about modern machines with 4, 6, 8, or 12 physical cores, since you might actually execute code on one of the CPUs uninterrupted if the system is under very little load. The important part here is that you can't know for sure and there is no guarantee that your code will be left to run uninterrupted.

Teaming up with the operating system

When you make a web request, you're not asking the CPU or the network card to do something for you – you're asking the operating system to talk to the network card for you.

There is no way for you as a programmer to make your system optimally efficient without playing to the strengths of the operating system. You basically don't have access to the hardware directly. *You must remember that the operating system is an abstraction over the hardware.*

However, this also means that to understand everything from the ground up, you'll also need to know how your operating system handles these tasks.

To be able to work with the operating system, you'll need to know how you can communicate with it, and that's exactly what we're going to go through next.

Communicating with the operating system

Communication with an operating system happens through what we call a **system call** (**syscall**). We need to know how to make system calls and understand why it's so important for us when we want to cooperate and communicate with the operating system. We also need to understand how the basic abstractions we use every day use system calls behind the scenes. We'll have a detailed walkthrough in *Chapter 3*, so we'll keep this brief for now.

A system call uses a public API that the operating system provides so that programs we write in 'userland' can communicate with the OS.

Most of the time, these calls are abstracted away for us as programmers by the language or the runtime we use.

Now, a syscall is an example of something that is unique to the kernel you're communicating with, but the **UNIX** family of kernels has many similarities. UNIX systems expose this through **libc**.

Windows, on the other hand, uses its own API, often referred to as **WinAPI**, and it can operate radically differently from how the UNIX-based systems operate.

Most often, though, there is a way to achieve the same things. In terms of functionality, you might not notice a big difference but as we'll see later, and especially when we dig into how **epoll**, **kqueue**, and **IOCP** work, they can differ a lot in how this functionality is implemented.

However, a syscall is not the only way we interact with our operating system, as we'll see in the following section.

The CPU and the operating system

Does the CPU cooperate with the operating system?

If you had asked me this question when I first thought I understood how programs work, I would most likely have answered *no*. We run programs on the CPU and we can do whatever we want if we know how to do it. Now, first of all, I wouldn't have thought this through, but unless you learn how CPUs and operating systems work together, it's not easy to know for sure.

What started to make me think I was very wrong was a segment of code that looked like what you're about to see. If you think inline assembly in Rust looks foreign and confusing, don't worry just yet. We'll go through a proper introduction to inline assembly a little later in this book. I'll make sure to go through each of the following lines until you get more comfortable with the syntax:

Repository reference: ch01/ac-assembly-dereference/src/main.rs

```
fn main() {
    let t = 100;
    let t_ptr: *const usize = &t;
    let x = dereference(t_ptr);
    println!("{}", x);
}

fn dereference(ptr: *const usize) -> usize {
    let mut res: usize;
    unsafe {
        asm!("mov {0}, [{1}]", out(reg) res, in(reg) ptr)
    };
    res
}
```

What you've just looked at is a dereference function written in assembly.

The `mov {0}, [{1}]` line needs some explanation. `{0}` and `{1}` are templates that tell the compiler that we're referring to the registers that `out(reg)` and `in(reg)` represent. The number is just an index, so if we had more inputs or outputs they would be numbered `{2}`, `{3}`, and so on. Since we only specify `reg` and not a specific register, we let the compiler choose what registers it wants to use.

The `mov` instruction instructs the CPU to take the first 8 bytes (if we're on a 64-bit machine) it gets when reading the memory location that `{1}` points to and place that in the register represented by `{0}`. The `[]` brackets will instruct the CPU to treat the data in that register as a memory address, and instead of simply copying the memory address itself to {0}, it will fetch what's at that memory location and move it over.

Anyway, we're just writing instructions to the CPU here. No standard library, no syscall; just raw instructions. There is no way the OS is involved in that dereference function, right?

If you run this program, you get what you'd expect:

```
100
```

Now, if you keep the `dereference` function but replace the `main` function with a function that creates a pointer to the 99999999999999 address, which we know is invalid, we get this function:

```
fn main() {
    let t_ptr = 99999999999999 as *const usize;
    let x = dereference(t_ptr);
    println!("{}", x);
}
```

Now, if we run that we get the following results.

This is the result on Linux:

```
Segmentation fault (core dumped)
```

This is the result on Windows:

```
error: process didn't exit successfully: `target\debug\ac-assembly-
dereference.exe` (exit code: 0xc0000005, STATUS_ACCESS_VIOLATION)
```

We get a segmentation fault. Not surprising, really, but as you also might notice, the error we get is different on different platforms. Surely, the OS is involved somehow. Let's take a look at what's really happening here.

Down the rabbit hole

It turns out that there is a great deal of cooperation between the OS and the CPU, but maybe not in the way you would naively think.

Many modern CPUs provide some basic infrastructure that operating systems use. This infrastructure gives us the security and stability we expect. Actually, most advanced CPUs provide a lot more options than operating systems such as Linux, BSD, and Windows actually use.

There are two in particular that I want to address here:

- How the CPU prevents us from accessing memory we're not supposed to access
- How the CPU handles asynchronous events such as I/O

We'll cover the first one here and the second in the next section.

How does the CPU prevent us from accessing memory we're not supposed to access?

As I mentioned, modern CPU architectures define some basic concepts by design. Some examples of this are as follows:

- Virtual memory
- Page table
- Page fault
- Exceptions
- Privilege level

Exactly how this works will differ depending on the specific CPU, so we'll treat them in general terms here.

Most modern CPUs have a **memory management unit** (**MMU**). This part of the CPU is often etched on the same dye, even. The MMU's job is to translate the virtual address we use in our programs to a physical address.

When the OS starts a process (such as our program), it sets up a page table for our process and makes sure a special register on the CPU points to this page table.

Now, when we try to dereference `t_ptr` in the preceding code, the address is at some point sent for translation to the MMU, which looks it up in the page table to translate it to a physical address in the memory where it can fetch the data.

In the first case, it will point to a memory address on our stack that holds the value `100`.

When we pass in `99999999999999` and ask it to fetch what's stored at that address (which is what dereferencing does), it looks for the translation in the page table but can't find it.

The CPU then treats this as a page fault.

At boot, the OS provided the CPU with an **interrupt descriptor table**. This table has a predefined format where the OS provides handlers for the predefined conditions the CPU can encounter.

Since the OS provided a pointer to a function that handles *page fault*, the CPU jumps to that function when we try to dereference `99999999999999` and thereby hands over control to the operating system.

The OS then prints a nice message for us, letting us know that we encountered what it calls a **segmentation fault**. This message will therefore vary depending on the OS you run the code on.

But can't we just change the page table in the CPU?

Now, this is where the *privilege level* comes in. Most modern operating systems operate with two *ring levels*: *ring 0*, the kernel space, and *ring 3*, the user space.

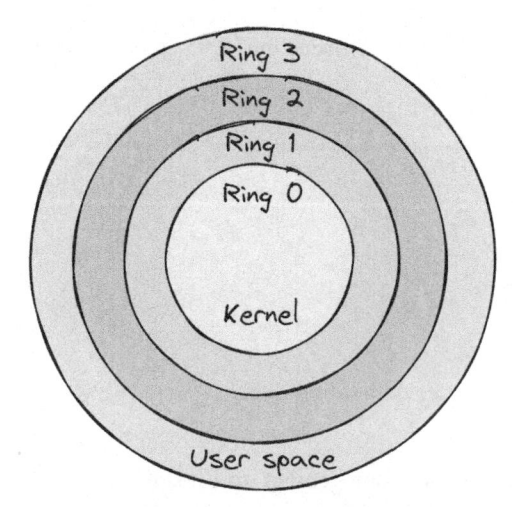

Figure 1.2 – Privilege rings

Most CPUs have a concept of more rings than what most modern operating systems use. This has historical reasons, which is also why *ring 0* and *ring 3* are used (and not 1 and 2).

Every entry in the page table has additional information about it. Amongst that information is the information about which ring it belongs to. This information is set up when your OS boots up.

Code executed in *ring 0* has almost unrestricted access to external devices and memory, and is free to change registers that provide security at the hardware level.

The code you write in *ring 3* will typically have extremely restricted access to I/O and certain CPU registers (and instructions). Trying to issue an instruction or setting a register from *ring 3* to change the page table will be prevented by the CPU. The CPU will then treat this as an exception and jump to the handler for that exception provided by the OS.

This is also the reason why you have no other choice than to cooperate with the OS and handle I/O tasks through syscalls. The system wouldn't be very secure if this wasn't the case.

So, to sum it up: yes, the CPU and the OS cooperate a great deal. Most modern desktop CPUs are built with an OS in mind, so they provide the hooks and infrastructure that the OS latches onto upon bootup. When the OS spawns a process, it also sets its privilege level, making sure that normal processes stay within the borders it defines to maintain stability and security.

Interrupts, firmware, and I/O

We're nearing the end of the general CS subjects in this book, and we'll start to dig our way out of the rabbit hole soon.

This part tries to tie things together and look at how the whole computer works as a system to handle I/O and concurrency.

Let's get to it!

A simplified overview

Let's look at some of the steps where we imagine that we read from a network card:

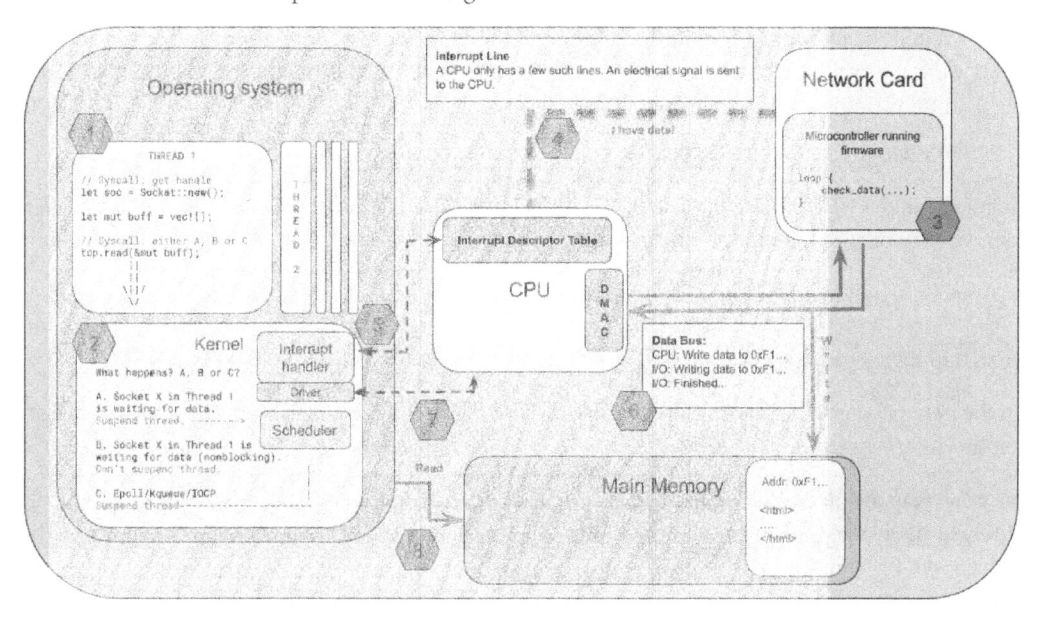

Remember that we're simplifying a lot here. This is a rather complex operation but we'll focus on the parts that are of most interest to us and skip a few steps along the way.

Step 1 – Our code

We register a socket. This happens by issuing a *syscall* to the OS. Depending on the OS, we either get a *file descriptor* (macOS/Linux) or a *socket* (Windows).

The next step is that we register our interest in Read events on that socket.

Step 2 – Registering events with the OS

This is handled in one of three ways:

1. We tell the operating system that we're interested in `Read` events but we want to wait for it to happen by `yielding` control over our thread to the OS. The OS then suspends our thread by storing the register state and switches to some other thread

   From our perspective, this will be blocking our thread until we have data to read.

2. We tell the operating system that we're interested in `Read` events but we just want a handle to a task that we can `poll` to check whether the event is ready or not.

   The OS will not suspend our thread, so this will not block our code.

3. We tell the operating system that we are probably going to be interested in many events, but we want to subscribe to one event queue. When we `poll` this queue, it will block our thread until one or more events occur.

   This will block our thread while we wait for events to occur.

Chapters 3 and 4 will go into detail about the third method, as it's the most used method for modern async frameworks to handle concurrency.

Step 3 – The network card

We're skipping some steps here, but I don't think they're vital to our understanding.

On the network card, there is a small microcontroller running specialized firmware. We can imagine that this microcontroller is polling in a busy loop, checking whether any data is incoming.

The exact way the network card handles its internals is a little different from what I suggest here, and will most likely vary from vendor to vendor. The important part is that there is a very simple but specialized CPU running on the network card doing work to check whether there are incoming events.

Once the firmware registers incoming data, it issues a *hardware interrupt*.

Step 4 – Hardware interrupt

A modern CPU has a set of **interrupt request line (IRQs)** for it to handle events that occur from external devices. A CPU has a fixed set of interrupt lines.

A hardware interrupt is an electrical signal that can occur at any time. The CPU immediately *interrupts* its normal workflow to handle the interrupt by saving the state of its registers and looking up the interrupt handler. The interrupt handlers are defined in the **interrupt descriptor table (IDT)**.

Step 5 – Interrupt handler

The IDT is a table where the OS (or a driver) registers handlers for different interrupts that may occur. Each entry points to a handler function for a specific interrupt. The handler function for a network card would typically be registered and handled by a *driver* for that card.

> **Note**
> The IDT is not stored on the CPU as it might seem in *Figure 1.3*. It's located in a fixed and known location in the main memory. The CPU only holds a pointer to the table in one of its registers.

Step 6 – Writing the data

This is a step that might vary a lot depending on the CPU and the firmware on the network card. If the network card and the CPU support **direct memory access** (**DMA**), which should be the standard on all modern systems today, the network card will write data directly to a set of buffers that the OS already has set up in the main memory.

In such a system, the *firmware* on the network card might issue an *interrupt* when the data is *written* to memory. DMA is very efficient, since the CPU is only notified when the data is already in memory. On older systems, the CPU needed to devote resources to handle the data transfer from the network card.

The **direct memory access controller** *(* **DMAC***) is added to the diagram since in such a system, it would control the access to memory. It's not part of the CPU as indicated in the previous diagram. We're deep enough in the rabbit hole now, and exactly where the different parts of a system are is not really important to us right now, so let's move on.*

Step 7 – The driver

The *driver* would normally handle the communication between the OS and the network card. At some point, the buffers are filled and the network card issues an interrupt. The CPU then jumps to the handler of that interrupt. The interrupt handler for this exact type of interrupt is registered by the driver, so it's actually the driver that handles this event and, in turn, informs the kernel that the data is ready to be read.

Step 8 – Reading the data

Depending on whether we chose method 1, 2, or 3, the OS will do as follows:

- Wake our thread
- Return **Ready** on the next poll
- Wake the thread and return a Read event for the handler we registered

Interrupts

As you know by now, there are two kinds of interrupts:

- Hardware interrupts
- Software interrupts

They are very different in nature.

Hardware interrupts

Hardware interrupts are created by sending an electrical signal through an IRQ. These hardware lines signal the CPU directly.

Software interrupts

These are interrupts issued from software instead of hardware. As in the case of a hardware interrupt, the CPU jumps to the IDT and runs the handler for the specified interrupt.

Firmware

Firmware doesn't get much attention from most of us; however, it's a crucial part of the world we live in. It runs on all kinds of hardware and has all kinds of strange and peculiar ways to make the computers we program on work.

Now, the firmware needs a microcontroller to be able to work. Even the CPU has firmware that makes it work. That means there are many more small 'CPUs' on our system than the cores we program against.

Why is this important? Well, you remember that concurrency is all about efficiency, right? Since we have many CPUs/microcontrollers already doing work for us on our system, one of our concerns is to not replicate or duplicate that work when we write code.

If a network card has firmware that continually checks whether new data has arrived, it's pretty wasteful if we duplicate that by letting our CPU continually check whether new data arrives as well. It's much better if we either check once in a while, or even better, get notified when data has arrived.

Summary

This chapter covered a lot of ground, so good job on doing all that legwork. We learned a little bit about how CPUs and operating systems have evolved from a historical perspective and the difference between non-preemptive and preemptive multitasking. We discussed the difference between concurrency and parallelism, talked about the role of the operating system, and learned that **system calls are the primary way for us to interact with the host operating system**. You've also seen how the CPU and the operating system cooperate through an infrastructure designed as part of the CPU.

Lastly, we went through a diagram on what happens when you issue a network call. You know there are at least three different ways for us to deal with the fact that the I/O call takes some time to execute, and we have to decide which way we want to handle that waiting time.

This covers most of the general background information we need so that we have the same definitions and overview before we go on. We'll go into more detail as we progress through the book, and the first topic that we'll cover in the next chapter is how programming languages model asynchronous program flow by looking into threads, coroutines and futures.

2
How Programming Languages Model Asynchronous Program Flow

In the previous chapter, we covered asynchronous program flow, concurrency, and parallelism in general terms. In this chapter, we'll narrow our scope. Specifically, we'll look into different ways to model and deal with concurrency in programming languages and libraries.

It's important to keep in mind that threads, futures, fibers, goroutines, promises, etc. are abstractions that give us a way to model an asynchronous program flow. They have different strengths and weaknesses, but they share a goal of giving programmers an easy-to-use (and importantly, hard to misuse), efficient, and expressive way of creating a program that handles tasks in a non-sequential, and often unpredictable, order.

The lack of precise definitions is prevalent here as well; many terms have a name that stems from a concrete implementation at some point in time but has later taken on a more general meaning that encompasses different implementations and varieties of the same thing.

We'll first go through a way of grouping different abstractions together based on their similarities before we go on to discuss the pros and cons of each of them. We'll also go through important definitions that we'll use throughout the book and discuss OS threads in quite some detail.

The topics we discuss here are quite abstract and complicated so don't feel bad if you don't understand everything immediately. As we progress through the book and you get used to the different terms and techniques by working through some examples, more and more pieces will fall into place.

Specifically, the following topics will be covered:

- Definitions
- Threads provided by the operating system
- Green threads/stackfull coroutines/fibers

- Callback based approaches
- Promises, futures, and async/await

Definitions

We can broadly categorize abstractions over concurrent operations into two groups:

1. **Cooperative**: These are tasks that yield voluntarily either by explicitly yielding or by calling a function that suspends the task when it can't progress further before another operation has finished (such as making a network call). Most often, these tasks yield to a scheduler of some sort. Examples of this are tasks generated by `async/await` in Rust and JavaScript.
2. **Non-cooperative**: Tasks that don't necessarily yield voluntarily. In such a system, the scheduler must be able to **pre-empt** a running task, meaning that the scheduler can stop the task and take control over the CPU even though the task would have been able to do work and progress. Examples of this are OS threads and Goroutines (after GO version 1.14).

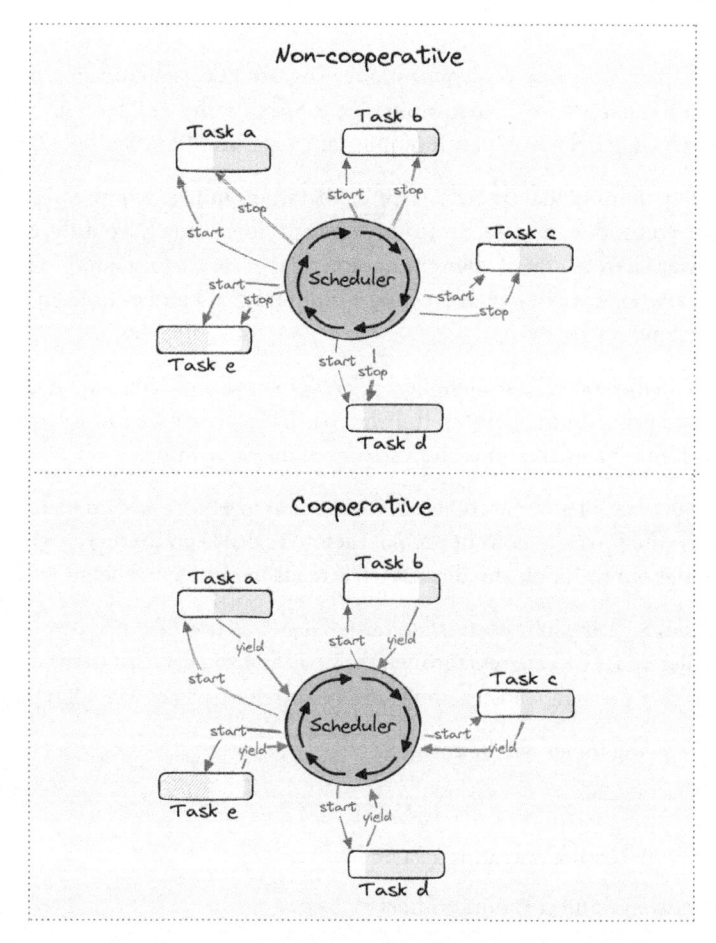

Figure 2.1 – Non-cooperative vs. cooperative multitasking

> **Note**
> In a system where the scheduler can pre-empt running tasks, tasks can also **yield voluntarily** as they do in a cooperative system, and it's rare with a system that *only* relies on pre-emption.

We can further divide these abstractions into two broad categories based on the characteristics of their implementation:

1. **Stackful**: Each task has its own call stack. This is often implemented as a stack that's similar to the stack used by the operating system for its threads. Stackful tasks can suspend execution at any point in the program as the whole stack is preserved.
2. **Stackless**: There is not a separate stack for each task; they all run sharing the same call stack. A task can't be suspended in the middle of a stack frame, limiting the runtime's ability to pre-empt the task. However, they need to store/restore less information when switching between tasks so they can be more efficient.

There are more nuances to these two categories that you'll get a deep understanding of when we implement an example of both a stackful coroutine (fiber) and a stackless coroutine (Rust futures generated by `async/await`) later in the book. For now, we keep the details to a minimum to just provide an overview.

Threads

We keep referring to threads all throughout this book, so before we get too far in, let's stop and give "thread" a good definition since it's one of those fundamental terms that causes a lot of confusion.

In the most general sense, a thread refers to a **thread of execution**, meaning a set of instructions that need to be executed sequentially. If we tie this back to the first chapter of this book, where we provided several definitions under the Concurrency vs. Parallelism subsection, a thread of execution is similar to what we defined as a **task** with multiple steps that need resources to progress.

The generality of this definition can be a cause of some confusion. A thread to one person can obviously refer to an OS thread, and to another person, it can simply refer to any abstraction that represents a thread of execution on a system.

Threads are often divided into two broad categories:

- **OS threads**: These threads are created by the OS and managed by the OS scheduler. On Linux, this is known as a **kernel thread**.
- **User-level threads**: These threads are created and managed by us as programmers without the OS knowing about them.

Now, this is where things get a bit tricky: OS threads on most modern operating systems have a lot of similarities. Some of these similarities are dictated by the design of modern CPUs. One example of this is that most CPUs assume that there is a stack it can perform operations on and that it has a register for the stack pointer and instructions for stack manipulation.

User-level threads can, in their broadest sense, refer to *any* implementation of a system (runtime) that creates and schedules tasks, and you can't make the same assumptions as you do with OS threads. They can closely resemble OS threads by using separate stacks for each task, as we'll see in *Chapter 5* when we go through our fiber/green threads example, or they can be radically different in nature, as we'll see when we go through how Rust models concurrent operations later on in Part 3 of this book.

No matter the definition, a set of tasks needs something that manages them and decides who gets what resources to progress. The most obvious resource on a computer system that all tasks need to progress is CPU time. We call the "something" that decides who gets CPU time to progress a **scheduler**.

Most likely, when someone refers to a "thread" without adding extra context, they refer to an OS thread/kernel thread, so that's what we'll do going forward.

I'll also keep referring to a thread of execution as simply a **task**. I find the topic of asynchronous programming easier to reason about when we limit the use of terms that have different assumptions associated with them depending on the context as much as possible.

With that out of the way, let's go through some defining characteristics of OS threads while we also highlight their limitations.

> **Important!**
>
> Definitions will vary depending on what book or article you read. For example, if you read about how a specific operating system works, you might see that processes or threads are abstractions that represent "tasks", which will seem to contradict the definitions we use here. As I mentioned earlier, the choice of reference frame is important, and it's why we take so much care to define the terms we use thoroughly as we encounter them throughout the book.
>
> The definition of a thread can also vary by operating system, even though most popular systems share a similar definition today. Most notably, Solaris (pre-Solaris 9, which was released in 2002) used to have a two-level thread system that differentiated between application threads, lightweight processes, and kernel threads. This was an implementation of what we call M:N threading, which we'll get to know more about later in this book. Just beware that if you read older material, the definition of a thread in such a system might differ significantly from the one that's commonly used today.

Now that we've gone through the most important definitions for this chapter, it's time to talk more about the most popular ways of handling concurrency when programming.

Threads provided by the operating system

> **Note!**
> We call this 1:1 threading. Each task is assigned one OS thread.
>
> Since this book will not focus specifically on OS threads as a way to handle concurrency going forward, we treat them more thoroughly here.

Let's start with the obvious. To use threads provided by the operating system, you need, well, an operating system. Before we discuss the use of threads as a means to handle concurrency, we need to be clear about what kind of operating systems we're talking about since they come in different flavors.

Embedded systems are more widespread now than ever before. This kind of hardware might not have the resources for an operating system, and if they do, you might use a radically different kind of operating system tailored to your needs, as the systems tend to be less general purpose and more specialized in nature.

Their support for threads, and the characteristics of how they schedule them, might be different from what you're used to in operating systems such as Windows or Linux.

Since covering all the different designs is a book on its own, we'll limit the scope to talk about treads, as they're used in Windows and Linux-based systems running on popular desktop and server CPUs.

OS threads are simple to implement and simple to use. We simply let the OS take care of everything for us. We do this by spawning a new OS thread for each task we want to accomplish and write code as we normally would.

The runtime we use to handle concurrency for us is the operating system itself. In addition to these advantages, you get parallelism for free. However, there are also some drawbacks and complexities resulting from directly managing parallelism and shared resources.

Creating new threads takes time

Creating a new OS thread involves some bookkeeping and initialization overhead, so while switching between two existing threads in the same process is pretty fast, creating new ones and discarding ones you don't use anymore involves work that takes time. All the extra work will limit throughput if a system needs to create and discard a lot of them. This can be a problem if you have huge amounts of small tasks that need to be handled concurrently, which often is the case when dealing with a lot of I/O.

Each thread has its own stack

We'll cover stacks in detail later in this book, but for now, it's enough to know that they occupy a fixed size of memory. Each OS thread comes with its own stack, and even though many systems allow this size to be configured, they're still fixed in size and can't grow or shrink. They are, after all, the cause of stack overflows, which will be a problem if you configure them to be too small for the tasks you're running.

If we have many small tasks that only require a little stack space but we reserve much more than we need, we will occupy large amounts of memory and possibly run out of it.

Context switching

As you now know, threads and schedulers are tightly connected. Context switching happens when the CPU stops executing one thread and proceeds with another one. Even though this process is highly optimized, it still involves storing and restoring the register state, which takes time. Every time that you yield to the OS scheduler, it can choose to schedule a thread from a different process on that CPU.

You see, threads created by these systems belong to a **process**. When you start a program, it starts a process, and the process creates at least one initial thread where it executes the program you've written. Each process can spawn multiple threads that share the same **address space**.

That means that threads within the same process can access shared memory and can access the same resources, such as files and file handles. One consequence of this is that when the OS switches contexts by stopping one thread and resuming another within the same process, it doesn't have to save and restore all the state associated with that process, just the state that's specific to that thread.

On the other hand, when the OS switches from a thread associated with one process to a thread associated with another, the new process will use a different address space, and the OS needs to take measures to make sure that process "A" doesn't access data or resources that belong to process "B". If it didn't, the system wouldn't be secure.

The consequence is that caches might need to be flushed and more state might need to be saved and restored. In a highly concurrent system under load, these context switches can take extra time and thereby limit the throughput in a somewhat unpredictable manner if they happen frequently enough.

Scheduling

The OS can schedule tasks differently than you might expect, and *every time you yield to the OS*, you're put in the same queue as all other threads and processes on the system.

Moreover, since there is no guarantee that the thread will resume execution on the same CPU core as it left off or that two tasks won't run in parallel and try to access the same data, you need to synchronize data access to prevent data races and other pitfalls associated with multicore programming.

Rust as a language will help you prevent many of these pitfalls, but synchronizing data access will require extra work and add to the complexity of such programs. We often say that using OS threads to handle concurrency gives us parallelism for free, but it isn't free in terms of added complexity and the need for proper data access synchronization.

The advantage of decoupling asynchronous operations from OS threads

Decoupling asynchronous operations from the concept of threads has a lot of benefits.

First of all, using OS threads as a means to handle concurrency requires us to use what essentially is an OS abstraction to represent our tasks.

Having a separate layer of abstraction to represent concurrent tasks gives us the freedom to choose how we want to handle concurrent operations. If we create an abstraction over concurrent operations such as a future in Rust, a promise in JavaScript, or a goroutine in GO, it is up to the runtime implementor to decide how these concurrent tasks are handled.

A runtime could simply map each concurrent operation to an OS thread, they could use fibers/green threads or state machines to represent the tasks. The programmer that writes the asynchronous code will not necessarily have to change anything in their code if the underlying implementation changes. In theory, the same asynchronous code could be used to handle concurrent operations on a microcontroller without an OS if there's just a runtime for it.

To sum it up, using threads provided by the operating system to handle concurrency has the following advantages:

- Simple to understand
- Easy to use
- Switching between tasks is reasonably fast
- You get parallelism for free

However, they also have a few drawbacks:

- OS-level threads come with a rather large stack. If you have many tasks waiting simultaneously (as you would in a web server under heavy load), you'll run out of memory pretty fast.
- Context switching can be costly and you might get an unpredictable performance since you let the OS do all the scheduling.
- The OS has many things it needs to handle. It might not switch back to your thread as fast as you'd wish.
- It is tightly coupled to an OS abstraction. This might not be an option on some systems.

Example

Since we'll not spend more time talking about OS threads in this book, we'll go through a short example so you can see how they're used:

ch02/aa-os-threads

```
use std::thread::{self, sleep};


fn main() {
    println!("So, we start the program here!");
    let t1 = thread::spawn(move || {
        sleep(std::time::Duration::from_millis(200));
        println!("The long running tasks finish last!");
    });


    let t2 = thread::spawn(move || {
        sleep(std::time::Duration::from_millis(100));
        println!("We can chain callbacks...");
        let t3 = thread::spawn(move || {
            sleep(std::time::Duration::from_millis(50));
            println!("...like this!");
        });
        t3.join().unwrap();
    });
    println!("The tasks run concurrently!");


    t1.join().unwrap();
    t2.join().unwrap();
}
```

In this example, we simply spawn several OS threads and put them to sleep. Sleeping is essentially the same as yielding to the OS scheduler with a request to be re-scheduled to run after a certain time has passed. To make sure our main thread doesn't finish and exit (which will exit the process) before our children thread has had time to run we `join` them at the end of our `main` function.

If we run the example, we'll see how the operations occur in a different order based on how long we yielded each thread to the scheduler:

```
So, we start the program here!
The tasks run concurrently!
We can chain callbacks...
...like this!
The long-running tasks finish last!
```

So, while using OS threads is great for a number of tasks, we also outlined a number of good reasons to look at alternatives by discussing their limitations and downsides. The first alternatives we'll look at are what we call fibers and green threads.

Fibers and green threads

> **Note!**
> This is an example of **M:N threading**. Many tasks can run concurrently on one OS thread. Fibers and green threads are often referred to as stackful coroutines.

The name "green threads" originally stems from an early implementation of an M:N threading model used in Java and has since been associated with different implementations of M:N threading. You will encounter different variations of this term, such as "green processes" (used in Erlang), which are different from the ones we discuss here. You'll also see some that define green threads more broadly than we do here.

The way we define green threads in this book makes them synonymous with fibers, so both terms refer to the same thing going forward.

The implementation of fibers and green threads implies that there is a runtime with a scheduler that's responsible for scheduling what task (M) gets time to run on the OS thread (N). There are many more tasks than there are OS threads, and such a system can run perfectly fine using only one OS thread. The latter case is often referred to as **M:1 threading**.

Goroutines is an example of a specific implementation of stackfull coroutines, but it comes with slight nuances. The term "coroutine" usually implies that they're cooperative in nature, but Goroutines can be pre-empted by the scheduler (at least since version 1.14), thereby landing them in somewhat of a grey area using the categories we present here.

Green threads and fibers use the same mechanisms as an OS, setting up a stack for each task, saving the CPU's state, and jumping from one task(thread) to another by doing a context switch.

We yield control to the scheduler (which is a central part of the runtime in such a system), which then continues running a different task.

The state of execution is stored in each stack, so in such a solution, there would be no need for `async`, `await`, `Future`, or `Pin`. In many ways, green threads mimic how an operating system facilitates concurrency, and implementing them is a great learning experience.

A runtime using fibers/green threads for concurrent tasks can have a high degree of flexibility. Tasks can, for example, be pre-empted and context switched at any time and at any point in their execution, so a long-running task that hogs the CPU could in theory be pre-empted by the runtime, acting as a safeguard from having tasks that end up blocking the whole system due to an edge-case or a programmer error.

This gives the runtime scheduler almost the same capabilities as the OS scheduler, which is one of the biggest advantages of systems using fibers/green threads.

The typical flow goes as follows:

- You run some non-blocking code
- You make a blocking call to some external resource
- The CPU jumps to the main thread, which schedules a different thread to run and jumps to that stack
- You run some non-blocking code on the new thread until a new blocking call or the task is finished
- The CPU jumps back to the main thread, schedules a new thread that is ready to make progress, and jumps to that thread

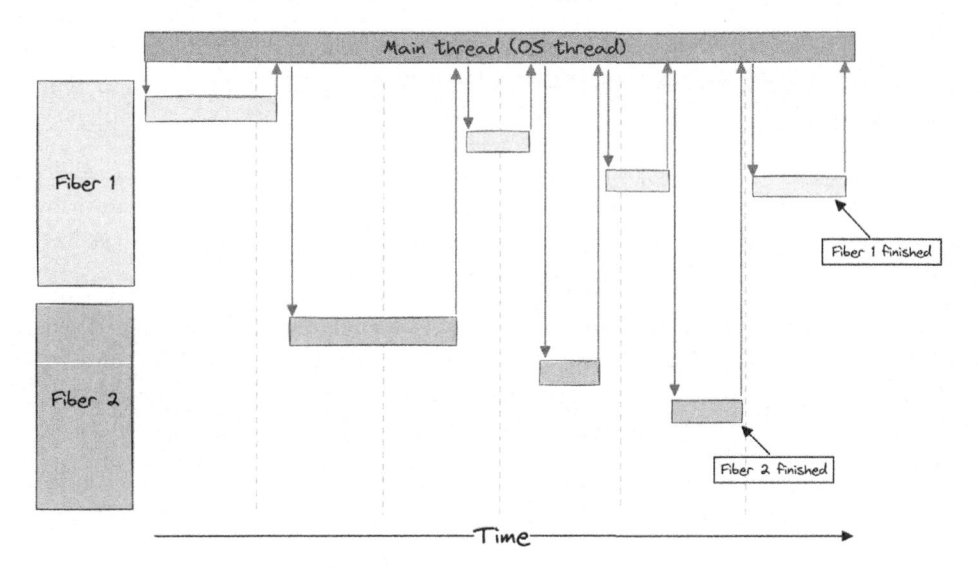

Figure 2.2 – Program flow using fibers/green threads

Each stack has a fixed space

As fibers and green threads are similar to OS threads, they do have some of the same drawbacks as well. Each task is set up with a stack of a fixed size, so you still have to reserve more space than you actually use. However, these stacks can be growable, meaning that once the stack is full, the runtime can grow the stack. While this sounds easy, it's a rather complicated problem to solve.

We can't simply grow a stack as we grow a tree. What actually needs to happen is one of two things:

1. You allocate a new piece of continuous memory and handle the fact that your stack is spread over two disjointed memory segments
2. You allocate a new larger stack (for example, twice the size of the previous stack), move all your data over to the new stack, and continue from there

The first solution sounds pretty simple, as you can leave the original stack as it is, and you can basically context switch over to the new stack when needed and continue from there. However, modern CPUs can work extremely fast if they can work on a contiguous piece of memory due to caching and their ability to predict what data your next instructions are going to work on. Spreading the stack over two disjointed pieces of memory will hinder performance. This is especially noticeable when you have a loop that happens to be just at the stack boundary, so you end up making up to two context switches for each iteration of the loop.

The second solution solves the problems with the first solution by having the stack as a contiguous piece of memory, but it comes with some problems as well.

First, you need to allocate a new stack and move all the data over to the new stack. But what happens with all pointers and references that point to something located on the stack when everything moves to a new location? You guessed it: every pointer and reference to anything located on the stack needs to be updated so they point to the new location. This is complex and time-consuming, but if your runtime already includes a garbage collector, you already have the overhead of keeping track of all your pointers and references anyway, so it might be less of a problem than it would for a non-garbage collected program. However, it does require a great deal of integration between the garbage collector and the runtime to do this every time the stack grows, so implementing this kind of runtime can get very complicated.

Secondly, you have to consider what happens if you have a lot of long-running tasks that only require a lot of stack space for a brief period of time (for example, if it involves a lot of recursion at the start of the task) but are mostly I/O bound the rest of the time. You end up growing your stack many times over only for one specific part of that task, and you have to make a decision whether you will accept that the task occupies more space than it needs or at some point move it back to a smaller stack. The impact this will have on your program will of course vary greatly based on the type of work you do, but it's still something to be aware of.

Context switching

Even though these fibers/green threads are lightweight compared to OS threads, you still have to save and restore registers at every context switch. This likely won't be a problem most of the time, but when compared to alternatives that don't require context switching, it can be less efficient.

Context switching can also be pretty complex to get right, especially if you intend to support many different platforms.

Scheduling

When a fiber/green thread yields to the runtime scheduler, the scheduler can simply resume execution on a new task that's ready to run. This means that you avoid the problem of being put in the same run queue as every other task in the system every time you yield to the scheduler. From the OS perspective, your threads are busy doing work all the time, so it will try to avoid pre-empting them if it can.

One unexpected downside of this is that most OS schedulers make sure all threads get some time to run by giving each OS thread a time slice where it can run before the OS pre-empts the thread and schedules a new thread on that CPU. A program using many OS threads might be allotted more time slices than a program with fewer OS threads. A program using M:N threading will most likely only use a few OS threads (one thread per CPU core seems to be the starting point on most systems). So, depending on whatever else is running on the system, your program might be allotted fewer time slices in total than it would be using many OS threads. However, with the number of cores available on most modern CPUs and the typical workload on concurrent systems, the impact from this should be minimal.

FFI

Since you create your own stacks that are supposed to grow/shrink under certain conditions and might have a scheduler that assumes it can pre-empt running tasks at any point, you will have to take extra measures when you use FFI. Most FFI functions will assume a normal OS-provided C-stack, so it will most likely be problematic to call an FFI function from a fiber/green thread. You need to notify the runtime scheduler, context switch to a different OS thread, and have some way of notifying the scheduler that you're done and the fiber/green thread can continue. This naturally creates overhead and added complexity both for the runtime implementor and the user making the FFI call.

Advantages

- It is simple to use for the user. The code will look like it does when using OS threads.
- Context switching is reasonably fast.
- Abundant memory usage is less of a problem when compared to OS threads.
- You are in full control over how tasks are scheduled and if you want you can prioritize them as you see fit.
- It's easy to incorporate pre-emption, which can be a powerful feature.

Drawbacks

- Stacks need a way to grow when they run out of space creating additional work and complexity
- You still need to save the CPU state on every context switch
- It's complicated to implement correctly if you intend to support many platforms and/or CPU architectures
- FFI can have a lot of overhead and add unexpected complexity

Callback based approaches

> **Note!**
> This is another example of M:N threading. Many tasks can run concurrently on one OS thread. Each task consists of a chain of callbacks.

You probably already know what we're going to talk about in the next paragraphs from JavaScript, which I assume most know.

The whole idea behind a callback-based approach is to save a pointer to a set of instructions we want to run later together with whatever state is needed. In Rust, this would be a closure.

Implementing callbacks is relatively easy in most languages. They don't require any context switching or pre-allocated memory for each task.

However, representing concurrent operations using callbacks requires you to write the program in a radically different way from the start. Re-writing a program that uses a normal sequential program flow to one using callbacks represents a substantial rewrite, and the same goes the other way.

Callback-based concurrency can be hard to reason about and can become very complicated to understand. It's no coincidence that the term "callback hell" is something most JavaScript developers are familiar with.

Since each sub-task must save all the state it needs for later, the memory usage will grow linearly with the number of callbacks in a task.

Advantages

- Easy to implement in most languages
- No context switching
- Relatively low memory overhead (in most cases)

Drawbacks

- Memory usage grows linearly with the number of callbacks.
- Programs and code can be hard to reason about.
- It's a very different way of writing programs and it will affect almost all aspects of the program since all yielding operations require one callback.
- Ownership can be hard to reason about. The consequence is that writing callback-based programs without a garbage collector can become very difficult.

- Sharing state between tasks is difficult due to the complexity of ownership rules.
- Debugging callbacks can be difficult.

Coroutines: promises and futures

> **Note!**
> This is another example of M:N threading. Many tasks can run concurrently on one OS thread. Each task is represented as a state machine.

Promises in JavaScript and **futures** in Rust are two different implementations that are based on the same idea.

There are differences between different implementations, but we'll not focus on those here. It's worth explaining promises a bit since they're widely known due to their use in JavaScript. Promises also have a lot in common with Rust's futures.

First of all, many languages have a concept of promises, but I'll use the one from JavaScript in the following examples.

Promises are one way to deal with the complexity that comes with a callback-based approach.

Instead of:

```
setTimer(200, () => {
  setTimer(100, () => {
    setTimer(50, () => {
      console.log("I'm the last one");
    });
  });
});
```

We can do:

```
function timer(ms) {
    return new Promise((resolve) => setTimeout(resolve, ms));
}

timer(200)
.then(() => timer(100))
.then(() => timer(50))
.then(() => console.log("I'm the last one"));
```

The latter approach is also referred to as **the continuation-passing style**. Each subtask calls a new one once it's finished.

The difference between callbacks and promises is even more substantial under the hood. You see, promises return a state machine that can be in one of three states: `pending`, `fulfilled`, or `rejected`.

When we call `timer(200)` in the previous example, we get back a promise in the `pending` state.

Now, the continuation-passing style does fix some of the issues related to callbacks, but it still retains a lot of them when it comes to complexity and the different ways of writing programs. However, they enable us to leverage the compiler to solve a lot of these problems, which we'll discuss in the next paragraph.

Coroutines and async/await

Coroutines come in two flavors: **asymmetric** and **symmetric**. Asymmetric coroutines yields to a scheduler, and they're the ones we'll focus on. Symmetric coroutines yield a specific destination; for example, a different coroutine.

While coroutines are a pretty broad concept in general, the introduction of coroutines as `objects` in programming languages is what really makes this way of handling concurrency rival the ease of use that OS threads and fibers/green threads are known for.

You see when you write `async` in Rust or JavaScript, the compiler re-writes what looks like a normal function call into a future (in the case of Rust) or a promise (in the case of JavaScript). **Await**, on the other hand, yields control to the runtime scheduler, and the task is suspended until the future/promise you're awaiting has finished.

This way, we can write programs that handle concurrent operations in almost the same way we write our normal sequential programs.

Our JavaScript program can now be written as follows:

```
async function run() {
    await timer(200);
    await timer(100);
    await timer(50);
    console.log("I'm the last one");
}
```

You can consider the `run` function as a pausable task consisting of several sub-tasks. On each "await" point, it yields control to the scheduler (in this case, it's the well-known JavaScript event loop).

Once one of the sub-tasks changes state to either `fulfilled` or `rejected`, the task is scheduled to continue to the next step.

When using Rust, you can see the same transformation happening with the function signature when you write something such as this:

```
async fn run() -> () { ... }
```

The function wraps the return object, and instead of returning the type (), it returns a `Future` with an output type of ():

```
Fn run() -> impl Future<Output = ()>
```

Syntactically, Rust's futures 0.1 was a lot like the promise example we just showed, and the Rust futures we use today have a lot in common with how `async/await` works in JavaScript..

This way of rewriting what look like normal functions and code into something else has a lot of benefits, but it's not without its drawbacks.

As with any stackless coroutine implementation, full pre-emption can be hard, or impossible, to implement. These functions have to yield at specific points, and there is no way to suspend execution in the middle of a stack frame in contrast to fibers/green threads. Some level of pre-emption is possible by having the runtime or compiler insert pre-emption points at every function call, for example, but it's not the same as being able to pre-empt a task at any point during its execution.

> **Pre-emption points**
>
> Pre-emption points can be thought of as inserting code that calls into the scheduler and asks it if it wishes to pre-empt the task. These points can be inserted by the compiler or the library you use before every new function call for example.

Furthermore, you need compiler support to make the most out of it. Languages that have metaprogramming abilities (such as macros) can emulate much of the same, but this will still not be as seamless as it will when the compiler is aware of these special async tasks.

Debugging is another area where care must be taken when implementing futures/promises. Since the code is re-written as state machines (or generators), you won't have the same stack traces as you do with normal functions. Usually, you can assume that the caller of a function is what precedes it both in the stack and in the program flow. For futures and promises, it might be the runtime that calls the function that progresses the state machine, so there might not be a good backtrace you can use to see what happened before calling the function that failed. There are ways to work around this, but most of them will incur some overhead.

Advantages

- You can write code and model programs the same way you normally would
- No context switching

- It can be implemented in a very memory-efficient way
- It's easy to implement for various platforms

Drawbacks

- Pre-emption can be hard, or impossible, to fully implement, as the tasks can't be stopped in the middle of a stack frame
- It needs compiler support to leverage its full advantages
- Debugging can be difficult both due to the non-sequential program flow and the limitations on the information you get from the backtraces.

Summary

You're still here? That's excellent! Good job on getting through all that background information. I know going through text that describes abstractions and code can be pretty daunting, but I hope you see why it's so valuable for us to go through these higher-level topics now at the start of the book. We'll get to the examples soon. I promise!

In this chapter, we went through a lot of information on how we can model and handle asynchronous operations in programming languages by using both OS-provided threads and abstractions provided by a programming language or a library. While it's not an extensive list, we covered some of the most popular and widely used technologies while discussing their advantages and drawbacks.

We spent quite some time going in-depth on threads, coroutines, fibers, green threads, and callbacks, so you should have a pretty good idea of what they are and how they're different from each other.

The next chapter will go into detail about how we do system calls and create cross-platform abstractions and what OS-backed event queues such as Epoll, Kqueue, and IOCP really are and why they're fundamental to most async runtimes you'll encounter out in the wild.

3
Understanding OS-Backed Event Queues, System Calls, and Cross-Platform Abstractions

In this chapter, we'll take a look at how an OS-backed event queue works and how three different operating systems handle this task in different ways. The reason for going through this is that most async runtimes I know of use OS-backed event queues such as this as a fundamental part of achieving high-performance I/O. You'll most likely hear references to these frequently when reading about how async code really works.

Event queues based on the technology we discuss in this chapter is used in many popular libraries like:

- mio (https://github.com/tokio-rs/mio), a key part of popular runtimes like Tokio
- polling (https://github.com/smol-rs/polling), the event queue used in Smol and async-std
- libuv (https://libuv.org/), the library used to create the event queue used in Node.js (a JavaScript runtime) and the Julia programming language
- C# for its asynchronous network calls
- Boost.Asio, a library for asynchronous network I/O for C++

All our interactions with the host operating system are done through **system calls** (**syscalls**). To make a system call using Rust, we need to know how to use Rust's **foreign function interface** (**FFI**).

In addition to knowing how to use FFI and make syscalls, we need to cover cross-platform abstractions. When creating an event queue, whether you create it yourself or use a library, you'll notice that the abstractions might seem a bit unintuitive if you only have a high-level overview of how, for example, IOCP works on Windows. The reason for this is that these abstractions need to provide one API that covers the fact that different operating systems handle the same task differently. This process often involves identifying a common denominator between the platforms and building a new abstraction on top of that.

Instead of using a rather complex and lengthy example to explain FFI, syscalls, and cross-platform abstractions, we'll ease into the topic using a simple example. When we encounter these concepts later on, we'll already know these subjects well enough, so we're well prepared for the more interesting examples in the following chapters.

In this chapter, we'll go through the following main topics:

- Why use an OS-backed event queue?
- Readiness-based event queues
- Completion-based event queues
- epoll
- kqueue
- IOCP
- Syscalls, FFI, and cross-platform abstractions

> **Note**
>
> There are popular, although lesser-used, alternatives you should know about even though we don't cover them here:
>
> **wepoll**: This uses specific APIs on Windows and wraps IOCP so it closely resembles how epoll works on Linux in contrast to regular IOCP. This makes it easier to create an abstraction layer with the same API on top of the two different technologies. It's used by both **libuv** and **mio**.
>
> **io_uring**: This is a relatively new API on Linux with many similarities to IOCP on Windows.
>
> I'm pretty confident that after you've gone through the next two chapters, you will have an easy time reading up on these if you want to learn more about them.

Technical requirements

This chapter doesn't require you to set up anything new, but since we're writing some low-level code for three different platforms, you need access to these platforms if you want to run all the examples.

The best way to follow along is to open the accompanying repository on your computer and navigate to the `ch03` folder.

This chapter is a little special since we build some basic understanding from the ground up, which means some of it is quite low-level and requires a specific operating system and CPU family to run. Don't worry; I've chosen the most used and popular CPU, so this shouldn't be a problem, but it is something you need to be aware of.

The machine must use a CPU using the x86-64 instruction set on Windows and Linux. Intel and AMD desktop CPUs use this architecture, but if you run Linux (or WSL) on a machine using an ARM processor you might encounter issues with some of the examples using inline assembly. On macOS, the example in the book targets the newer M-family of chips, but the repository also contains examples targeting the older Intel-based Macs.

Unfortunately, some examples targeting specific platforms require that specific operating system to run. However, this will be the only chapter where you need access to three different platforms to run all the examples. Going forward, we'll create examples that will run on all platforms either natively or using **Windows Subsystem for Linux** (**WSL**), but to understand the basics of cross-platform abstractions, we need to actually create examples that target these different platforms.

Running the Linux examples

If you don't have a Linux machine set up, you can run the Linux example on the Rust Playground, or if you're on a Windows system, my suggestion is to set up WSL and run the code there. You can find the instructions on how to do that at `https://learn.microsoft.com/en-us/windows/wsl/install`. Remember, you have to install Rust in the WSL environment as well, so follow the instructions in the *Preface* section of this book on how to install Rust on Linux.

If you use VS Code as your editor, there is a very simple way of switching your environment to WSL. Press *Ctrl+Shift+P* and write `Reopen folder in WSL`. This way, you can easily open the example folder in WSL and run the code examples using Linux there.

Why use an OS-backed event queue?

You already know by now that we need to cooperate closely with the OS to make I/O operations as efficient as possible. Operating systems such as Linux, macOS, and Windows provide several ways of performing I/O, both blocking and non-blocking.

I/O operations need to go through the operating system since they are dependent on resources that our operating system abstracts over. This can be the disk drive, the network card, or other peripherals. Especially in the case of network calls, we're not only dependent on our own hardware, but we also depend on resources that might reside far away from our own, causing a significant delay.

In the previous chapter, we covered different ways to handle asynchronous operations when programming, and while they're all different, they all have one thing in common: they need control over when and if they should yield to the OS scheduler when making a syscall.

In practice, this means that syscalls that normally would yield to the OS scheduler (blocking calls) needs to be avoided and we need to use non-blocking calls instead. We also need an efficient way to know the status of each call so we know when the task that made the otherwise blocking call is ready to progress. This is the main reason for using an OS-backed event queue in an asynchronous runtime.

We'll look at three different ways of handling an I/O operation as an example.

Blocking I/O

When we ask the operating system to perform a blocking operation, it will suspend the OS thread that makes the call. It will then store the CPU state it had at the point where we made the call and go on to do other things. When data arrives for us through the network, it will wake up our thread again, restore the CPU state, and let us resume as if nothing has happened.

Blocking operations are the least flexible to use for us as programmers since we yield control to the OS at every call. The big advantage is that our thread gets woken up once the event we're waiting for is ready so we can continue. If we take the whole system running on the OS into account, it's a pretty efficient solution since the OS will give threads that have work to do time on the CPU to progress. However, if we narrow the scope to look at our process in isolation, we find that every time we make a blocking call, we put a thread to sleep, even if we still have work that our process could do. This leaves us with the choice of spawning new threads to do work on or just accepting that we have to wait for the blocking call to return. We'll go a little more into detail about this later.

Non-blocking I/O

Unlike a blocking I/O operation, the OS will not suspend the thread that made an I/O request, but instead give it a handle that the thread can use to ask the operating system if the event is ready or not.

We call the process of querying for status **polling**.

Non-blocking I/O operations give us as programmers more freedom, but, as usual, that comes with a responsibility. If we poll too often, such as in a loop, we will occupy a lot of CPU time just to ask for an updated status, which is very wasteful. If we poll too infrequently, there will be a significant delay between an event being ready and us doing something about it, thus limiting our throughput.

Event queuing via epoll/kqueue and IOCP

This is a sort of hybrid of the previous approaches. In the case of a network call, the call itself will be non-blocking. However, instead of polling the handle regularly, we can add that handle to an event queue, and we can do that with thousands of handles with very little overhead.

As programmers, we now have a new choice. We can either query the queue with regular intervals to check if any of the events we added have changed status or we can make a blocking call to the queue, telling the OS that we want to be woken up when at least one event in our queue has changed status so that the task that was waiting for that specific event can continue.

This allows us to only yield control to the OS when there is no more work to do and all tasks are waiting for an event to occur before they can progress. We can decide exactly when we want to issue such a blocking call ourselves.

> Note
> We will not cover methods such as **poll** and **select**. Most operating systems have methods that are older and not widely used in modern async runtimes today. Just know that there are other calls we can make that essentially seek to give the same flexibility as the event queues we just discussed.

Readiness-based event queues

epoll and **kqueue** are known as **readiness-based event queues**, which means they let you know when an action is ready to be performed. An example of this is a socket that is ready to be read from.

To give an idea about how this works in practice, we can take a look at what happens when we read data from a socket using epoll/kqueue:

1. We create an event queue by calling the syscall `epoll_create` or `kqueue`.
2. We ask the OS for a file descriptor representing a network socket.
3. Through another syscall, we register an interest in `Read` events on this socket. It's important that we also inform the OS that we'll be expecting to receive a notification when the event is ready in the event queue we created in *step 1*.
4. Next, we call `epoll_wait` or `kevent` to wait for an event. This will block (suspend) the thread it's called on.
5. When the event is ready, our thread is unblocked (resumed) and we return from our `wait` call with data about the event that occurred.

6. We call `read` on the socket we created in *step 2*.

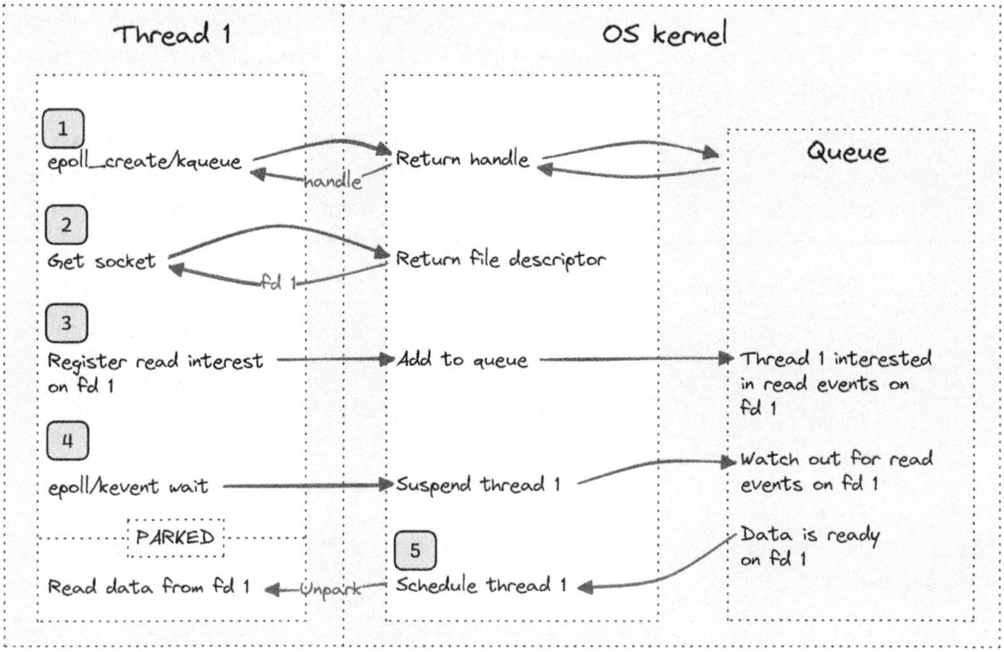

Figure 3.1 – A simplified view of the epoll and kqueue flow

Completion-based event queues

IOCP stands for **input/output completion port**. This is a completion-based event queue. This type of queue notifies you when events are completed. An example of this is when data has been read into a buffer.

The following is a basic breakdown of what happens in this type of event queue:

1. We create an event queue by calling the syscall `CreateIoCompletionPort`.
2. We create a buffer and ask the OS to give us a handle to a socket.
3. We register an interest in `Read` events on this socket with another syscall, but this time we also pass in the buffer we created in (step 2), which the data will be read to.
4. Next, we call `GetQueuedCompletionStatusEx`, which will block until an event has been completed.

5. Our thread is unblocked and our buffer is now filled with the data we're interested in.

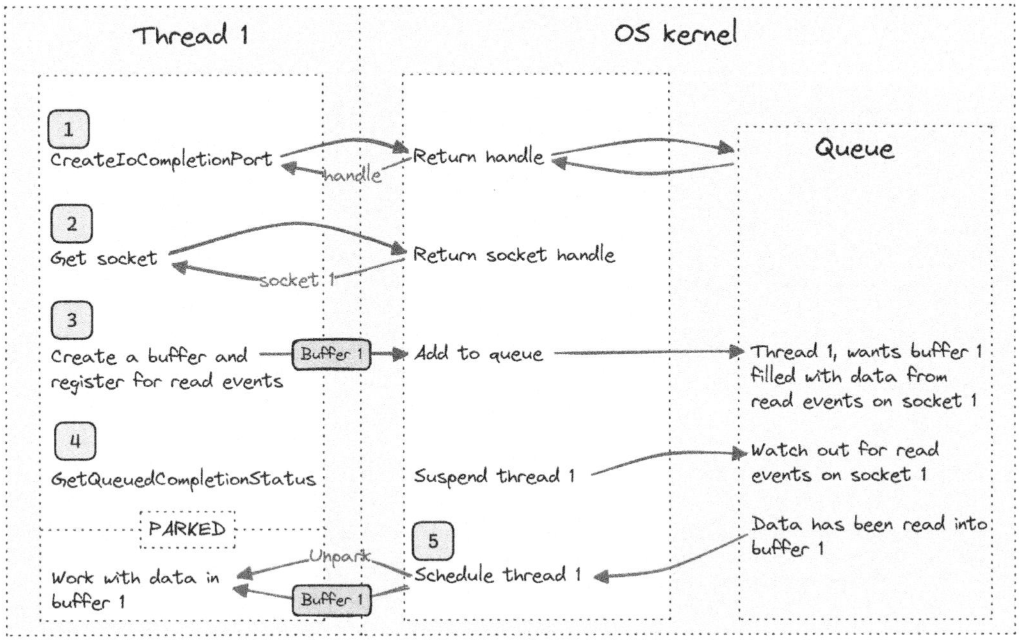

Figure 3.2 – A simplified view of the IOCP flow

epoll, kqueue, and IOCP

epoll is the Linux way of implementing an event queue. In terms of functionality, it has a lot in common with kqueue. The advantage of using epoll over other similar methods on Linux, such as select or poll, is that epoll was designed to work very efficiently with a large number of events.

kqueue is the macOS way of implementing an event queue (which originated from BSD) in operating systems such as FreeBSD and OpenBSD. In terms of high-level functionality, it's similar to epoll in concept but different in actual use.

IOCP is the way Windows handle this type of event queue. In Windows, a **completion port** will let you know when an event has been completed. Now, this might sound like a minor difference, but it's not. This is especially apparent when you want to write a library since abstracting over both means you'll either have to model IOCP as readiness-based or model epoll/kqueue as completion-based.

Lending out a buffer to the OS also provides some challenges since it's very important that this buffer stays untouched while waiting for an operation to return.

Windows	Linux	macOS
IOCP	epoll	kqueue
Completion based	Readiness based	Readiness based

Table 3.1 – Different platforms and event queues

Cross-platform event queues

When creating a cross-platform event queue, you have to deal with the fact that you have to create one unified API that's the same whether it's used on Windows (IOCP), macOS (kqueue), or Linux (epoll). The most obvious difference is that IOCP is completion-based while kqueue and epoll are readiness-based.

This fundamental difference means that you have to make a choice:

- You can create an abstraction that treats kqueue and epoll as completion-based queues, or
- You can create an abstraction that treats IOCP as a readiness-based queue

From my personal experience, it's a lot easier to create an abstraction that mimics a completion-based queue and handle the fact that kqueue and epoll are readiness-based behind the scenes than the other way around. The use of wepoll, as I alluded to earlier, is one way of creating a readiness-based queue on Windows. It will simplify creating such an API greatly, but we'll leave that out for now because it's less well known and not an approach that's officially documented by Microsoft.

Since IOCP is completion-based, it needs a buffer to read data into since it returns when data is read into that buffer. Kqueue and epoll, on the other hand, don't require that. They'll only return when you can read data into a buffer without blocking.

By requiring the user to supply a buffer of their preferred size to our API, we let the user control how they want to manage their memory. The user defines the size of the buffers, and the re-usages and controls all the aspects of the memory that will be passed to the OS when using IOCP.

In the case of epoll and kqueue in such an API, you can simply call read for the user and fill the same buffers, making it appear to the user that the API is completion-based.

If you wanted to present a readiness-based API instead, you have to create an illusion of having two separate operations when doing I/O on Windows. First, request a notification when the data is ready to be read on a socket, and then actually read the data. While possible to do, you'll most likely find yourself having to create a very complex API or accept some inefficiencies on Windows platforms due to having intermediate buffers to keep the illusion of having a readiness-based API.

We'll leave the topic of event queues for when we go on to create a simple example showing how exactly they work. Before we do that, we need to become really comfortable with FFI and syscalls, and we'll do that by writing an example of a syscall on three different platforms.

We'll also use this opportunity to talk about abstraction levels and how we can create a unified API that works on the three different platforms.

System calls, FFI, and cross-platform abstractions

We'll implement a very basic syscall for the three architectures: **BSD/macOS**, **Linux**, and **Windows**. We'll also see how this is implemented in three levels of abstraction.

The syscall we'll implement is the one used when we write something to the **standard output (stdout)** since that is such a common operation and it's interesting to see how it really works.

We'll start off by looking at the lowest level of abstraction we can use to make system calls and build our understanding of them from the ground up.

The lowest level of abstraction

The lowest level of abstraction is to write what is often referred to as a "raw" syscall. A raw syscall is one that bypasses the OS-provided library for making syscalls and instead relies on the OS having a stable **syscall ABI**. A stable syscall ABI means it guarantees that if you put the right data in certain registers and call a specific CPU instruction that passes control to the OS, it will always do the same thing.

To make a raw syscall, we need to write a little **inline assembly**, but don't worry. Even though we introduce it abruptly here, we'll go through it line by line, and in *Chapter 5*, we'll introduce inline assembly in more detail so you become familiar with it.

At this level of abstraction, we need to write different code for BSD/macOS, Linux, and Windows. We also need to write different code if the OS is running on different CPU architectures.

Raw syscall on Linux

On Linux and macOS, the syscall we want to invoke is called `write`. Both systems operate based on the concept of **file descriptors**, and `stdout` is already present when you start a process.

If you don't run Linux on your machine, you have some options to run this example. You can copy and paste the code into the Rust Playground or you can run it using WSL in Windows.

As mentioned in the introduction, I'll list what example you need to go to at the start of each example and you can run the example there by writing `cargo run`. The source code itself is always located in the example folder at `src/main.rs`.

The first thing we do is to pull in the standard library module that gives us access to the `asm!` macro.

Repository reference: ch03/a-raw-syscall

```rust
use std::arch::asm;
```

The next step is to write our syscall function:

```rust
#[inline(never)]
fn syscall(message: String) {
    let msg_ptr = message.as_ptr();
    let len = message.len();

    unsafe {
        asm!(
            "mov rax, 1",
            "mov rdi, 1",
            "syscall",
            in("rsi") msg_ptr,
            in("rdx") len,
            out("rax") _,
            out("rdi") _,
            lateout("rsi") _,
            lateout("rdx") _
        );
    }
}
```

We'll go through this first one line by line. The next ones will be pretty similar, so we only need to cover this in great detail once.

First, we have an attribute named `#[inline(never)]` that tells the compiler that we never want this function to be inlined during optimization. Inlining is when the compiler omits the function call and simply copies the body of the function instead of calling it. In this case, we don't want that to ever happen.

Next, we have our function call. The first two lines in the function simply get the raw pointer to the memory location where our text is stored and the length of the text buffer.

The next line is an unsafe block since there is no way to call assembly such as this safely in Rust.

The first line of assembly puts the value 1 in the `rax` register. When the CPU traps our call later on and passes control to the OS, the kernel knows that a value of one in `rax` means that we want to make a `write`.

The second line puts the value 1 in the `rdi` register. This tells the kernel where we want to write to, and a value of one means that we want to write to `stdout`.

The third line calls the `syscall` instruction. This instruction issues a software interrupt, and the CPU passes on control to the OS.

Rust's inline assembly syntax will look a little intimidating at first, but bear with me. We'll cover this in detail a little later in this book so that you get comfortable with it. For now, I'll just briefly explain what it does.

The fourth line writes the address to the buffer where our text is stored in the `rsi` register.

The fifth line writes the length (in bytes) of our text buffer to the `rdx` register.

The next four lines are not instructions to the CPU; they're meant to tell the compiler that it can't store anything in these registers and assume the data is untouched when we exit the inline assembly block. We do that by telling the compiler that there will be some unspecified data (indicated by the underscore) written to these registers.

Finally, it's time to call our raw syscall:

```
fn main() {
    let message = "Hello world from raw syscall!\n";
    let message = String::from(message);
    syscall(message);
}
```

This function simply creates a `String` and calls our `syscall` function, passing it in as an argument.

If you run this on Linux, you should now see the following message in your console:

```
Hello world from raw syscall!
```

Raw syscall on macOS

Now, since we use instructions that are specific to the CPU architecture, we'll need different functions depending on if you run an older Mac with an intel CPU or if you run a newer Mac with an Arm 64-based CPU. We only present the one working for the new M series of chips using an ARM 64 architecture, but don't worry, if you've cloned the Github repository, you'll find code that works on both versions of Mac there.

Since there are only minor changes, I'll present the whole example here and just go through the differences.

Remember, you need to run this code on a machine with macOS and an M-series chip. You can't try this in the Rust playground.

ch03/a-raw-syscall

```rust
use std::arch::asm;
fn main() {
    let message = "Hello world from raw syscall!\n";
    let message = String::from(message);
    syscall(message);
}

#[inline(never)]
fn syscall(message: String) {
    let ptr = message.as_ptr();
    let len = message.len();

    unsafe {
        asm!(
            "mov x16, 4",
            "mov x0, 1",
            "svc 0",
            in("x1") ptr,
            in("x2") len,
            out("x16") _,
            out("x0") _,
            lateout("x1") _,
            lateout("x2") _
        );
    }
}
```

Aside from different register naming, there is not that much difference from the one we wrote for Linux, with the exception of the fact that a `write` operation has the code 4 on macOS instead of 1 as it did on Linux. Also, the CPU instruction that issues a software interrupt is `svc 0` instead of `syscall`.

Again, if you run this on macOS, you'll get the following printed to your console:

```
Hello world from raw syscall!
```

What about raw syscalls on Windows?

This is a good opportunity to explain why writing raw syscalls, as we just did, is a bad idea if you want your program or library to work across platforms.

You see, if you want your code to work far into the future, you have to worry about what guarantees the OS gives. Linux guarantees that, for example, the value 1 written to the `rax` register will always refer to `write`, but Linux works on many platforms, and not everyone uses the same CPU architecture. We have the same problem with macOS that just recently changed from using an Intel-based x86_64 architecture to an ARM 64-based architecture.

Windows gives absolutely zero guarantees when it comes to low-level internals such as this. Windows has changed its internals numerous times and provides no official documentation on this matter. The only things we have are reverse-engineered tables that you can find on the internet, but these are not a robust solution since what was a `write` syscall can be changed to a `delete` syscall the next time you run Windows update. Even if that's unlikely, you have no guarantee, which in turn makes it impossible for you to guarantee to users of your program that it's going to work in the future.

So, while raw syscalls in theory do work and are good to be familiar with, they mostly serve as an example of why we'd rather link to the libraries that the different operating systems supply for us when making syscalls. The next segment will show how we do just that.

The next level of abstraction

The next level of abstraction is to use the API, which all three operating systems provide for us.

We'll soon see that this abstraction helps us remove some code. In this specific example, the syscall is the same on Linux and on macOS, so we only need to worry if we're on Windows. We can differentiate between the platforms by using the `#[cfg(target_family = "windows")]` and `#[cfg(target_family = "unix")]` conditional compilation flags. You'll see these used in the example in the repository.

Our main function will look the same as it did before:

ch03/b-normal-syscall

```
use std::io;
fn main() {
```

```
        let message = "Hello world from syscall!\n";
        let message = String::from(message);
        syscall(message).unwrap();
}
```

The only difference is that instead of pulling in the `asm` module, we pull in the `io` module.

Using the OS-provided API in Linux and macOS

You can run this code directly in the Rust playground since it runs on Linux, or you can run it locally on a Linux machine using WSL or on macOS:

ch03/b-normal-syscall

```
#[cfg(target_family = "unix")]
#[link(name = "c")]
extern "C" {
    fn write(fd: u32, buf: *const u8, count: usize) -> i32;
}

fn syscall(message: String) -> io::Result<()> {
    let msg_ptr = message.as_ptr();
    let len = message.len();
    let res = unsafe { write(1, msg_ptr, len) };

    if res == -1 {
        return Err(io::Error::last_os_error());
    }
    Ok(())
}
```

Let's go through the different steps one by one. Knowing how to do a proper syscall will be very useful for us later on in this book.

```
#[link(name = "c")]
```

Every Linux (and macOS) installation comes with a version of `libc`, which is a C library for communicating with the operating system. Having `libc`, with a consistent API, allows us to program the same way without worrying about the underlying platform architecture. Kernel developers can also make changes to the underlying ABI without breaking everyone's program. This flag tells the compiler to link to the `"c"` library on the system.

Next up is the definition of what functions in the linked library we want to call:

```
extern "C" {
  fn write(fd: u32, buf: *const u8, count: usize);
}
```

`extern "C"` (sometimes written without the `"C"`, since `"C"` is assumed if nothing is specified) means we want to use the `"C"` **calling convention** when calling the function `write` in the `"C"` library we're linking to. This function needs to have the exact same name as the function in the library we're linking to. The parameters don't have to have the same name, but they must be in the same order. It's good practice to name them the same as in the library you're linking to.

Here, we use Rusts FFI, so when you read about using FFI to call external functions, it's exactly what we're doing here.

The `write` function takes a file descriptor, `fd`, which in this case is a handle to `stdout`. In addition, it expects us to provide a pointer to an array of u8, `buf` values and the length of that buffer, `count`.

> **Calling convention**
>
> This is the first time we've encountered this term, so I'll go over a brief explanation, even though we dive deeper into this topic later in the book.
>
> A calling convention defines how function calls are performed and will, amongst other things, specify:
>
> - How arguments are passed into the function
>
> - What registers the function is expected to store at the start and restore before returning
>
> - How the function returns its result
>
> - How the stack is set up (we'll get back to this one later)
>
> So, before you call a foreign function you need to specify what calling convention to use since there is no way for the compiler to know if we don't tell it. The C calling convention is by far the most common one to encounter.

Next, we wrap the call to our linked function in a normal Rust function.

ch03/b-normal-syscall

```
#[cfg(target_family = "unix")]
fn syscall(message: String) -> io::Result<()> {
    let msg_ptr = message.as_ptr();
    let len = message.len();
    let res = unsafe { write(1, msg_ptr, len) };

    if res == -1 {
        return Err(io::Error::last_os_error());
    }
    Ok(())
}
```

You'll probably be familiar with the first two lines now, as they're the same as we wrote for our raw syscall example. We get the pointer to the buffer where our text is stored and the length of that buffer.

Next is our call to the `write` function in `libc`, which needs to be wrapped in an `unsafe` block since Rust can't guarantee safety when calling external functions.

You might wonder how we know that the value `1` refers to the file handle of `stdout`.

You'll meet this situation a lot when writing syscalls from Rust. Usually, constants are defined in the C header files, so we need to manually search them up and look for these definitions. `1` is always the file handle to `stdout` on UNIX systems, so it's easy to remember.

> **Note**
>
> Wrapping the `libc` functions and providing these constants is exactly what the create `libc` (https://github.com/rust-lang/libc) provides for us. Most of the time, you can use that instead of doing all the manual work of linking to and defining functions as we do here.

Lastly, we have the error handling, and you'll see this all the time when using FFI. C functions often use a specific integer to indicate if the function call was successful or not. In the case of this `write` call, the function will either return the number of bytes written or, if there is an error, it will return the value -1. You'll find this information easily by reading the *man-pages* (https://man7.org/linux/man-pages/index.html) for Linux.

If there is an error, we use the built-in function in Rust's standard library to query the OS for the last error it reported for this process and convert that to a rust `io::Error` type.

If you run this function using `cargo run`, you will see this output:

```
Hello world from syscall!
```

Using Windows API

On Windows, things work a bit differently. While UNIX models almost everything as "files" you interact with, Windows uses other abstractions. On Windows, you get a **handle** that represents some object you can interact with in specific ways depending on exactly what kind of handle you have.

We will use the same `main` function as before, but we need to link to different functions in the Windows API and make changes to our `syscall` function.

ch03/b-normal-syscall

```
#[link(name = "kernel32")]
extern "system" {
    fn GetStdHandle(nStdHandle: i32) -> i32;
    fn WriteConsoleW(
```

```
        hConsoleOutput: i32,
        lpBuffer: *const u16,
        numberOfCharsToWrite: u32,
        lpNumberOfCharsWritten: *mut u32,
        lpReserved: *const std::ffi::c_void,
    ) -> i32;
}
```

The first thing you notice is that we no longer link to the "C" library. Instead, we link to the kernel32 library. The next change is the use of the system calling convention. This calling convention is a bit peculiar. You see, Windows uses different calling conventions depending on whether you write for a 32-bit x86 Windows version or a 64-bit x86_64 Windows version. Newer Windows versions running on x86_64 use the "C" calling convention, so if you have a newer system you can try changing that out and see that it still works. "Specifying system" lets the compiler figure out the right one to use based on the system.

We link to two different syscalls in Windows:

- GetStdHandle: This retrieves a reference to a standard device like stdout
- WriteConsoleW: WriteConsole comes in two types. WriteConsoleW takes Unicode text and WriteConsoleA takes ANSI-encoded text. We're using the one that takes Unicode text in our program.

Now, **ANSI-encoded** text works fine if you only write English text, but as soon as you write text in other languages, you might need to use special characters that are not possible to represent in ANSI but possible in **Unicode**. If you mix them up, your program will not work as you expect.

Next is our new syscall function:

ch03/b-normal-syscall

```
fn syscall(message: String) -> io::Result<()> {
    let msg: Vec<u16> = message.encode_utf16().collect();
    let msg_ptr = msg.as_ptr();
    let len = msg.len() as u32;

    let mut output: u32 = 0;
        let handle = unsafe { GetStdHandle(-11) };
        if handle == -1 {
            return Err(io::Error::last_os_error())
        }
        let res = unsafe {
            WriteConsoleW(
                handle,
```

```
                msg_ptr,
                len,
                &mut output,
                std::ptr::null()
            )};
            
        if res == 0 {
            return Err(io::Error::last_os_error());
        }
    Ok(())
}
```

The first thing we do is convert the text to utf-16-encoded text, which Windows uses. Fortunately, Rust has a built-in function to convert our utf-8-encoded text to utf-16 code points. encode_utf16 returns an iterator over u16 code points that we can collect to a Vec.

The next two lines should be familiar by now. We get the pointer to where the text is stored and the length of the text in bytes.

The next thing we do is call GetStdHandle and pass in the value -11. The values we need to pass in for the different standard devices are described together with the GetStdHandle documentation at https://learn.microsoft.com/en-us/windows/console/getstdhandle. This is convenient, as we don't have to dig through C header files to find all the constant values we need.

The return code to expect is also documented thoroughly for all functions, so we handle potential errors here in the same way as we did for the Linux/macOS syscalls.

Finally, we have the call to the WriteConsoleW function. There is nothing too fancy about this, and you'll notice similarities with the write syscall we used for Linux. One difference is that the output is not returned from the function but written to an address location we pass in in the form of a pointer to our output variable.

> **Note**
> Now that you've seen how we create cross-platform syscalls, you will probably also understand why we're not including the code to make every example in this book cross-platform. It's simply the case that the book would be extremely long if we did, and it's not apparent that all that extra information will actually benefit our understanding of the key concepts.

The highest level of abstraction

This is simple, but I wanted to add this just for completeness. Rust standard library wraps the calls to the underlying OS APIs for us, so we don't have to care about what syscalls to invoke.

```
fn main() {
  println!("Hello world from the standard library");
}
```

Congratulations! You've now written the same syscall using three levels of abstraction. You now know what FFI looks like, you've seen some inline assembly (which we'll cover in greater detail later), and you've made a proper syscall to print something to the console. You've also seen one of the things our standard library tries to solve by wrapping these calls for different platforms so we don't have to know these syscalls to print something to the console.

Summary

In this chapter, we went through what OS-backed event queues are and gave a high-level overview of how they work. We also went through the defining characteristics of epoll, kqueue, and IOCP and focused on how they differ from each other.

In the last half of this chapter, we introduced some examples of syscalls. We discussed raw syscalls, and "normal" syscalls so that you know what they are and have seen examples of both. We also took the opportunity to talk about abstraction levels and the advantages of relying on good abstractions when they're available to us.

As a part of making system calls, you also got an introduction to Rusts FFI.

Finally, we created a cross-platform abstraction. You also saw some of the challenges that come with creating a unifying API that works across several operating systems.

The next chapter will walk you through an example using epoll to create a simple event queue, so you get to see exactly how this works in practice. In the repository, you'll also find the same example for both Windows and macOS, so you have that available if you ever want to implement an event queue for either of those platforms.

Part 2: Event Queues and Green Threads

In this part, we'll present two examples. The first example demonstrates the creation of an event queue using epoll. We will design the API to closely resemble the one used by mio, allowing us to grasp the fundamentals of both mio and epoll. The second example illustrates the use of fibers/green threads, similar to the approach employed by Go. This method is one of the popular alternatives to Rust's asynchronous programming using futures and async/await. Rust also utilized green threads before reaching version 1.0, making it a part of Rust's asynchronous history. Throughout the exploration, we will delve into fundamental programming concepts such as ISAs, ABIs, calling conventions, stacks, and touch on assembly programming. This section comprises the following chapters:

- *Chapter 4, Create Your Own Event Queue*
- *Chapter 5, Creating Our Own Fibers*

4
Create Your Own Event Queue

In this chapter, we'll create a simple version of an event queue using epoll. We'll take inspiration from **mio** (https://github.com/tokio-rs/mio), a low-level I/O library written in Rust that underpins much of the Rust async ecosystem. Taking inspiration from mio has the added benefit of making it easier to dive into their code base if you wish to explore how a real production-ready library works.

By the end of this chapter, you should be able to understand the following:

- The difference between blocking and non-blocking I/O
- How to use epoll to make your own event queue
- The source code of cross-platform event queue libraries such as mio
- Why we need an abstraction layer on top of epoll, kqueue, and IOCP if we want a program or library to work across different platforms

We've divided the chapter into the following sections:

- Design and introduction to epoll
- The ffi module
- The Poll module
- The main program

Technical requirements

This chapter focuses on epoll, which is specific to Linux. Unfortunately, epoll is not part of the **Portable Operating System Interface** (**POSIX**) standard, so this example will require you to run Linux and won't work with macOS, BSD, or Windows operating systems.

If you're on a machine running Linux, you're already set and can run the examples without any further steps.

If you're on Windows, my recommendation is to set up **WSL** (`https://learn.microsoft.com/en-us/windows/wsl/install`), if you haven't already, and install Rust on the Linux operating system running on WSL.

If you're using Mac, you can create a **virtual machine** (**VM**) running Linux, for example, by using the **QEMU**-based **UTM** application (`https://mac.getutm.app/`) or any other solution for managing VMs on a Mac.

A last option is to rent a Linux server (there are even some providers with a free layer), install Rust, and either use an editor such as Vim or Emacs in the console or develop on the remote machine using VS Code through SSH (`https://code.visualstudio.com/docs/remote/ssh`). I personally have good experience with Linode's offering (`https://www.linode.com/`), but there are many, many other options out there.

It's theoretically possible to run the examples on the Rust playground, but since we need a delay server, we would have to use a remote delay server service that accepts plain HTTP requests (not HTTPS) and modify the code so that the modules are all in one file instead. It's possible in a clinch but not really recommended.

> **The delay server**
>
> This example relies on calls made to a server that delays the response for a configurable duration. In the repository, there is a project named `delayserver` in the root folder.
>
> You can set up the server by simply entering the folder in a separate console window and writing `cargo run`. Just leave the server running in a separate, open terminal window as we'll use it in our example.
>
> The `delayserver` program is cross-platform, so it works without any modification on all platforms that Rust supports. If you're running WSL on Windows, I recommend running the `delayserver` program in WSL as well. Depending on your setup, you might get away with running the server in a Windows console and still be able to reach it when running the example in WSL. Just be aware that it might not work out of the box.
>
> The server will listen to port `8080` by default and the examples there assume this is the port used. You can change the listening port in the `delayserver` code before you start the server, but just remember to make the same corrections in the example code.
>
> The actual code for `delayserver` is less than 30 lines, so going through the code should only take a few minutes if you want to see what the server does.

Design and introduction to epoll

Okay, so this chapter will be centered around one main example you can find in the repository under `ch04/a-epoll`. We'll start by taking a look at how we design our example.

As I mentioned at the start of this chapter, we'll take our inspiration from `mio`. This has one big upside and one downside. The upside is that we get a gentle introduction to how `mio` is designed, making it much easier to dive into that code base if you want to learn more than what we cover in this example. The downside is that we introduce an overly thick abstraction layer over epoll, including some design decisions that are very specific to `mio`.

I think the upsides outweigh the downsides for the simple reason that if you ever want to implement a production-quality event loop, you'll probably want to look into the implementations that are already out there, and the same goes for if you want to dig deeper into the building blocks of asynchronous programming in Rust. In Rust, `mio` is one of the important libraries underpinning much of the async ecosystem, so gaining a little familiarity with it is an added bonus.

It's important to note that `mio` is a cross-platform library that creates an abstraction over epoll, kqueue, and IOCP (through Wepoll, as we described in *Chapter 3*). Not only that, `mio` supports iOS and Android, and in the future, it will likely support other platforms as well. So, leaving the door open to unify an API over so many different systems is bound to also come with some compromises if you compare it to what you can achieve if you only plan to support one platform.

> **mio**
>
> mio describes itself as a *"fast, low-level I/O library for Rust focusing on non-blocking APIs and event notification for building performance I/O apps with as little overhead as possible over the OS abstractions."*
>
> mio drives the event queue in Tokio, which is one of the most popular and widely used asynchronous runtimes in Rust. This means that mio is driving I/O for popular frameworks such as Actix Web (https://actix.rs/), Warp (https://github.com/seanmonstar/warp), and Rocket (https://rocket.rs/).
>
> The version of mio we'll use as design inspiration in this example is version **0.8.8**. The API has changed in the past and may change in the future, but the parts of the API we cover here have been stable since 2019, so it's a good bet that there will not be significant changes to it in the near future.

As is the case with all cross-platform abstractions, it's often necessary to go the route of choosing the least common denominator. Some choices will limit flexibility and efficiency on one or more platforms in the pursuit of having a unified API that works with all of them. We'll discuss some of those choices in this chapter.

Before we go further, let's create a blank project and give it a name. We'll refer to it as `a-epoll` going forward, but you will of course need to replace that with the name you choose.

Enter the folder and type the `cargo init` command.

In this example, we'll divide the project into a few modules, and we'll split the code up into the following files:

```
src
 |-- ffi.rs
 |-- main.rs
 |-- poll.rs
```

Their descriptions are as follows:

- `ffi.rs`: This module will contain the code related to the syscalls we need to communicate with the host operating system
- `main.rs`: This is the example program itself
- `poll.rs`: This module contains the main abstraction, which is a thin layer over epoll

Next, create the four files, mentioned in the preceding list, in the `src` folder.

In `main.rs`, we need to declare the modules as well:

a-epoll/src/main.rs

```rust
mod ffi;
mod poll;
```

Now that we have our project set up, we can start by going through how we'll design the API we'll use. The main abstraction is in `poll.rs`, so go ahead and open that file.

Let's start by stubbing out the structures and functions we need. It's easier to discuss them when we have them in front of us:

a-epoll/src/poll.rs

```rust
use std::{io::{self, Result}, net::TcpStream, os::fd::AsRawFd};
use crate::ffi;

type Events = Vec<ffi::Event>;

pub struct Poll {
    registry: Registry,
}

impl Poll {
    pub fn new() -> Result<Self> {
        todo!()
```

```rust
    }

    pub fn registry(&self) -> &Registry {
        &self.registry
    }

    pub fn poll(&mut self, events: &mut Events, timeout: Option<i32>) -> Result<()> {
        todo!()
    }
}

pub struct Registry {
    raw_fd: i32,
}

impl Registry {
    pub fn register(&self, source: &TcpStream, token: usize, interests: i32) -> Result<()>
    {
        todo!()
    }
}
impl Drop for Registry {
    fn drop(&mut self) {
        todo!()
    }
}
```

We've replaced all the implementations with `todo!()` for now. This macro will let us compile the program even though we've yet to implement the function body. If our execution ever reaches `todo!()`, it will panic.

The first thing you'll notice is that we'll pull the `ffi` module in scope in addition to some types from the standard library.

We'll also use the `std::io::Result` type as our own `Result` type. It's convenient since most errors will stem from one of our calls into the operating system, and an operating system error can be mapped to an `io::Error` type.

There are two main abstractions over epoll. One is a structure called `Poll` and the other is called `Registry`. The name and functionality of these functions are the same as they are in `mio`. Naming abstractions such as these is surprisingly difficult, and both constructs could very well have had a different name, but let's lean on the fact that someone else has spent time on this before us and decided to go with these in our example.

`Poll` is a struct that represents the event queue itself. It has a few methods:

- `new`: Creates a new event queue
- `registry`: Returns a reference to the registry that we can use to register interest to be notified about new events
- `poll`: Blocks the thread it's called on until an event is ready or it times out, whichever occurs first

`Registry` is the other half of the equation. While `Poll` represents the event queue, `Registry` is a handle that allows us to register interest in new events.

`Registry` will only have one method: `register`. Again, we mimic the API mio uses (https://docs.rs/mio/0.8.8/mio/struct.Registry.html), and instead of accepting a predefined list of methods for registering different interests, we accept an `interests` argument, which will indicate what kind of events we want our event queue to keep track of.

One more thing to note is that we won't use a generic type for all sources. We'll only implement this for `TcpStream`, even though there are many things we could potentially track with an event queue.

This is especially true when we want to make this cross-platform since, depending on the platforms you want to support, there are many types of event sources we might want to track.

mio solves this by having `Registry::register` accept an object implementing the `Source` trait that mio defines. As long as you implement this trait for the source, you can use the event queue to track events on it.

In the following pseudo-code, you'll get an idea of how we plan to use this API:

```
let queue = Poll::new().unwrap();
let id = 1;

// register interest in events on a TcpStream
queue.registry().register(&stream, id, ...).unwrap();
let mut events = Vec::with_capacity(1);

// This will block the curren thread
queue.poll(&mut events, None).unwrap();
//...data is ready on one of the tracked streams
```

You might wonder why we need the `Registry` struct at all.

To answer that question, we need to remember that mio abstracts over epoll, kqueue, and IOCP. It does this by making `Registry` wrap around a `Selector` object. The `Selector` object is conditionally compiled so that every platform has its own `Selector` implementation corresponding to the relevant syscalls to make IOCP, kqueue, and epoll do the same thing.

`Registry` implements one important method we won't implement in our example, called `try_clone`. The reason we won't implement this is that we don't need it to understand how an event loop like this works and we want to keep the example simple and easy to understand. However, this method is important for understanding why the responsibility of registering events and the queue itself is divided.

> **Important note**
>
> By moving the concern of registering interests to a separate struct like this, users can call `Registry::try_clone` to get an owned `Registry` instance. This instance can be passed to, or shared through `Arc<Registry>` with, other threads, allowing multiple threads to register interest to the same `Poll` instance even when `Poll` is blocking another thread while waiting for new events to happen in `Poll::poll`.

`Poll::poll` requires exclusive access since it takes a `&mut self`, so when we're waiting for events in `Poll::poll`, there is no way to register interest from a different thread at the same time if we rely on using `Poll` to register interest, since that will be prevented by Rust's type system.

It also makes it effectively impossible to have multiple threads waiting for events by calling `Poll::poll` on the same instance in any meaningful way since it would require synchronization that essentially would make each call sequential anyway.

The design lets users interact with the queue from potentially many threads by registering interest, while one thread makes the blocking call and handles the notifications from the operating system.

> **Note**
>
> The fact that `mio` doesn't enable you to have multiple threads that are blocked on the same call to `Poll::poll` isn't a limitation due to epoll, kqueue, or IOCP. They all allow for the scenario that many threads will call `Poll::poll` on the same instance and get notifications on events in the queue. epoll even allows specific flags to dictate whether the operating system should wake up only one or all threads that wait for notification (specifically the `EPOLLEXCLUSIVE` flag).
>
> The problem is partly about how the different platforms decide which threads to wake when there are many of them waiting for events on the same queue, and partly about the fact that there doesn't seem to be a huge interest in that functionality. For example, epoll will, by default, wake all threads that block on `Poll`, while Windows, by default, will only wake up one thread. You can modify this behavior to some extent, and there have been ideas on implementing a `try_clone` method on `Poll` as well in the future. For now, the design is like we outlined, and we will stick to that in our example as well.

This brings us to another topic we should cover before we start implementing our example.

Is all I/O blocking?

Finally, a question that's easy to answer. The answer is a big, resounding... maybe. The thing is that not all I/O operations will block in the sense that the operating system will park the calling thread and it will be more efficient to switch to another task. The reason for this is that the operating system is smart and will cache a lot of information in memory. If information is in the cache, a syscall requesting that information would simply return immediately with the data, so forcing a context switch or any rescheduling of the current task might be less efficient than just handling the data synchronously. The problem is that there is no way to know for sure whether I/O is blocking and it depends on what you're doing.

Let me give you two examples.

DNS lookup

When creating a TCP connection, one of the first things that happens is that you need to convert a typical address such as www.google.com to an IP address such as 216.58.207.228. The operating system maintains a mapping of local addresses and addresses it's previously looked up in a cache and will be able to resolve them almost immediately. However, the first time you look up an unknown address, it might have to make a call to a DNS server, which takes a lot of time, and the OS will park the calling thread while waiting for the response if it's not handled in a non-blocking manner.

File I/O

Files on the local filesystem are another area where the operating system performs quite a bit of caching. Smaller files that are frequently read are often cached in memory, so requesting that file might not block at all. If you have a web server that serves static files, there is most likely a rather limited set of small files you'll be serving. The chances are that these are cached in memory. However, there is no way to know for sure – if an operating system is running low on memory, it might have to map memory pages to the hard drive, which makes what would normally be a very fast memory lookup excruciatingly slow. The same is true if there is a huge number of small files that are accessed randomly, or if you serve very large files since the operating system will only cache a limited amount of information. You'll also encounter this kind of unpredictability if you have many unrelated processes running on the same operating system as it might not cache the information that's important to you.

A popular way of handling these cases is to forget about non-blocking I/O, and actually make a blocking call instead. You don't want to do these calls in the same thread that runs a Poll instance (since every small delay will block all tasks), but you would probably relegate that task to a **thread pool**. In the thread pool, you have a limited number of threads that are tasked with making regular blocking calls for things such as DNS lookups or file I/O.

An example of a runtime that does exactly this is libuv (http://docs.libuv.org/en/v1.x/threadpool.html#threadpool). libuv is the asynchronous I/O library that Node.js is built upon.

While its scope is larger than mio (which only cares about non-blocking I/O), libuv is to Node in JavaScript what mio is to Tokio in Rust.

> **Note**
> The reason for doing file I/O in a thread pool is that there have historically been poor cross-platform APIs for non-blocking file I/O. While it's true that many runtimes choose to relegate this task to a thread pool making blocking calls to the OS, it might not be true in the future as the OS APIs evolve over time.

Creating a thread pool to handle these cases is outside the scope of this example (even mio considers this outside its scope, just to be clear). We'll focus on showing how epoll works and mention these topics in the text, even though we won't actually implement a solution for them in this example.

Now that we've covered a lot of basic information about epoll, mio, and the design of our example, it's time to write some code and see for ourselves how this all works in practice.

The ffi module

Let's start with the modules that don't depend on any others and work our way from there. The ffi module contains mappings to the syscalls and data structures we need to communicate with the operating system. We'll also explain how epoll works in detail once we have presented the syscalls.

It's only a few lines of code, so I'll place the first part here so it's easier to keep track of where we are in the file since there's quite a bit to explain. Open the ffi.rs file and write the following lines of code:

ch04/a-epoll/src/ffi.rs

```rust
pub const EPOLL_CTL_ADD: i32 = 1;
pub const EPOLLIN: i32 = 0x1;
pub const EPOLLET: i32 = 1 << 31;

#[link(name = "c")]
extern "C" {
    pub fn epoll_create(size: i32) -> i32;
    pub fn close(fd: i32) -> i32;
    pub fn epoll_ctl(epfd: i32, op: i32, fd: i32, event: *mut Event) -> i32;
    pub fn epoll_wait(epfd: i32, events: *mut Event, maxevents: i32, timeout: i32) -> i32;
}
```

The first thing you'll notice is that we declare a few constants called EPOLL_CTL_ADD, EPOLLIN, and EPOLLET.

I'll get back to explaining what these constants are in a moment. Let's first take a look at the syscalls we need to make. Fortunately, we've already covered syscalls in detail, so you already know the basics of ffi and why we link to C in the preceding code:

- epoll_create is the syscall we make to create an epoll queue. You can find the documentation for it at https://man7.org/linux/man-pages/man2/epoll_create.2.html. This method accepts one argument called size, but size is there only for historical reasons. The argument will be ignored but must have a value larger than 0.

- close is the syscall we need to close the file descriptor we get when we create our epoll instance, so we release our resources properly. You can read the documentation for the syscall at https://man7.org/linux/man-pages/man2/close.2.html.

- epoll_ctl is the control interface we use to perform operations on our epoll instance. This is the call we use to register interest in events on a source. It supports three main operations: *add*, *modify*, or *delete*. The first argument, epfd, is the epoll file descriptor we want to perform operations on. The second argument, op, is the argument where we specify whether we want to perform an *add*, *modify*, or *delete* operation

- In our case, we're only interested in adding interest for events, so we'll only pass in EPOLL_CTL_ADD, which is the value to indicate that we want to perform an *add* operation. epoll_event is a little more complicated, so we'll discuss it in more detail. It does two important things for us: first, the events field indicates what kind of events we want to be notified of and it can also modify the behavior of *how* and *when* we get notified. Second, the data field passes on a piece of data to the kernel that it will return to us when an event occurs. The latter is important since we need this data to identify exactly what event occurred since that's the only information we'll receive in return that can identify what source we got the notification for. You can find the documentation for this syscall here: https://man7.org/linux/man-pages/man2/epoll_ctl.2.html.

- epoll_wait is the call that will block the current thread and wait until one of two things happens: we receive a notification that an event has occurred or it times out. epfd is the epoll file descriptor identifying the queue we made with epoll_create. events is an array of the same Event structure we used in epoll_ctl. The difference is that the events field now gives us information about what event *did* occur, and importantly the data field contains the same data that we passed in when we registered interest

- For example, the data field lets us identify which file descriptor has data that's ready to be read. The maxevents arguments tell the kernel how many events we have reserved space for in our array. Lastly, the timeout argument tells the kernel how long we will wait for events before it will wake us up again so we don't potentially block forever. You can read the documentation for epoll_wait at https://man7.org/linux/man-pages/man2/epoll_wait.2.html.

The last part of the code in this file is the `Event` struct:

ch04/a-epoll/src/ffi.rs

```
#[derive(Debug)]
#[repr(C, packed)]
pub struct Event {
    pub(crate) events: u32,
    // Token to identify event
    pub(crate) epoll_data: usize,
}
impl Event {
    pub fn token(&self) -> usize {
        self.epoll_data
    }
}
```

This structure is used to communicate to the operating system in `epoll_ctl`, and the operating system uses the same structure to communicate with us in `epoll_wait`.

Events are defined as a `u32`, but it's more than just a number. This field is what we call a **bitmask**. I'll take the time to explain bitmasks in a later section since it's common in most syscalls and not something everyone has encountered before. In simple terms, it's a way to use the bit representation as a set of yes/no flags to indicate whether an option has been chosen or not.

The different options are described in the link I provided for the `epoll_ctl` syscall. I won't explain all of them in detail here, but just cover the ones we'll use:

- `EPOLLIN` represents a bitflag indicating we're interested in read operations on the file handle
- `EPOLLET` represents a bitflag indicating that we're interested in getting events notified with epoll set to an edge-triggered mode

We'll get back to explaining bitflags, bitmasks, and what edge-triggered mode really means in a moment, but let's just finish with the code first.

The last field on the `Event` struct is `epoll_data`. This field is defined as a union in the documentation. A union is much like an enum, but in contrast to Rust's enums, it doesn't carry any information on what type it is, so it's up to us to make sure we know what type of data it holds.

We use this field to simply hold a `usize` so we can pass in an integer identifying each event when we register interest using `epoll_ctl`. It would be perfectly fine to pass in a pointer instead – just as long as we make sure that the pointer is still valid when it's returned to us in `epoll_wait`.

We can think of this field as a token, which is exactly what `mio` does, and to keep the API as similar as possible, we copy `mio` and provide a `token` method on the struct to get this value.

> **What does #[repr(packed)] do?**
>
> The `#[repr(packed)]` annotation is new to us. Usually, a struct will have padding either between fields or at the end of the struct. This happens even when we've specified `#[repr(C)]`.
>
> The reason has to do with efficient access to the data stored in the struct by not having to make multiple fetches to get the data stored in a struct field. In the case of the `Event` struct, the usual padding would be adding 4 bytes of padding at the end of the `events` field. When the operating system expects a packed struct for `Event`, and we give it a padded one, it will write parts of `event_data` to the padding between the fields. When you try to read `event_data` later on, you'll end up only reading the last part of `event_data`, which happened to overlap and get the wrong data
>
> *[Diagram illustrating packed vs non-packed struct layouts: showing "We create a the 'Event' struct and pass it to the OS", "The OS writes: events: ABCD, epoll_data: EFGHIJKL", and "We read the data". In the packed case, events = ABCD and epoll_data = EFGHIJKL. In the non-packed case with padding, events = ABCD but epoll_data = IJKL — NB! Wrong data]*
>
> The fact that the operating system expects a packed `Event` struct isn't obvious by reading the manpages for Linux, so you have to read the appropriate C header files to know for sure. You could of course simply rely on the `libc` crate (https://github.com/rust-lang/libc), which we would do too if we weren't here to learn things like this for ourselves.

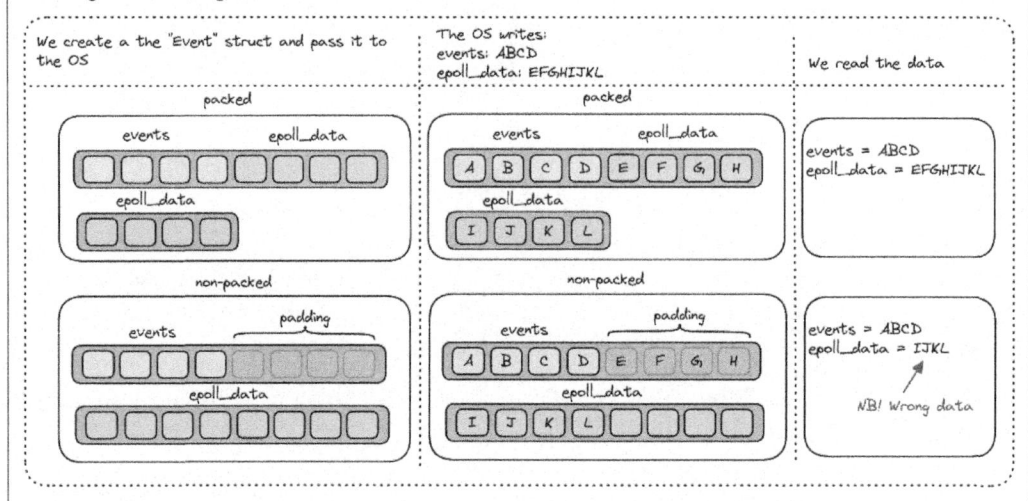

So, now that we've finished walking through the code, there are a few topics that we promised to get back to.

Bitflags and bitmasks

You'll encounter this all the time when making syscalls (in fact, the concept of bitmasks is pretty common in low-level programming). A bitmask is a way to treat each bit as a switch, or a flag, to indicate that an option is either enabled or disabled.

An integer, such as `i32`, can be expressed as 32 bits. `EPOLLIN` has the hex value of `0x1` (which is simply 1 in decimal). Represented in bits, this would look like 00000000000000000000000000000001.

`EPOLLET`, on the other hand, has a value of `1 << 31`. This simply means the bit representation of the decimal number 1, shifted 31 bits to the left. The decimal number 1 is incidentally the same as `EPOLLIN`, so by looking at that representation and shifting the bits 31 times to the left, we get a number with the bit representation of 10000000000000000000000000000000.

The way we use bitflags is that we use the OR operator, `|`, and by OR'ing the values together, we get a bitmask with each flag we OR'ed set to 1. In our example, the bitmask would look like 10000000000000000000000000000001.

The receiver of the bitmask (in this case, the operating system) can then do an opposite operation, check which flags are set, and act accordingly.

We can create a very simple example in code to show how this works in practice (you can simply run this in the Rust playground or create a new empty project for throwaway experiments such as this):

```rust
fn main() {
    let bitflag_a: i32 = 1 << 31;
    let bitflag_b: i32 = 0x1;
    let bitmask: i32 = bitflag_a | bitflag_b;
    println!("{bitflag_a:032b}");
    println!("{bitflag_b:032b}");
    println!("{bitmask:032b}");
    check(bitmask);
}

fn check(bitmask: i32) {
    const EPOLLIN: i32 = 0x1;
    const EPOLLET: i32 = 1 << 31;
    const EPOLLONESHOT: i32 = 0x40000000;

    let read = bitmask & EPOLLIN != 0;
    let et = bitmask & EPOLLET != 0;
    let oneshot = bitmask & EPOLLONESHOT != 0;

    println!("read_event? {read}, edge_triggered: {et}, oneshot?: {oneshot}")
}
```

This code will output the following:

```
10000000000000000000000000000000
00000000000000000000000000000001
```

```
10000000000000000000000000000001
read_event? true, edge_triggered: true, oneshot?: false
```

The next topic we will introduce in this chapter is the concept of edge-triggered events, which probably need some explanation.

Level-triggered versus edge-triggered events

In a perfect world, we wouldn't need to discuss this, but when working with epoll, it's almost impossible to avoid having to know about the difference. It's not obvious by reading the documentation, especially not if you haven't had previous experience with these terms before. The interesting part of this is that it allows us to create a parallel between how events are handled in epoll and how events are handled at the hardware level.

epoll can notify events in a **level-triggered** or **edge-triggered** mode. If your main experience is programming in high-level languages, this must sound very obscure (it did to me when I first learned about it), but bear with me. In the `events` bitmask on the `Event` struct, we set the `EPOLLET` flag to get notified in edge-triggered mode (the default if you specify nothing is level-triggered).

This way of modeling event notification and event handling has a lot of similarities to how computers handle interrupts.

Level-triggered means that the answer to the question "Has an event happened" is true as long as the electrical signal on an interrupt line is reported as high. If we translate this to our example, *a read event has occurred as long as there is data in the buffer associated with the file handle*.

When handling interrupts, you would clear the interrupt by servicing whatever hardware caused it, or you could mask the interrupt, which simply disables interrupts on that line until it's explicitly unmasked later on.

In our example, we clear the *interrupt* by draining all the data in the buffer by reading it. When the buffer is drained, the answer to our question changes to *false*.

When using epoll in its default mode, which is level-triggered, we can encounter a case where we get multiple notifications on the same event since we haven't had time to drain the buffer yet (remember, as long as there is data in the buffer, epoll will notify you over and over again). This is especially apparent when we have one thread that reports events and then delegates the task of handling the event (reading from the stream) to other worker threads since epoll will happily report that an event is ready even though we're in the process of handling it.

To remedy this, epoll has a flag named `EPOLLONESHOT`.

EPOLLONESHOT tells epoll that once we receive an event on this file descriptor, it should disable the file descriptor in the interest list. It won't remove it, but we won't get any more notifications on that file descriptor unless we explicitly reactivate it by calling `epoll_ctl` with the `EPOLL_CTL_MOD` argument and a new bitmask.

If we didn't add this flag, the following could happen: if *thread 1* is the thread where we call `epoll_wait`, then once it receives a notification about a read event, it starts a task in *thread 2* to read from that file descriptor, and then calls `epoll_wait` again to get notifications on new events. In this case, the call to `epoll_wait` would return again and tell us that data is ready on the same file descriptor since we haven't had the time to drain the buffer on that file descriptor yet. We know that the task is taken care of by `thread 2`, but we still get a notification. Without additional synchronization and logic, we could end up giving the task of reading from the same file descriptor to *thread 3*, which could cause problems that are quite hard to debug.

Using EPOLLONESHOT solves this problem since *thread 2* will have to reactivate the file descriptor in the event queue once it's done handling its task, thereby telling our epoll queue that it's finished with it and that we are interested in getting notifications on that file descriptor again.

To go back to our original analogy of hardware interrupts, EPOLLONESHOT could be thought of as masking an interrupt. You haven't actually cleared the source of the event notification yet, but you don't want further notifications until you've done that and explicitly unmask it. In epoll, the EPOLLONESHOT flag will disable notifications on the file descriptor until you explicitly enable it by calling `epoll_ctl` with the op argument set to `EPOLL_CTL_MOD`.

Edge-triggered means that the answer to the question "Has an event happened" is true only if the electrical signal has *changed* from low to high. If we translate this to our example: a read event has occurred when the buffer has changed from *having no data* to *having data*. As long as there is data in the buffer, no new events will be reported. You still handle the event by draining all the data from the socket, but you won't get a new notification until the buffer is fully drained and then filled with new data.

Edge-triggered mode also comes with some pitfalls. The biggest one is that if you don't drain the buffer properly, you will never receive a notification on that file handle again.

Lines in red/dotted lines indicates when the answer to the question «has event happened» equals true.

Note that edge-triggered events could potentially trigger on a falling edge (from high-to-low), but for the purpose of explaining epoll we only consider events triggered by a rising edge to get an intuitive understanding. The same goes for level-triggered events.

Edge-triggered (rising edge) | **Level-triggered (high level)**

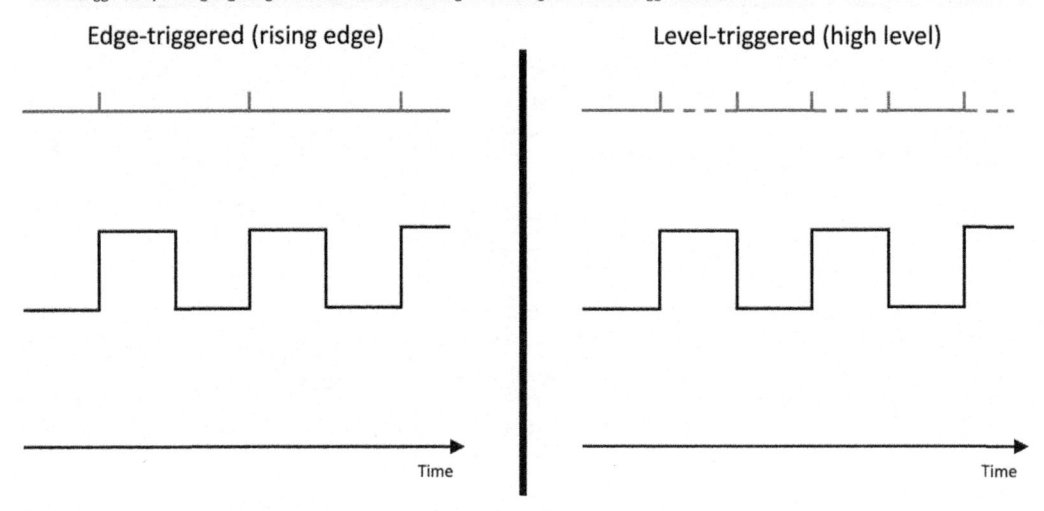

Figure 4.1 – Edge-triggered versus level-triggered events

mio doesn't, at the time of writing, support `EPOLLONESHOT` and uses epoll in an edge-triggered mode, which we will do as well in our example.

> **What about waiting on epoll_wait in multiple threads?**
>
> As long as we only have one `Poll` instance, we avoid the problems and subtleties of having multiple threads calling `epoll_wait` on the same epoll instance. Using level-triggered events will wake up all threads that are waiting in the `epoll_wait` call, causing all of them to try to handle the event (this is often referred to as the problem of the thundering heard). epoll has another flag you can set, called `EPOLLEXCLUSIVE`, that solves this issue. Events that are set to be edge-triggered will only wake up one of the threads blocking in `epoll_wait` by default and avoid this issue.
>
> Since we only use one `Poll` instance from a single thread, this will not be an issue for us.

I know and understand that this sounds very complex. The general concept of event queues is rather simple, but the details can get a bit complex. That said, epoll is one of the most complex APIs in my experience since the API has clearly been evolving over time to adapt the original design to suit modern requirements, and there is really no easy way to actually use and understand it correctly without covering at least the topics we covered here.

One word of comfort here is that both kqueue and IOCP have APIs that are easier to understand. There is also the fact that Unix has a new asynchronous I/O interface called `io_uring` that will be more and more and more common in the future.

Now that we've covered the hard part of this chapter and gotten a high-level overview of how epoll works, it's time to implement our mio-inspired API in `poll.rs`.

The Poll module

If you haven't written or copied the code we presented in the *Design and introduction to epoll* section, it's time to do it now. We'll implement all the functions where we just had `todo!()` earlier.

We start by implementing the methods on our `Poll` struct. First up is opening the `impl Poll` block and implementing the `new` function:

ch04/a-epoll/src/poll.rs

```rust
impl Poll {
    pub fn new() -> Result<Self> {
        let res = unsafe { ffi::epoll_create(1) };
        if res < 0 {
            return Err(io::Error::last_os_error());
        }

        Ok(Self {
            registry: Registry { raw_fd: res },
        })
    }
```

Given the thorough introduction to epoll in the *The ffi module* section, this should be pretty straightforward. We call `ffi::epoll_create` with an argument of 1 (remember, the argument is ignored but must have a non-zero value). If we get any errors, we ask the operating system to report the last error for our process and return that. If the call succeeds, we return a new `Poll` instance that simply wraps around our registry that holds the epoll file descriptor.

Next up is our registry method, which simply hands out a reference to the inner `Registry` struct:

ch04/a-epoll/src/poll.rs

```rust
    pub fn registry(&self) -> &Registry {
        &self.registry
    }
```

The last method on `Poll` is the most interesting one. It's the `poll` function, which will park the current thread and tell the operating system to wake it up when an event has happened on a source we're tracking, or the timeout has elapsed, whichever comes first. We also close the `impl Poll` block here:

ch04/a-epoll/src/poll.rs

```rust
    pub fn poll(&mut self, events: &mut Events, timeout: Option<i32>) -> Result<()> {
        let fd = self.registry.raw_fd;
        let timeout = timeout.unwrap_or(-1);
        let max_events = events.capacity() as i32;
        let res = unsafe { ffi::epoll_wait(fd, events.as_mut_ptr(), max_events, timeout) };

        if res < 0 {
            return Err(io::Error::last_os_error());
        };

        unsafe { events.set_len(res as usize) };
        Ok(())
    }
}
```

The first thing we do is to get the raw file descriptor for the event queue and store it in the `fd` variable.

Next is our `timeout`. If it's `Some`, we unwrap that value, and if it's `None`, we set it to `-1`, which is the value that tells the operating system that we want to block until an event occurs even though that might never happen.

At the top of the file, we defined `Events` as a type alias for `Vec<ffi::Event>`, so the next thing we do is to get the capacity of that `Vec`. It's important that we don't rely on `Vec::len` since that reports how many items we have in the `Vec`. `Vec::capacity` reports the space we've allocated and that's what we're after.

Next up is the call to `ffi::epoll_wait`. This call will return successfully if it has a value of 0 or larger, telling us how many events have occurred.

> **Note**
> We would get a value of 0 if a timeout elapses before an event has happened.

The last thing we do is to make an unsafe call to `events.set_len(res as usize)`. This function is unsafe since we could potentially set the length so that we would access memory that's not been initialized yet in safe Rust. We know from the guarantee the operating system gives us that the number of events it returns is pointing to valid data in our `Vec`, so this is safe in our case.

Next up is our `Registry` struct. We will only implement one method, called `register`, and lastly, we'll implement the `Drop` trait for it, closing the epoll instance:

ch04/a-epoll/src/poll.rs

```rust
impl Registry {
    pub fn register(&self, source: &TcpStream, token: usize, interests: i32) -> Result<()>
    {
        let mut event = ffi::Event {
            events: interests as u32,
            epoll_data: token,
        };

        let op = ffi::EPOLL_CTL_ADD;
        let res = unsafe {
            ffi::epoll_ctl(self.raw_fd, op, source.as_raw_fd(), &mut event)
        };

        if res < 0 {
            return Err(io::Error::last_os_error());
        }
        Ok(())
    }
}
```

The register function takes a `&TcpStream` as a source, a token of type `usize`, and a bitmask named `interests`, which is of type `i32`.

> **Note**
> This is where mio does things differently. The source argument is specific to each platform. Instead of having the implementation of register on `Registry`, it's handled in a platform-specific way in the source argument it receives.

The first thing we do is to create an `ffi::Event` object. The `events` field is simply set to the bitmask we received and named `interests`, and `epoll_data` is set to the value we passed in the `token` argument.

The operation we want to perform on the epoll queue is adding interest in events on a new file descriptor. Therefore, we set the op argument to the ffi::EPOLL_CTL_ADD constant value.

Next up is the call to ffi::epoll_ctl. We pass in the file descriptor to the epoll instance first, then we pass in the op argument to indicate what kind of operation we want to perform. The last two arguments are the file descriptor we want the queue to track and the Event object we created to indicate what kind of events we're interested in getting notifications for.

The last part of the function body is simply the error handling, which should be familiar by now.

The last part of poll.rs is the Drop implementation for Registry:

ch04/a-epoll/src/poll.rs

```
impl Drop for Registry {
    fn drop(&mut self) {
        let res = unsafe { ffi::close(self.raw_fd) };
        if res < 0 {
            let err = io::Error::last_os_error();
            eprintln!("ERROR: {err:?}");
        }
    }
}
```

The Drop implementation simply calls ffi::close on the epoll file descriptor. Adding a panic to drop is rarely a good idea since drop can be called within a panic already, which will cause the process to simply abort. mio logs errors if they occur in its Drop implementation but doesn't handle them in any other way. For our simple example, we'll just print the error so we can see if anything goes wrong since we don't implement any kind of logging here.

The last part is the code for running our example, and that leads us to main.rs.

The main program

Let's see how it all works in practice. Make sure that delayserver is up and running, because we'll need it for these examples to work.

The goal is to send a set of requests to delayserver with varying delays and then use epoll to wait for the responses. Therefore, we'll only use epoll to track read events in this example. The program doesn't do much more than that for now.

The first thing we do is to make sure our `main.rs` file is set up correctly:

ch04/a-epoll/src/main.rs

```
use std::{io::{self, Read, Result, Write}, net::TcpStream};


use ffi::Event;
use poll::Poll;


mod ffi;
mod poll;
```

We import a few types from our own crate and from the standard library, which we'll need going forward, as well as declaring our two modules.

We'll be working directly with `TcpStream`s in this example, and that means that we'll have to format the HTTP requests we make to our `delayserver` ourselves.

The server will accept `GET` requests, so we create a small helper function to format a valid HTTP GET request for us:

ch04/a-epoll/src/main.rs

```
fn get_req(path: &str) -> Vec<u8> {
    format!(
        "GET {path} HTTP/1.1\r\n\
         Host: localhost\r\n\
         Connection: close\r\n\
         \r\n"
    )
}
```

The preceding code simply takes a path as an input argument and formats a valid GET request with it. The *path* is the part of the URL after the scheme and host. In our case, the path would be everything in bold in the following URL: http://localhost:8080/**2000/hello-world**.

Next up is our `main` function. It's divided into two parts:

- Setup and sending requests
- Wait and handle incoming events

The first part of the `main` function looks like this:

```
fn main() -> Result<()> {
    let mut poll = Poll::new()?;
    let n_events = 5;

    let mut streams = vec![];
    let addr = "localhost:8080";

    for i in 0..n_events {
        let delay = (n_events - i) * 1000;
        let url_path = format!("/{delay}/request-{i}");
        let request = get_req(&url_path);
        let mut stream = std::net::TcpStream::connect(addr)?;
        stream.set_nonblocking(true)?;

        stream.write_all(request.as_bytes())?;
        poll.registry()
            .register(&stream, i, ffi::EPOLLIN | ffi::EPOLLET)?;

        streams.push(stream);
    }
}
```

The first thing we do is to create a new `Poll` instance. We also specify what number of events we want to create and handle in our example.

The next step is creating a variable to hold a collection of `Vec<TcpStream>` objects.

We also store the address to our local `delayserver` in a variable called `addr`.

The next part is where we create a set of requests that we issue to our `delayserver`, which will eventually respond to us. For each request, we expect a read event to happen sometime later on in the `TcpStream` we sent the request on.

The first thing we do in the loop is set the delay time in milliseconds. Setting the delay to `(n_events - i) * 1000` simply sets the first request we make to have the longest timeout, so we should expect the responses to arrive in the reverse order from which they were sent.

> **Note**
> For simplicity, we use the index the event will have in the `streams` collection as its ID. This ID will be the same as the `i` variable in our loop. For example, in the first loop, `i` will be 0; it will also be the first stream to be pushed to our `streams` collection, so the index will be 0 as well. We therefore use 0 as the identification for this stream/event throughout since retrieving the `TcpStream` associated with this event will be as simple as indexing to that location in the `streams` collection.

The next line, `format!("/{delay}/request-{i}")`, formats the *path* for our GET request. We set the timeout as described previously, and we also set a message where we store the identifier for this event, `i`, so we can track this event on the server side as well.

Next up is creating a `TcpStream`. You've probably noticed that the `TcpStream` in Rust doesn't accept `&str` but an argument that implements the `ToSocketAddrs` trait. This trait is implemented for `&str` already, so that's why we can simply write it like we do in this example.

Before `Tcpstream::connect` actually opens a socket, it will try to parse the address we pass in as an IP address. If it fails, it will parse it as a domain address and a port number, and then ask the operating system to do a DNS lookup for that address, which it then can use to actually connect to our server. So, you see, there is potentially quite a bit going on when we do a simple connection.

You probably remember that we discussed some of the nuances of the DNS lookup earlier and the fact that such a call could either be very fast since the operating system already has the information stored in memory or block while waiting for a response from the DNS server. This is a potential downside if you use `TcpStream` from the standard library if you want full control over the entire process.

> **TcpStream in Rust and Nagle's algorithm**
>
> Here is a little fact for you (I originally intended to call it a "fun fact," but realized that's stretching the concept of "fun" just a little too far!). In Rust's `TcpStream`, and, more importantly, most APIs that aim to mimic the standard library's `TcpStream` such as mio or Tokio, the stream is created with the `TCP_NODELAY` flag set to `false`. In practice, this means that Nagle's algorithm is used, which can cause some issues with latency outliers and possibly reduced throughput on some workloads.
>
> Nagle's algorithm is an algorithm that aims to reduce network congestion by pooling small network packages together. If you look at non-blocking I/O implementations in other languages, many, if not most, disable this algorithm by default. This is not the case in most Rust implementations and is worth being aware of. You can disable it by simply calling `TcpStream::set_nodelay(true)`. If you try to create your own async library or rely on Tokio/mio, and observe lower throughput than expected or latency problems, it's worth checking whether this flag is set to `true` or not.

To continue with the code, the next step is setting `TcpStream` to non-blocking by calling `TcpStream::set_nonblocking(true)`.

After that, we write our request to the server before we register interest in read events by setting the `EPOLLIN` flag bit in the `interests` bitmask.

For each iteration, we push the stream to the end of our `streams` collection.

The next part of the `main` function is handling incoming events.

Let's take a look at the last part of our `main` function:

```
let mut handled_events = 0;
    while handled_events < n_events {
        let mut events = Vec::with_capacity(10);
        poll.poll(&mut events, None)?;

        if events.is_empty() {
            println!("TIMEOUT (OR SPURIOUS EVENT NOTIFICATION)");
            continue;
        }

        handled_events += handle_events(&events, &mut streams)?;
    }

    println!("FINISHED");
    Ok(())
}
```

The first thing we do is create a variable called `handled_events` to track how many events we have handled.

Next is our event loop. We loop as long as the handled events are less than the number of events we expect. Once all events are handled, we exit the loop.

Inside the loop, we create a `Vec<Event>` with the capacity to store 10 events. It's important that we create this using `Vec::with_capacity` since the operating system will assume that we pass it memory that we've allocated. We could choose any number of events here and it would work just fine, but setting too low a number would limit how many events the operating system could notify us about on each wakeup.

Next is our blocking call to `Poll::poll`. As you know, this will actually tell the operating system to park our thread and wake us up when an event has occurred.

If we're woken up, but there are no events in the list, it's either a timeout or a spurious event (which could happen, so we need a way to check whether a timeout has actually elapsed if that's important to us). If that's the case, we simply call `Poll::poll` once more.

If there are events to be handled, we pass these on to the `handle_events` function together with a mutable reference to our `streams` collection.

The last part of `main` is simply to write `FINISHED` to the console to let us know we exited `main` at that point.

The last bit of code in this chapter is the `handle_events` function. This function takes two arguments, a slice of `Event` structs and a mutable slice of `TcpStream` objects.

Let's take a look at the code before we explain it:

```rust
fn handle_events(events: &[Event], streams: &mut [TcpStream]) -> Result<usize> {
    let mut handled_events = 0;
    for event in events {
        let index = event.token();
        let mut data = vec![0u8; 4096];

        loop {
            match streams[index].read(&mut data) {
                Ok(n) if n == 0 => {
                    handled_events += 1;
                    break;
                }
                Ok(n) => {
                    let txt = String::from_utf8_lossy(&data[..n]);

                    println!("RECEIVED: {:?}", event);
                    println!("{txt}\n------\n");
                }
                // Not ready to read in a non-blocking manner. This could
                // happen even if the event was reported as ready
                Err(e) if e.kind() == io::ErrorKind::WouldBlock => break,
                Err(e) => return Err(e),
            }
        }
    }

    Ok(handled_events)
}
```

The first thing we do is to create a variable, `handled_events`, to track how many events we consider handled on each wakeup. The next step is looping through the events we received.

In the loop, we retrieve the *token* that identifies which `TcpStream` we received an event for. As we explained earlier in this example, this *token* is the same as the index for that particular stream in the `streams` collection, so we can simply use it to index into our `streams` collection and retrieve the right `TcpStream`.

Before we start reading data, we create a buffer with a size of 4,096 bytes (you can, of course, allocate a larger or smaller buffer for this if you want to).

We create a loop since we might need to call `read` multiple times to be sure that we've actually drained the buffer. *Remember how important it is to fully drain the buffer when using epoll in edge-triggered mode.*

We match on the result of calling `TcpStream::read` since we want to take different actions based on the result:

- If we get `Ok(n)` and the value is 0, we've drained the buffer; we consider the event as handled and break out of the loop.
- If we get `Ok(n)` with a value larger than 0, we read the data to a `String` and print it out with some formatting. We do not break out of the loop yet since we have to call `read` until 0 is returned (or an error) to be sure that we've drained the buffers fully.
- If we get `Err` and the error is of the `io::ErrorKind::WouldBlock` type, we simply break out of the loop. We don't consider the event handled yet since `WouldBlock` indicates that the data transfer is not complete, but there is no data ready right now.
- If we get any other error, we simply return that error and consider it a failure.

> **Note**
> There is one more error condition you'd normally want to cover, and that is `io::ErrorKind::Interrupted`. Reading from a stream could be interrupted by a signal from the operating system. This should be expected and probably not considered a failure. The way to handle this is the same as what we do when we get an error of the `WouldBlock` type.

If the `read` operation is successful, we return the number of events handled.

> **Be careful with using TcpStream::read_to_end**
> You should be careful with using `TcpStream::read_to_end` or any other function that fully drains the buffer for you when using non-blocking buffers. If you get an error of the `io::WouldBlock` type, it will report that as an error even though you had several successful reads before you got that error. You have no way of knowing how much data you read successfully other than observing any changes to the `&mut Vec` you passed in.

The main program

Now, if we run our program, we should get the following output:

```
RECEIVED: Event { events: 1, epoll_data: 4 }
HTTP/1.1 200 OK
content-length: 9
connection: close
content-type: text/plain; charset=utf-8
date: Wed, 04 Oct 2023 15:29:09 GMT

request-4
------

RECEIVED: Event { events: 1, epoll_data: 3 }
HTTP/1.1 200 OK
content-length: 9
connection: close
content-type: text/plain; charset=utf-8
date: Wed, 04 Oct 2023 15:29:10 GMT

request-3
------

RECEIVED: Event { events: 1, epoll_data: 2 }
HTTP/1.1 200 OK
content-length: 9
connection: close
content-type: text/plain; charset=utf-8
date: Wed, 04 Oct 2023 15:29:11 GMT

request-2
------

RECEIVED: Event { events: 1, epoll_data: 1 }
HTTP/1.1 200 OK
content-length: 9
connection: close
content-type: text/plain; charset=utf-8
date: Wed, 04 Oct 2023 15:29:12 GMT

request-1
------

RECEIVED: Event { events: 1, epoll_data: 0 }
HTTP/1.1 200 OK
```

```
content-length: 9
connection: close
content-type: text/plain; charset=utf-8
date: Wed, 04 Oct 2023 15:29:13 GMT

request-0
------

FINISHED
```

As you see, the responses are sent in reverse order. You can easily confirm this by looking at the output on the terminal on running the `delayserver` instance. The output should look like this:

```
#1 - 5000ms: request-0
#2 - 4000ms: request-1
#3 - 3000ms: request-2
#4 - 2000ms: request-3
#5 - 1000ms: request-4
```

The ordering might be different sometimes as the server receives them almost simultaneously, and can choose to handle them in a slightly different order.

Say we track events on the stream with ID 4:

1. In `send_requests`, we assigned the ID 4 to the last stream we created.
2. Socket 4 sends a request to `delayserver`, setting a delay of 1,000 ms and a message of `request-4` so we can identify it on the server side.
3. We register socket 4 with the event queue, making sure to set the `epoll_data` field to 4 so we can identify on what stream the event occurred.
4. `delayserver` receives that request and delays the response for 1,000 ms before it sends an `HTTP/1.1 200 OK` response back, together with the message we originally sent.
5. `epoll_wait` wakes up, notifying us that an event is ready. In the `epoll_data` field of the `Event` struct, we get back the same data that we passed in when registering the event. This tells us that it was an event on stream 4 that occurred.
6. We then read data from stream 4 and print it out.

In this example, we've kept things at a very low level even though we used the standard library to handle the intricacies of establishing a connection. Even though you've actually made a raw HTTP request to your own local server, you've set up an epoll instance to track events on a `TcpStream` and you've used epoll and syscalls to handle incoming events.

That's no small feat – congratulations!

Before we leave this example, I wanted to point out how few changes we need to make to have our example use mio as the event loop instead of the one we created.

In the repository under `ch04/b-epoll-mio`, you'll see an example where we do the exact same thing using mio instead. It only requires importing a few types from mio instead of our own modules and making *only five minor changes to our code*!

Not only have you replicated what mio does, but you pretty much know how to use mio to create an event loop as well!

Summary

The concept of epoll, kqueue, and IOCP is pretty simple at a high level, but the devil is in the details. It's just not that easy to understand and get it working correctly. Even programmers who work on these things will often specialize in one platform (epoll/kqueue or Windows). It's rare that one person will know all the intricacies of all platforms, and you could probably write a whole book about this subject alone.

If we summarize what you've learned and got firsthand experience with in this chapter, the list is quite impressive:

- You learned a lot about how mio is designed, enabling you to go to that repository and know what to look for and how to get started on that code base much easier than before reading this chapter
- You learned a lot about making syscalls on Linux
- You created an epoll instance, registered events with it, and handled those events
- You learned quite a bit about how epoll is designed and its API
- You learned about edge-triggering and level-triggering, which are extremely low-level, but useful, concepts to have an understanding of outside the context of epoll as well
- You made a raw HTTP request
- You saw how non-blocking sockets behave and how error codes reported by the operating system can be a way of communicating certain conditions that you're expected to handle
- You learned that not all I/O is equally "blocking" by looking at DNS resolution and file I/O

That's pretty good for a single chapter, I think!

If you dive deeper into the topics we covered here, you'll soon realize that there are gotchas and rabbit holes everywhere – especially if you expand this example to abstract over epoll, kqueue, and IOCP. You'll probably end up reading Linus Torvald's emails on how edge-triggered mode was supposed to work on pipes before you know it.

At least you now have a good foundation for further exploration. You can expand on our simple example and create a proper event loop that handles connecting, writing, timeouts, and scheduling; you can dive deeper into kqueue and IOCP by looking at how `mio` solves that problem; or you can be happy that you don't have to directly deal with it again and appreciate the effort that went into libraries such as `mio`, `polling`, and `libuv`.

By this point, we've gained a lot of knowledge about the basic building blocks of asynchronous programming, so it's time to start exploring how different programming languages create abstractions over asynchronous operations and use these building blocks to give us as programmers efficient, expressive, and productive ways to write our asynchronous programs.

First off is one of my favorite examples, where we'll look into how fibers (or green threads) work by implementing them ourselves.

You've earned a break now. Yeah, go on, the next chapter can wait. Get a cup of tea or coffee and reset so you can start the next chapter with a fresh mind. I promise it will be both fun and interesting.

5
Creating Our Own Fibers

In this chapter, we take a deep dive into a very popular way of handling concurrency. There is no better way of getting a fundamental understanding of the subject than doing it yourself. Fortunately, even though the topic is a little complex, we only need around 200 lines of code to get a fully working example in the end.

What makes the topic complex is that it requires quite a bit of fundamental understanding of how CPUs, operating systems, and assembly work. This complexity is also what makes this topic so interesting. If you explore and work through this example in detail, you will be rewarded with an eye-opening understanding of topics you might only have heard about or only have a rudimentary understanding of. You will also get the chance to get to know a few aspects of the Rust language that you haven't seen before, expanding your knowledge of both Rust and programming in general.

We start off by introducing a little background knowledge that we need before we start writing code. Once we have that in place, we'll start with some small examples that will allow us to show and discuss the most technical and difficult parts of our example in detail so we can introduce the topics gradually. Lastly, we'll build on the knowledge we've gained and create our main example, which is a working example of fibers implemented in Rust.

As a bonus, you'll get two expanded versions of the example in the repository to inspire you to go on and change, adapt, and build upon what we've created to make it your own.

I'll list the main topics here so you can refer to them later on:

- How to use the repository alongside the book
- Background information
- An example we can build upon
- The stack
- Implementing our own fibers
- Final thoughts

> **Note**
> In this chapter, we'll use the terms "fibers" and "green threads" to refer to this exact implementation of stackful coroutines. The term "threads" in this chapter, which is used in the code we write, will refer to the green threads/fibers we implement in our example and not OS threads.

Technical requirements

To run the examples, you will need a computer running on a CPU using the x86-64 instruction set. Most popular desktop, server, and laptop CPUs out there today use this instruction set, as do most modern CPUs from Intel and AMD (which are most CPU models from these manufacturers produced in the last 10–15 years).

One caveat is that the modern M-series Macs use the ARM ISA (instruction set), which won't be compatible with the examples we write here. However, older Intel-based Macs do, so you should be able to use a Mac to follow along if you don't have the latest version.

If you don't have a computer using this instruction set available, you have a few options to install Rust and run the examples:

- Mac users on M-series chips can use Rosetta (which ships with newer MacOS versions) and get the examples working with just four simple steps. You'll find the instructions in the repository under `ch05/How-to-MacOS-M.md`.
- `https://mac.getutm.app/Rent` (some even have a free layer) a remote server running Linux on x86-64. I have experience with Linode's offering (`https://www.linode.com/`), but there are many more options out there.

To follow along with the examples in the book, you also need a Unix-based operating system. The example code will work natively on any Linux and BSD operating system (such as Ubuntu or macOS) as long as it's running on an x86-64 CPU.

If you're on Windows, there is a version of the example in the repository that works natively with Windows too, but to follow along with the book, my clear recommendation is to set up **Windows Subsystem for Linux** (**WSL**) (`https://learn.microsoft.com/en-us/windows/wsl/install`), install Rust, and follow along using Rust on WSL.

I personally use VS Code as my editor, as it makes it very easy to switch between using a Linux version on WSL and Windows—simply press *Ctrl* + *Shift* + *P* and search for the `Reopen folder in WSL`.

How to use the repository alongside the book

The recommended way to read this chapter is to have the repository open alongside the book. In the repository, you'll find three different folders that correspond to the examples we go through in this chapter:

- `ch05/a-stack swap`

- `ch05/b-show-stack`
- `ch05/c-fibers`

In addition, you will get two more examples that I refer to in the book but that should be explored in the repository:

- `ch05/d-fibers-closure`: This is an extended version of the first example that might inspire you to do more complex things yourself. The example tries to mimic the API used in the Rust standard library using `std::thread::spawn`.
- `ch05/e-fibers-windows`: This is a version of the example that we go through in this book that works on both Unix-based systems and Windows. There is a quite detailed explanation in the README of the changes we make for the example work on Windows. I consider this recommended reading if you want to dive deeper into the topic, but it's not important to understand the main concepts we go through in this chapter.

Background information

We are going to interfere with and control the CPU directly. This is not very portable since there are many kinds of CPUs out there. While the overall implementation will be the same, there is a small but important part of the implementation that will be very specific to the CPU architecture we're programming for. Another aspect that limits the portability of our code is that operating systems have different ABIs that we need to adhere to, and those same pieces of code will have to change based on the different ABIs. Let's explain exactly what we mean here before we go further so we know we're on the same page.

Instruction sets, hardware architectures, and ABIs

Okay, before we start, we need to know the differences between an **application binary interface** (**ABI**), a **CPU architecture**, and an **instruction set architecture** (**ISA**). We need this to write our own stack and make the CPU jump over to it. Fortunately, while this might sound complex, we only need to know a few specific things for our example to run. The information presented here is useful in many more circumstances than just our example, so it's worthwhile to cover it in some detail.

An ISA describes an abstract model of a CPU that defines how the CPU is controlled by the software it runs. We often simply refer to this as the *instruction set*, and it defines what instructions the CPU can execute, what registers programmers can use, how the hardware manages memory, etc. Examples of ISAs are **x86-64**, **x86**, and the **ARM ISA** (used in Mac M-series chips).

ISAs are broadly classified into two subgroups, **complex instruction set computers** (**CISC**) and **reduced instruction set computers** (**RISC**), based on their complexity. CISC architectures offer a lot of different instructions that the hardware must know how to execute, resulting in some instructions that are very specialized and rarely used by programs. RISC architectures accept fewer instructions but require some operations to be handled by software that could be directly handled by the hardware in a CISC architecture. The x86-64 instruction set we'll focus on is an example of a CISC architecture.

To add a little complexity (you know, it's not fun if it's too easy), there are different names that refer to the same ISA. For example, the x86-64 instruction set is also referred to as the AMD64 instruction set and the Intel 64 instruction set, so no matter which one you encounter, just know that they refer to the same thing. In our book, we'll simply call it the x86-64 instruction set.

> **Tip**
>
> To find the architecture on your current system, run one of the following commands in your terminal:
>
> On Linux and MacOS: `arch` or `uname -m`
>
> On Windows PowerShell: `$env:PROCESSOR_ARCHITECTURE`
>
> On Windows Command Prompt: `echo %PROCESSOR_ARCHITECTURE%`

The instruction set just defines how a program can interface with the CPU. The concrete implementation of an ISA can vary between different manufacturers, and a specific implementation is referred to as a CPU architecture, such as Intel Core processors. However, in practice, these terms are often used interchangeably since they all perform the same functions from a programmer's perspective and there is seldom a need to target a specific implementation of an ISA.

The ISA specifies the minimum set of instructions the CPU must be able to execute. Over time, there have been extensions to this instruction set, such as **Streaming SIMD Extensions** (**SSE**), that add more instructions and registers that programmers can take advantage of.

For the examples in this chapter, we will target the x86-64 ISA, a popular architecture used in most desktop computers and servers today.

So, we know that a processor architecture presents an interface that programmers can use. Operating system implementors use this infrastructure to create operating systems.

Operating systems such as Windows and Linux define an ABI that specifies a set of rules that the programmer has to adhere to for their programs to work correctly on that platform. Examples of operating system ABI's are **System V ABI** (Linux) and **Win64** (Windows). The ABI specifies how the operating system expects a stack to be set up, how you should call a function, how you create a file that will load and run as a program, the name of the function that will be called once the program has loaded, etc.

A very important part of the ABI that operating systems must specify is its **calling convention**. The calling convention defines how the stack is used and how functions are called.

Let's illustrate this with an example of how Linux and Windows handle arguments to a function on x86-64; for example, a function with a signature such as `fn foo(a: i64, b: i64)`.

The x86-64 ISA defines 16 general-purpose registers. These are registers the CPU provides for programmers to use for whatever they see fit. Note that *programmers* here include the ones that write the operating system, and they can lay additional restrictions on what registers you can use for what when you create a program to run on their operating system. In our specific example, Windows and Unix-based systems have different requirements for where to place the arguments for a function:

- Linux specifies that a function that takes two arguments should place the first argument to the function in the `rdi` register and the second one in the `rsi` register
- Windows requires that the first two arguments be passed in the registers `rcx` and `rdx`

This is just one of many ways in which a program that is written for one platform won't work on another. Usually, these details are the concern of compiler developers, and the compiler will handle the different calling conventions when you compile for a specific platform.

So to sum it up, CPUs implement an instruction set. The instruction set defines what instructions the CPU can execute and the infrastructure it should provide to programmers (such as registers). An operating system uses this infrastructure in different ways, and it provides additional rules that a programmer must obey to run their program correctly on their platform. Most of the time, the only programmers that need to care about these details are the ones who write operating systems or compilers. However, when we write low-level code ourselves, we need to know about the ISA *and* the OS ABI to have our code work correctly.

Since we need to write this kind of code to implement our own fibers/green threads, we must potentially write different code for each OS ABI/ISA combination that exists. That means one for Windows/x86-64, one for Windows/ARM, one for MacOS/x86-64, one for Macos/M, etc.

As you understand, this is also one major contributor to the complexity of using fibers/green threads for handling concurrency. It has a lot of advantages once it's correctly implemented for an ISA/OS ABI combination, but it requires a lot of work to get it right.

For the purpose of the examples in this book, we will only focus on one such combination: the System V ABI for x86-64.

> Note!
> In the accompanying repository, you will find a version of the main example for this chapter for Windows x86-64. The changes we have to make to make it work on Windows are explained in the README.

The System V ABI for x86-64

As mentioned earlier, this architecture of the CPU features a set of 16 general-purpose 64-bit registers, 16 SSE registers with 128-bit width, and 8 floating point registers with 80-bit width:

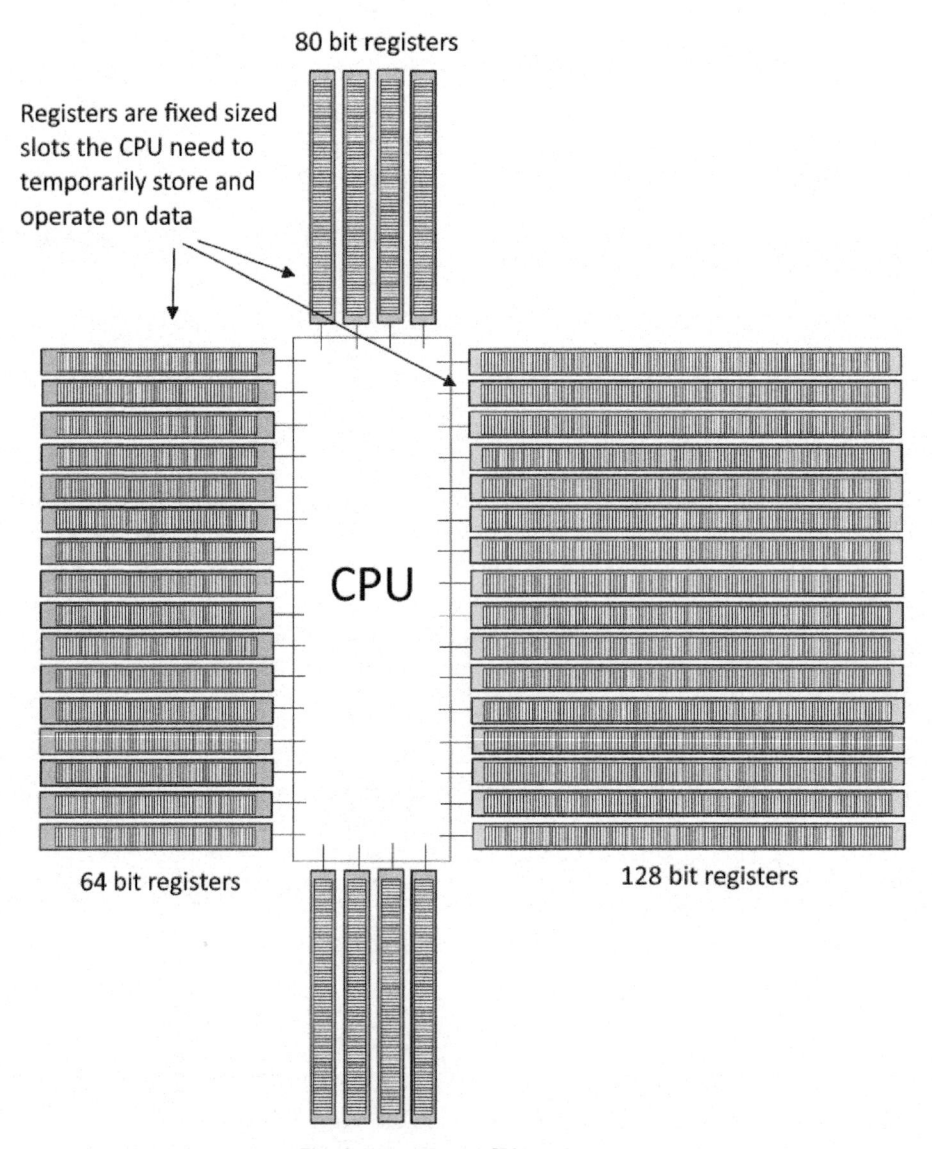

Figure 5.1 – x86-64 CPU registers

There are architectures that build upon this base and extend it, such as the Intel **Advanced Vector Extensions** (**AVX**), which provide an additional 16 registers of 256 bits in width. Let's take a look at a page from the System V ABI specification:

Background information   101

Register	Usage	callee saved
%rax	tempory register, with variable arguments passes information about the number of vector registers used; 1st return register	No
%rbx	callee-saved register	Yes
%rcx	used to pass 4th integer argument to functions	No
%rdx	used to pass 3rd argument to functions; 2nd return register	No
%rsp	stack pointer	Yes
%rbp	callee-saved register; optionally used a frame pointer	Yes
%rsi	used to pass 2nd argument to functions	No
%rdi	used to pass 1st argument to functions	No
%r8	used to pass 5th argument to functions	No
%r9	used to pass 6th argument to functions	No
%r10	temporay register, used for passing a funtion's statis chain pointer	No
%r11	temporary register	No
%r12-r14	callee-saved registers	Yes
%r15	callee-saved register; optionally used as GOT base pointer	Yes
%xmm0-%xmm1	used to pass and return floating point arguments	No
%xmm2-%xmm7	used to pass floating point arguments	No
%xmm8-%xmm15	temporary registers	No
%mm0-%mm7	temporary registers	No
%k0-%k7	temporary registers	No
%st0, %st1	temporary registers, used to return long double arguments	No
%st2, %st7	temporary registers	No
%fs	Reserved for system (as thread specific data register)	No
mscsr	SSE2 control and status word	partial
x87 SW	x87 status word	No
x87 SW	x87 control word	Yes

Figure 3.4: Register Usage

Figure 5.2 – Register usage

Figure 5.1 shows an overview of the general-purpose registers in the x86-64 architecture. Out of special interest for us right now are the registers marked as *callee saved*. These are the registers we need to keep track of our context across function calls. It includes the next instructions to run, the base pointer, the stack pointer, and so on. While the registers themselves are defined by the ISA, the rules on what is considered callee saved are defined by the System V ABI. We'll get to know this more in detail later.

> **Note**
>
> Windows has a slightly different convention. On Windows, the register XMM6:XMM15 is also calle-saved and must be saved and restored if our functions use them. The code we write in this first example runs fine on Windows since we don't really adhere to any ABI yet and just focus on how we'll instruct the CPU to do what we want.

If we want to issue a very specific set of commands to the CPU directly, we need to write small pieces of code in assembly. Fortunately, we only need to know some very basic assembly instructions for our first mission. Specifically, we need to know how to move values to and from registers:

```
mov rax, rsp
```

A quick introduction to Assembly language

First and foremost, **Assembly** language isn't particularly portable since it's the lowest level of human-readable instructions we can write to the CPU, and the instructions we write in assembly will vary from architecture to architecture. Since we will only write assembly targeting the x86-64 architecture going forward, we only need to learn a few instructions for this particular architecture.

Before we go too deep into the specifics, you need to know that there are two popular dialects used in assembly: the **AT&T dialect** and the **Intel dialect**.

The Intel dialect is the standard when writing inline assembly in Rust, but in Rust, we can specify that we want to use the AT&T dialect instead if we want to. Rust has its own take on how to do inline assembly that at first glance looks foreign to anyone used to inline assembly in C. It's well thought through though, and I'll spend a bit of time explaining it in more detail as we go through the code, so both readers with experience with the C-type inline assembly and readers who have no experience should be able to follow along.

> **Note**
> We will use the Intel dialect in our examples.

Assembly has strong backward compatibility guarantees. That's why you will see that the same registers are addressed in different ways. Let's look at the rax register we used as an example as an explanation:

```
rax     # 64 bit register (8 bytes)
eax     # 32 low bits of the "rax" register
ax      # 16 low bits of the "rax" register
ah      # 8 high bits of the "ax" part of the "rax" register
al      # 8 low bits of the "ax" part of the "rax" register
```

As you can see, this is basically like watching the history of CPUs evolve in front of us. Since most CPUs today are 64 bits, we will use the 64-bit versions in our code.

The word size in the assembly also has historical reasons. It stems from the time when the CPU had 16-bit data buses, so a word is 16 bits. This is relevant because you will see many instructions suffixed with q (quad word) or l (long word). So, a movq would mean a move of 4 * 16 bits, which is 64 bits.

A plain mov will use the size of the register you target on most modern assemblers. This is the one you will see most used in both AT&T and the Intel dialect when writing inline assembly, and it's the one we will use in our code.

One more thing to note is that the **stack alignment** on x86-64 is 16 bytes. Just remember this for later.

An example we can build upon

This is a short example where we will create our own stack and make our CPU return out of its current execution context and over to the stack we just created. We will build on these concepts in the following chapters.

Setting up our project

First, let's start a new project by creating a folder named `a-stack-swap`. Enter the new folder and run the following:

```
cargo init
```

> **Tip**
> You can also navigate to the folder called `ch05/a-stack-swap` in the accompanying repository and see the whole example there.

In our `main.rs`, we start by importing the `asm!` macro:

ch05/a-stack-swap/src/main.rs

```rust
use core::arch::asm;
```

Let's set a small stack size of only 48 bytes here so that we can print the stack and look at it before we switch contexts after we get the first example to work:

```rust
const SSIZE: isize = 48;
```

> **Note**
> There seems to be an issue in macOS using such a small stack. The minimum for this code to run is a stack size of 624 bytes. The code works on the Rust Playground, at https://play.rust-lang.org, if you want to follow this exact example (however, you'll need to wait roughly 30 seconds for it to time out due to our loop in the end).

Then let's add a struct that represents our CPU state. We'll only focus on the register that stores the stack pointer for now since that is all we need:

```rust
#[derive(Debug, Default)]
#[repr(C)]
struct ThreadContext {
    rsp: u64,
}
```

In later examples, we will use all the registers marked as *callee saved* in the specification document I linked to. These are the registers described in the System V x86-64 ABI that we'll need to save our context, but right now, we only need one register to make the CPU jump over to our stack.

Note that this needs to be #[repr(C)] because of how we access the data in our assembly. Rust doesn't have a stable language ABI, so there is no way for us to be sure that this will be represented in memory with rsp as the first 8 bytes. C has a stable language ABI and that's exactly what this attribute tells the compiler to use. Granted, our struct only has one field right now, but we will add more later.

For this very simple example, we will define a function that just prints out a message and then loops forever:

```
fn hello() -> ! {
    println!("I LOVE WAKING UP ON A NEW STACK!");
    loop {}
}
```

Next up is our inline assembly, where we switch over to our own stack:

```
unsafe fn gt_switch(new: *const ThreadContext) {
    asm!(
        "mov rsp, [{0} + 0x00]",
        "ret",
        in(reg) new,
    );
}
```

At first glance, you might think that there is nothing special about this piece of code, but let's stop and consider what happens here for a moment.

If we refer back to *Figure 5.1*, we'll see that rsp is the register that stores the **stack pointer** that the CPU uses to figure out the current location on the stack.

Now, what we actually want to do if we want the CPU to swap to a different stack is to set the register for the stack pointer (rsp) to the top of our new stack and set the instruction pointer (rip) on the CPU to point to the address hello.

The instruction pointer, or program counter as it's sometimes called on different architectures, points to the *next* instruction to run. If we can manipulate it directly, the CPU would fetch the instruction pointed to by the rip register and execute the first instruction we wrote in our hello function. The CPU will then push/pop data on the new stack using the address pointed to by the stack pointer and simply leave our old stack as it was.

Now, this is where it gets a little difficult. On the x86-64 instruction set, there is no way for us to manipulate rip directly, so we have to use a little trick.

The first thing we do is set up the new stack and write the address to the function we want to run at a 16-byte offset from the top of the stack (the ABI dictates a 16-byte stack alignment, so the top of our stack frame must start at a 16-byte offset). We'll see how to create a continuous piece of memory a little later, but it's a rather straightforward process.

Next, we pass the address of the first byte in which we stored this address on our newly created stack to the `rsp` register (the address we set to `new.rsp` will point to an address located on our own stack, which in turn is an address that leads to the `hello` function). Got it?

The `ret` keyword transfers program control to what would normally be the return address located on top of the stack frame it's currently in. Since we placed the address to `hello` on our new stack and set the `rsp` register to point to our new stack, the CPU will think `rsp` now points to the return address of the function it's currently running, but instead, it's pointing to a location on our new stack.

When the CPU executes the `ret` instruction it will pop the first value of the stack (which is conveniently the address to our `hello` function) and place that address in the rip register for us. On the next cycle, the CPU will fetch the instructions located at that function pointer and start executing those instructions. Since `rsp` now points to our new stack, it will use that stack going forward.

> **Note**
>
> If you feel a little confused right now, that's very understandable. These details are hard to understand and get right, and it takes time to get comfortable with how it works. As we'll see later in this chapter, there is a little more data that we need to save and restore (right now, we don't have a way to resume the stack we just swapped from), but the technical details on how the stack swap happens are the same as described previously.

Before we explain how we set up the new stack, we'll use this opportunity to go line by line and explain how the inline assembly macro works.

An introduction to Rust inline assembly macro

We'll use the body of our `gt_switch` function as a starting point by going through everything step by step.

If you haven't used inline assembly before, this might look foreign, but we'll use an extended version of the example later to switch contexts, so we need to understand what's going on.

`unsafe` is a keyword that indicates that Rust cannot enforce the safety guarantees in the function we write. Since we are manipulating the CPU directly, this is most definitely unsafe. The function will also take a pointer to an instance of our `ThreadContext` from which we will only read one field:

```
unsafe gt_switch(new: *const ThreadContext)
```

The next line is the asm! macro in the Rust standard library. It will check our syntax and provide an error message if it encounters something that doesn't look like valid Intel (by default) assembly syntax.

```
asm!(
```

The first thing the macro takes as input is the assembly template:

```
"mov rsp, [{0} + 0x00]",
```

This is a simple instruction that moves the value stored at `0x00` offset (that means no offset at all in hex) from the memory location at `{0}` to the `rsp` register. Since the `rsp` register usually stores a pointer to the most recently pushed value on the stack, we effectively push the address to `hello` on top of the current stack so that the CPU will return to that address instead of resuming where it left off in the previous stack frame.

> **Note**
> Note that we don't need to write `[{0} + 0x00]` when we don't want an offset from the memory location. Writing `mov rsp, [{0}]` would be perfectly fine. However, I chose to introduce how we do an offset here as we'll need it later on when we want to access more fields in our `ThreadContext` struct.

Note that the **Intel syntax** is a little backward. You might be tempted to think `mov a, b` means "move what's at `a` to `b`", but the Intel dialect usually dictates that the destination register is first and the source is second.

To make this confusing, this is the opposite of what's typically the case with the **AT&T syntax**, where reading it as "move a to b" is the correct thing to do. This is one of the fundamental differences between the two dialects, and it's useful to be aware of.

You will not see `{0}` used like this in normal assembly. This is part of the assembly template and is a placeholder for the value passed as the first parameter to the macro. You'll notice that this closely matches how string templates are formatted in Rust using `println!` or the like. The parameters are numbered in ascending order starting from 0. We only have one input parameter here, which corresponds to `{0}`.

You don't really have to index your parameters like this; writing `{}` in the correct order would suffice (as you would do using the `println!` macro). However, using an index improves readability and I would strongly recommend doing it that way.

The `[]` basically means "get what's at this memory location", you can think of it as the same as dereferencing a pointer.

Let's try to sum up what we do here with words:

Move what's at the + 0x00 offset from the memory location that {compiler_chosen_general_purpose_register} points to to the rsp register.

The next line is the ret keyword, which instructs the CPU to pop a memory location off the stack and then makes an unconditional jump to that location. In effect, we have hijacked our CPU and made it return to our stack.

Next up is the first non-assembly argument to the asm! macro is our input parameter:

```
in(reg) new,
```

When we write in(reg), we let the compiler decide on a general-purpose register to store the value of new. out(reg) means that the register is an output, so if we write out(reg) new, we need new to be mut so we can write a value to it. You'll also find other versions such as inout and lateout.

Options

The last thing we need to introduce to get a minimal understanding of Rust's inline assembly for now is the options keyword. After the input and output parameters, you'll often see something like options(att_syntax), which specifies that the assembly is written with the AT&T syntax instead of the Intel syntax. Other options include pure, nostack, and several others.

I'll refer you to the documentation for you to read about them since they're explained in detail there:

https://doc.rust-lang.org/nightly/reference/inline-assembly.html#options

Inline assembly is quite complex, so we'll take this step by step and introduce more details on how it works along the way through our examples.

Running our example

The last bit we need is the main function to run our example. I'll present the whole function and we'll walk through it step by step:

```
fn main() {
    let mut ctx = ThreadContext::default();
    let mut stack = vec![0_u8; SSIZE as usize];

    unsafe {
        let stack_bottom = stack.as_mut_ptr().offset(SSIZE);
        let sb_aligned = (stack_bottom as usize & !15) as *mut u8;
        std::ptr::write(sb_aligned.offset(-16) as *mut u64, hello as u64);
        ctx.rsp = sb_aligned.offset(-16) as u64;
        gt_switch(&mut ctx);
```

```
        }
}
```

So, in this function, we're actually creating our new stack. `hello` is a pointer already (a function pointer), so we can cast it directly as an `u64` since all pointers on 64-bit systems will be, well, 64-bit. Then, we write this pointer to our new stack.

> **Note**
> We'll talk more about the stack in the next segment, but one thing we need to know now is that the stack grows downwards. If our 48-byte stack starts at index 0 and ends on index 47, index 32 will be the first index of a 16-byte offset from the start/base of our stack.

Make note that we write the pointer to an offset of 16 bytes from the base of our stack.

> **What does the line let sb_aligned = (stack_bottom as usize &! 15) as *mut u8; do?**
> When we ask for memory like we do when creating a `Vec<u8>`, there is no guarantee that the memory we get is 16-byte-aligned when we get it. This line of code essentially rounds our memory address down to the nearest 16-byte-aligned address. If it's already 16 byte-aligned, it does nothing. This way, we know that we end up at a 16-byte-aligned address if we simply subtract 16 from the base of our stack.

We cast the address to `hello` as a pointer to a `u64` instead of a pointer to a `u8`. We want to write to position "32, 33, 34, 35, 36, 37, 38, 39", which is the 8-byte space we need to store our `u64`. If we don't do this cast, we try to write a `u64` only to position 32, which is not what we want.

When we run the example by writing `cargo run` in our terminal, we get:

```
Finished dev [unoptimized + debuginfo] target(s) in 0.58s
Running `target\debug\a-stack-swap`
I LOVE WAKING UP ON A NEW STACK!
```

> **Tip**
> As we end the program in an endless loop, you'll have to exit by pressing *Ctrl + C*.

OK, so what happened? We didn't call the function `hello` at any point, but it still executed.

What happened is that we actually made the CPU jump over to our own stack, and since it thinks it returns from a function, it will read the address to `hello` and start executing the instructions it points to. We have taken the first step toward implementing a context switch.

In the next sections, we will talk about the stack in a bit more detail before we implement our fibers. It will be easier now that we have covered so much of the basics.

The stack

A stack is nothing more than a piece of contiguous memory.

This is important to know. A computer only has memory, it doesn't have a special stack memory and a heap memory; it's all part of the same memory.

The difference is how this memory is accessed and used. The stack supports simple push/pop instructions on a contiguous part of memory, that's what makes it fast to use. The heap memory is allocated by a memory allocator on demand and can be scattered around in different locations.

We'll not go through the differences between the stack and the heap here since there are numerous articles explaining them in detail, including a chapter in *The Rust Programming Language* at `https://doc.rust-lang.org/stable/book/ch04-01-what-is-ownership.html#the-stack-and-the-heap`.

What does the stack look like?

Let's start with a simplified view of the stack. A 64-bit CPU will read 8 bytes at a time. Even though the natural way for us to see a stack is a long line of `u8` as shown in *Figure 5.2*, the CPU will treat it more like a long line of `u64` instead since it won't be able to read less than 8 bytes when it makes a load or a store.

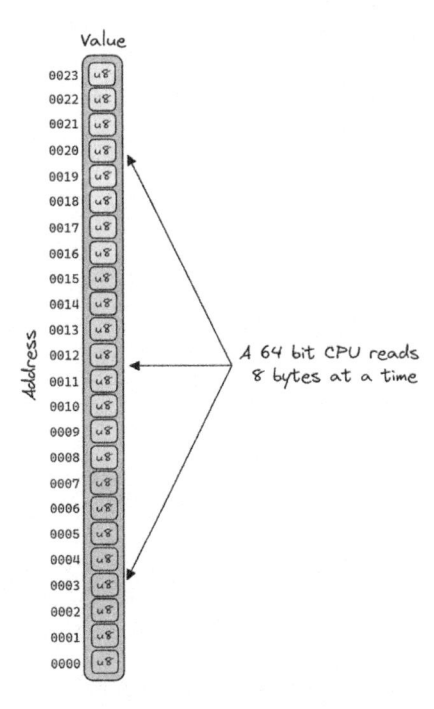

Figure 5.3 – The stack

When we pass a pointer, we need to make sure we pass in a pointer to either address 0016, 0008, or 0000 in the example.

The stack grows downwards, so we start at the top and work our way down.

When we set the **stack pointer** in a 16-byte aligned stack, we need to make sure to put our stack pointer to an address that is a *multiple* of 16. In the example, the only address that satisfies this requirement is 0008 (remember the stack starts on the top).

If we add the following lines of code to our example in the last chapter just before we do the switch in our `main` function, we can effectively print out our stack and have a look at it:

ch05/b-show-stack

```
for i in 0..SSIZE {
    println!("mem: {}, val: {}",
    sb_aligned.offset(-i as isize) as usize,
    *sb_aligned.offset(-i as isize))
}
```

The output we get is as follows:

```
mem: 2643866716720, val: 0
mem: 2643866716719, val: 0
mem: 2643866716718, val: 0
mem: 2643866716717, val: 0
mem: 2643866716716, val: 0
mem: 2643866716715, val: 0
mem: 2643866716714, val: 0
mem: 2643866716713, val: 0
mem: 2643866716712, val: 0
mem: 2643866716711, val: 0
mem: 2643866716710, val: 0
mem: 2643866716709, val: 127
mem: 2643866716708, val: 247
mem: 2643866716707, val: 172
mem: 2643866716706, val: 15
mem: 2643866716705, val: 29
mem: 2643866716704, val: 240
mem: 2643866716703, val: 0
mem: 2643866716702, val: 0
mem: 2643866716701, val: 0
mem: 2643866716700, val: 0
mem: 2643866716699, val: 0
...
```

```
mem: 2643866716675, val: 0
mem: 2643866716674, val: 0
mem: 2643866716673, val: 0
I LOVE WAKING UP ON A NEW STACK!
```

I've printed out the memory addresses as u64 here, so it's easier to parse if you're not very familiar with hex.

The first thing to note is that this is just a contiguous piece of memory, starting at address 2643866716673 and ending at 2643866716720.

The addresses 2643866716704 to 2643866716712 are of special interest to us. The first address is the address of our stack pointer, the value we write to the rsp register of the CPU. The range represents the values we wrote to the stack before we made the switch.

> Note
> The actual addresses you get will be different every time you run the program.

In other words, the values 240, 205, 252, 56, 67, 86, 0, 0 represent the pointer to our hello() function written as u8 values.

> Endianness
>
> An interesting side note here is that the order the CPU writes an u64 as a set of 8 u8 bytes is dependent on its endianness. In other words, a CPU can write our pointer address as 240, 205, 252, 56, 67, 86, 0, 0 if it's little-endian or 0, 0, 86, 67, 56, 252, 205, 240 if it's big-endian. Think of it like how Hebrew, Arabic, and Persian languages read and write from right to left, while Latin, Greek, and Indic languages read and write from left to right. It doesn't really matter as long as you know it in advance, and the results will be the same.
>
> The x86-64 architecture uses a little-endian format, so if you try to parse the data manually, you'll have to bear this in mind.

As we write more complex functions, our extremely small 48-byte stack will soon run out of space. You see, as we run the functions we write in Rust, the CPU will now push and pop values on our new stack to execute our program and it's left to the programmer to make sure they don't overflow the stack. This brings us to our next topic: stack sizes.

Stack sizes

We touched upon this topic earlier in *Chapter 2*, but now that we've created our own stack and made our CPU jump over to it, you might get a better sense of the issue. One of the advantages of creating our own green threads is that we can freely choose how much space we reserve for each stack.

When you start a process in most modern operating systems, the standard stack size is normally 8 MB, but it can be configured differently. This is enough for most programs, but it's up to the programmer to make sure we don't use more than we have. This is the cause of the dreaded stack overflow that most of us have experienced.

However, when we can control the stacks ourselves, we can choose the size we want. 8 MB for each task is way more than we need when running simple functions in a web server, for example, so by reducing the stack size, we can have millions of fibers/green threads running on a machine. We run out of memory a lot sooner using stacks provided by the operating system.

Anyway, we need to consider how to handle the stack size, and most production systems such as **Boost.Coroutine** or the one you find in **Go** will use either segmented stacks or growable stacks. We will make this simple for ourselves and use a fixed stack size going forward.

Implementing our own fibers

Before we start, I want to make sure you understand that the code we write is quite unsafe and is not a "best practice" when writing Rust. I want to try to make this as safe as possible without introducing a lot of unnecessary complexity, but there is no way to avoid the fact that there will be a lot of unsafe code in this example. We will also prioritize focusing on *how* this works and explain it as simply as possible, which will be enough of a challenge in and of itself, so the focus on best practices and safety will have to take the back seat on this one.

Let's start off by creating a whole new project called `c-fibers` and removing the code in `main.rs` so we start with a blank sheet.

> **Note**
>
> You will also find this example in the repository under the `ch05/c-fibers` folder. This example, as well as `ch05/d-fibers-closure` and `ch05/e-fibers-windows`, needs to be compiled using the nightly compiler since we use an unstable feature. You can do this in one of two ways:
>
> • Override the default toolchain for the entire directory you're in by writing `rustup override set nightly` (I personally prefer this option).
>
> • Tell cargo to use the nightly toolchain every time you compile or run the program using `cargo +nightly run`.
>
> We'll create a simple runtime with a very simple scheduler. Our fibers will save/restore their state so they can be stopped and resumed at any point during execution. Each fiber will represent a task that we want to progress concurrently, and we simply create a new fiber for each task we want to run.

We start off the example by enabling a specific feature we need, importing the `asm` macro, and defining a few constants:

ch05/c-fibers/main.rs

```rust
#![feature(naked_functions)]
use std::arch::asm;

const DEFAULT_STACK_SIZE: usize = 1024 * 1024 * 2;
const MAX_THREADS: usize = 4;
static mut RUNTIME: usize = 0;
```

The feature we want to enable is called the `naked_functions` feature. Let's explain what a naked function is right away.

> **Naked functions**
>
> If you remember when we talked about the operating system ABI and calling conventions earlier, you probably remember that each architecture and OS have different requirements. This is especially important when creating new stack frames, which is what happens when you call a function. So, the compiler knows about what each architecture/OS requires and adjusts layout, and parameter placement on the stack and saves/restores certain registers to make sure we satisfy the ABI on the platform we're on. This happens both when we enter and exit a function and is often called a function **prologue** and **epilogue**.
>
> In Rust, we can enable this feature and mark a function as `#[naked]`. A naked function tells the compiler that we don't want it to create a function prologue and epilogue and that we want to take care of this ourselves. Since we do the trick where we return over to a new stack and want to resume the old one at a later point we don't want the compiler to think it manages the stack layout at these points. It worked in our first example since we never switched back to the original stack, but it won't work going forward.

Our `DEFAULT_STACK_SIZE` is set to 2 MB, which is more than enough for our use. We also set `MAX_THREADS` to 4 since we don't need more for our example.

The last static constant, `RUNTIME`, is a pointer to our runtime (yeah, I know, it's not pretty with a mutable global variable, but it's making it easier for us to focus on the important parts of the example later on).

The next thing we do is set up some data structures to represent the data we'll be working with:

```rust
pub struct Runtime {
    threads: Vec<Thread>,
    current: usize,
}
```

```rust
#[derive(PartialEq, Eq, Debug)]
enum State {
    Available,
    Running,
    Ready,
}

struct Thread {
    stack: Vec<u8>,
    ctx: ThreadContext,
    state: State,
}

#[derive(Debug, Default)]
#[repr(C)]
struct ThreadContext {
    rsp: u64,
    r15: u64,
    r14: u64,
    r13: u64,
    r12: u64,
    rbx: u64,
    rbp: u64,
}
```

`Runtime` is going to be our main entry point. We are basically going to create a very small runtime with a very simple scheduler and switch between our threads. The runtime holds an array of `Thread` structs and a `current` field to indicate which thread we are currently running.

`Thread` holds data for a thread. The **stack** is similar to what we saw in our first example in earlier chapters. The `ctx` field is a context representing the data our CPU needs to resume where it left off on a stack and a `state` field that holds our thread state.

`State` is an **enum** representing the states our threads can be in:

- `Available` means the thread is available and ready to be assigned a task if needed
- `Running` means the thread is running
- `Ready` means the thread is ready to move forward and resume execution

`ThreadContext` holds data for the registers that the CPU needs to resume execution on a stack.

> **Note**
>
> The registers we save in our `ThreadContext` struct are the registers that are marked as *callee saved* in *Figure 5.1*. We need to save these since the ABI states that the *callee* (which will be our `switch` function from the perspective of the OS) needs to restore them before the *caller* is resumed.

Next up is how we initialize the data to a newly created thread:

```
impl Thread {
    fn new() -> Self {
        Thread {
            stack: vec![0_u8; DEFAULT_STACK_SIZE],
            ctx: ThreadContext::default(),
            state: State::Available,
        }
    }
}
```

This is pretty easy. A new thread starts in the `Available` state, indicating it is ready to be assigned a task.

One thing I want to point out here is that we allocate our stack here. That is not needed and is not an optimal use of our resources since we allocate memory for threads we might need instead of allocating on first use. However, this lowers the complexity in the parts of our code that have a more important focus than allocating memory for our stack.

> **Note**
>
> Once a stack is allocated it must not move! No `push()` on the vector or any other methods that might trigger a reallocation. If the stack is reallocated, any pointers that we hold to it are invalidated.
>
> It's worth mentioning that `Vec<T>` has a method called `into_boxed_slice()`, which returns a reference to an allocated slice `Box<[T]>`. Slices can't grow, so if we store that instead, we can avoid the reallocation problem. There are several other ways to make this safer, but we'll not focus on those in this example.

Implementing the runtime

The first thing we need to do is to initialize a new runtime to a base state. The next code segments all belong to the `impl Runtime` block, and I'll make sure to let you know when the block ends since it can be hard to spot the closing bracket when we divide it up as much as we do here.

The first thing we do is to implement a `new` function on our `Runtime` struct:

```
impl Runtime {
  pub fn new() -> Self {
    let base_thread = Thread {
      stack: vec![0_u8; DEFAULT_STACK_SIZE],
      ctx: ThreadContext::default(),
      state: State::Running,
    };

    let mut threads = vec![base_thread];
    let mut available_threads: Vec<Thread> = (1..MAX_THREADS).map(|_| Thread::new()).collect();
    threads.append(&mut available_threads);

    Runtime {
      threads,
      current: 0,
    }
  }
}
```

When we instantiate our `Runtime`, we set up a base thread. This thread will be set to the `Running` state and will make sure we keep the runtime running until all tasks are finished.

Then, we instantiate the rest of the threads and set the current thread (the base thread) to `0`.

The next thing we do is admittedly a little bit hacky since we do something that's usually a no-go in Rust. As I mentioned when we went through the constants, we want to access our runtime struct from anywhere in our code so that we can call yield on it at any point in our code. There are ways to do this safely, but the topic at hand is already complex, so even though we're juggling with knives here, I will do everything I can to keep everything that's not the main focal point of this example as simple as it can be.

After we call initialize on the Runtime, we have to make sure we don't do anything that can invalidate the pointer we take to `self` once it's initialized.

```
pub fn init(&self) {
    unsafe {
        let r_ptr: *const Runtime = self;
        RUNTIME = r_ptr as usize;
    }
}
```

This is where we start running our runtime. It will continually call `t_yield()` until it returns `false`, which means that there is no more work to do and we can exit the process:

```
pub fn run(&mut self) -> ! {
    while self.t_yield() {}
    std::process::exit(0);
}
```

> **Note**
>
> `yield` is a reserved word in Rust, so we can't name our function that. If that was not the case, it would be my preferred name for it over the slightly more cryptic `t_yield`.

This is the return function that we call when a thread is finished. `return` is another reserved keyword in Rust, so we name this `t_return()`. Make a note that the user of our threads does not call this; we set up our stack so this is called when the task is done:

```
fn t_return(&mut self) {
    if self.current != 0 {
        self.threads[self.current].state = State::Available;
        self.t_yield();
    }
}
```

If the calling thread is the `base_thread`, we won't do anything. Our runtime will call `t_yield` for us on the base thread. If it's called from a spawned thread, we know it's finished since all threads will have a `guard` function on top of their stack (which we'll show further down), and the only place where this function is called is on our `guard` function.

We set its state to `Available`, letting the runtime know it's ready to be assigned a new task, and then immediately call `t_yield`, which will schedule a new thread to be run.

So, finally, we get to the heart of our runtime: the `t_yield` function.

The first part of this function is our scheduler. We simply go through all the threads and see if any are in the `Ready` state, which indicates that it has a task it is ready to make progress. This could be a database call that has returned in a real-world application.

If no thread is `Ready`, we're all done. This is an extremely simple scheduler using only a round-robin algorithm. A real scheduler might have a much more sophisticated way of deciding what task to run next.

If we find a thread that's ready to be run, we change the state of the current thread from `Running` to `Ready`.

Let's present the function before we go on to explain the last part of it:

```
#[inline(never)]
fn t_yield(&mut self) -> bool {
    let mut pos = self.current;
    while self.threads[pos].state != State::Ready {
        pos += 1;
        if pos == self.threads.len() {
            pos = 0;
        }
        if pos == self.current {
            return false;
        }
    }

    if self.threads[self.current].state != State::Available {
        self.threads[self.current].state = State::Ready;
    }

    self.threads[pos].state = State::Running;
    let old_pos = self.current;
    self.current = pos;

    unsafe {
        let old: *mut ThreadContext = &mut self.threads[old_pos].ctx;
        let new: *const ThreadContext = &self.threads[pos].ctx;
        asm!("call switch", in("rdi") old, in("rsi") new, clobber_abi("C"));
    }
    self.threads.len() > 0
}
```

The next thing we do is to call the function `switch`, which will save the current context (the old context) and load the new context into the CPU. The new context is either a new task or all the information the CPU needs to resume work on an existing task.

Our `switch` function, which we will cover a little further down, takes two arguments and is marked as `#[naked]`. Naked functions are not like normal functions. They don't accept formal arguments, for example, so we can't simply call it in Rust as a normal function like `switch(old, new)`.

You see, usually, when we call a function with two arguments, the compiler will place each argument in a register described by the calling convention for the platform. However, when we call a `#[naked]` function, we need to take care of this ourselves. Therefore, we pass in the address to our old and new `ThreadContext` using assembly. `rdi` is the register for the first argument in the System V ABI calling convention and `rsi` is the register used for the second argument.

The `#[inline(never)]` attribute prevents the compiler from simply substituting a call to our function with a copy of the function content wherever it's called (this is what inlining means). This is almost never a problem on debug builds, but in this case, our program will fail if the compiler **inlines** this function in a release build. The issue manifests itself by the runtime exiting before all the tasks are finished. Since we store Runtime as a static usize that we then cast as a *mut pointer (which is almost guaranteed to cause UB), it's *most likely* caused by the compiler making the wrong assumptions when this function is inlined and called by casting and dereferencing RUNTIME in one of the helper methods that will be outlined. Just make a note that this is probably avoidable if we change our design; it's not something worth dwelling on for too long in this specific case.

> **More inline assembly**
>
> We need to explain the new concepts we introduced here. The assembly calls the function switch (the function is tagged with #[no_mangle] so we can call it by name). The in("rdi") old and in("rsi") new arguments place the value of old and new to the rdi and rsi registers, respectively. The System V ABI for x86-64 states that the rdi register holds the first argument to a function and rsi holds the second argument.
>
> The clobber_abi("C") argument tells the compiler that it may not assume any that any general-purpose registers are preserved across the asm! block. The compiler will emit instructions to push the registers it uses to the stack and restore them when resuming after the asm! block.
>
> If you take one more look at the list in *Figure 5.1*, we already know that we need to take special care with registers that are marked as *callee saved*. When calling a normal function, the compiler will insert code* to save/restore all the non-callee-saved, or caller saved, registers before calling a function so it can resume with the correct state when the function returns. Since we marked the function we're calling as #[naked], we explicitly told the compiler to not insert this code, so the safest thing is to make sure the compiler doesn't assume that it can rely on any register being untouched when it resumes after the call we make in our asm! block.
>
> *In some instances, the compiler will know that a register is untouched by the function call since it controls the register usage in both the caller and the callee and it will not emit any special instructions to save/restore registers they know will be untouched when the function returns

The self.threads.len() > 0 line at the end is just a way for us to prevent the compiler from optimizing our code away. This happens to me on Windows but not on Linux, and it is a common problem when running benchmarks, for example. There are other ways of preventing the compiler from optimizing this code, but I chose the simplest way I could find. As long as it's commented, it should be OK to do. The code never reaches this point anyway.

Next up is our spawn function. I'll present the function first and guide you through it after:

```
pub fn spawn(&mut self, f: fn()) {
    let available = self
        .threads
        .iter_mut()
        .find(|t| t.state == State::Available)
        .expect("no available thread.");
```

```
            let size = available.stack.len();
            unsafe {
                let s_ptr = available.stack.as_mut_ptr().offset(size as isize);
                let s_ptr = (s_ptr as usize & !15) as *mut u8;
                std::ptr::write(s_ptr.offset(-16) as *mut u64, guard as u64);
                std::ptr::write(s_ptr.offset(-24) as *mut u64, skip as u64);
                std::ptr::write(s_ptr.offset(-32) as *mut u64, f as u64);
                available.ctx.rsp = s_ptr.offset(-32) as u64;
            }
            available.state = State::Ready;
        }
} // We close the `impl Runtime` block here
```

> **Note**
> I promised to point out where we close the `impl Runtime` block, and we do that after the `spawn` function. The upcoming functions are "free" functions that don't belong to a struct.

While I think `t_yield` is the logically interesting function in this example, I think `spawn` is the most interesting one technically.

The first thing to note is that the function takes one argument: `f: fn()`. This is simply a function pointer to the function we take as an argument. This function is the task we want to run concurrently with other tasks. If this was a library, this is the function that users actually pass to us and want our runtime to handle concurrently.

In this example, we take a simple function as an argument, but if we modify the code slightly we can also accept a closure.

> **Tip**
> In example `ch05/d-fibers-closure`, you can see a slightly modified example that accepts a closure instead, making it more flexible than the one we walk through here. I would really encourage you to check that one out once you've finished this example.

The rest of the function is where we set up our stack as we discussed in the previous chapter and make sure our stack looks like the one specified in the System V ABI stack layout.

When we spawn a new fiber (or userland thread), we first check if there are any available userland threads (threads in Available state). If we run out of threads, we panic in this scenario, but there are several (better) ways to handle that. We'll keep things simple for now.

When we find an available thread, we get the stack length and a pointer to our u8 byte array.

In the next segment, we have to use some unsafe functions. We'll explain the functions we refer to here later, but this is where we set them up in our new stack so that they're called in the right order for our runtime to work.

First, we make sure that the memory segment we'll use is 16-byte-aligned. Then, we write the address to our guard function that will be called when the task we provide finishes and the function returns.

Second, we'll write the address to a skip function, which is there just to handle the gap when we return from f, so that guard will get called on a 16-byte boundary. The next value we write to the stack is the address to f.

> **Why do we need the skip function?**
>
> Remember how we explained how the stack works? We want the f function to be the first to run, so we set the base pointer to f and make sure it's 16-byte aligned. We then push the address to the skip function and lastly the guard function. Since, skip is simply one instruction, ret, doing this makes sure that our call to guard is 16-byte aligned so that we adhere to the ABI requirements.

After we've written our function pointers to the stack, we set the value of rsp, which is the stack pointer to the address of our provided function, so we start executing that first when we are scheduled to run.

Lastly, we set the state to Ready, which means we have work to do and that we are ready to do it. Remember, it's up to our scheduler to actually start up this thread.

We're now finished implementing our Runtime, if you got all this, you basically understand how fibers/green threads work. However, there are still a few details needed to make it all work.

Guard, skip, and switch functions

There are a few functions we've referred to that are really important for our Runtime to actually work. Fortunately, all but one of them are extremely simple to understand. We'll start with the guard function:

```
fn guard() {
    unsafe {
        let rt_ptr = RUNTIME as *mut Runtime;
        (*rt_ptr).t_return();
    };
}
```

The `guard` function is called when the function that we passed in, `f`, has returned. When `f` returns, it means our task is finished, so we de-reference our `Runtime` and call `t_return()`. We could have made a function that does some additional work when a thread is finished, but right now, our `t_return()` function does all we need. It marks our thread as `Available` (if it's not our base thread) and yields so we can resume work on a different thread.

Next is our `skip` function:

```
#[naked]
unsafe extern "C" fn skip() {
    asm!("ret", options(noreturn))
}
```

There is not much happening in the `skip` function. We use the `#[naked]` attribute so that this function essentially compiles down to just `ret` instruction. `ret` will just pop off the next value from the stack and jump to whatever instructions that address points to. In our case, this is the `guard` function.

Next up is a small helper function named `yield_thread`:

```
pub fn yield_thread() {
    unsafe {
        let rt_ptr = RUNTIME as *mut Runtime;
        (*rt_ptr).t_yield();
    };
}
```

This helper function lets us call `t_yield` on our `Runtime` from an arbitrary place in our code without needing any references to it. This function is very unsafe, and it's one of the places where we make big shortcuts to make our example slightly simpler to understand. If we call this and our Runtime is not initialized yet or the runtime is dropped, it will result in undefined behavior. However, making this safer is not a priority for us just to get our example up and running.

We are very close to the finish line; just one more function to go. The last bit we need is our `switch` function, and you already know the most important parts of it already. Let's see how it looks and explain how it differs from our first stack swap function:

```
#[naked]
#[no_mangle]
unsafe extern "C" fn switch() {
    asm!(
        "mov [rdi + 0x00], rsp",
        "mov [rdi + 0x08], r15",
        "mov [rdi + 0x10], r14",
        "mov [rdi + 0x18], r13",
        "mov [rdi + 0x20], r12",
        "mov [rdi + 0x28], rbx",
        "mov [rdi + 0x30], rbp",
```

```
            "mov rsp, [rsi + 0x00]",
            "mov r15, [rsi + 0x08]",
            "mov r14, [rsi + 0x10]",
            "mov r13, [rsi + 0x18]",
            "mov r12, [rsi + 0x20]",
            "mov rbx, [rsi + 0x28]",
            "mov rbp, [rsi + 0x30]",
            "ret", options(noreturn)
        );
}
```

So, this is our full stack switch function. You probably remember from our first example that this is just a bit more elaborate. We first read out the values of all the registers we need and then set all the register values to the register values we saved when we suspended execution on the new thread.

This is essentially all we need to do to save and resume the execution.

Here we see the #[naked] attribute used again. Usually, every function has a prologue and an epilogue and we don't want that here since this is all assembly and we want to handle everything ourselves. If we don't include this, we will fail to switch back to our stack the second time.

You can also see us using the offset we introduced earlier in practice:

```
0x00[rdi] # 0
0x08[rdi] # 8
0x10[rdi] # 16
0x18[rdi] # 24
```

These are hex numbers indicating the offset from the memory pointer to which we want to read/write. I wrote down the base 10 numbers as comments, so as you can see, we only offset the pointer in 8-byte steps, which is the same size as the u64 fields on our ThreadContext struct.

This is also why it's important to annotate ThreadContext with #[repr(C)]; it tells us that the data will be represented in memory in this exact way so we write to the right field. The Rust ABI makes no guarantee that they are represented in the same order in memory; however, the C-ABI does.

Finally, there is one new option added to the asm! block. option(noreturn) is a requirement when writing naked functions and we will receive a compile error if we don't add it. Usually, the compiler will assume that a function call will return, but naked functions are not anything like the functions we're used to. They're more like labeled containers of assembly that we can call, so we don't want the compiler to emit ret instructions at the end of the function or make any assumptions that we return to the previous stack frame. By using this option, we tell the compiler to treat the assembly block as if it never returns, and we make sure that we never fall through the assembly block by adding a ret instruction ourselves.

Next up is our main function, which is pretty straightforward, so I'll simply present the code here:

```
fn main() {
    let mut runtime = Runtime::new();
    runtime.init();
    runtime.spawn(|| {
        println!("THREAD 1 STARTING");
        let id = 1;
        for i in 0..10 {
            println!("thread: {} counter: {}", id, i);
            yield_thread();
        }
        println!("THREAD 1 FINISHED");
    });
    runtime.spawn(|| {
        println!("THREAD 2 STARTING");
        let id = 2;
        for i in 0..15 {
            println!("thread: {} counter: {}", id, i);
            yield_thread();
        }
        println!("THREAD 2 FINISHED");
    });
    runtime.run();
}
```

As you see here, we initialize our runtime and spawn two threads: one that counts to 10 and yields between each count and one that counts to 15. When we `cargo run` our project, we should get the following output:

```
Finished dev [unoptimized + debuginfo] target(s) in 2.17s
Running `target/debug/green_threads`
THREAD 1 STARTING
thread: 1 counter: 0
THREAD 2 STARTING
thread: 2 counter: 0
thread: 1 counter: 1
thread: 2 counter: 1
thread: 1 counter: 2
thread: 2 counter: 2
thread: 1 counter: 3
thread: 2 counter: 3
thread: 1 counter: 4
thread: 2 counter: 4
thread: 1 counter: 5
thread: 2 counter: 5
thread: 1 counter: 6
thread: 2 counter: 6
thread: 1 counter: 7
```

```
thread: 2 counter: 7
thread: 1 counter: 8
thread: 2 counter: 8
thread: 1 counter: 9
thread: 2 counter: 9
THREAD 1 FINISHED.
thread: 2 counter: 10
thread: 2 counter: 11
thread: 2 counter: 12
thread: 2 counter: 13
thread: 2 counter: 14
THREAD 2 FINISHED.
```

Beautiful! Our threads alternate since they yield control on each count until THREAD 1 finishes and THREAD 2 counts the last numbers before it finishes its task.

Finishing thoughts

I want to round off this chapter by pointing out some of the advantages and disadvantages of this approach, which we went through in *Chapter 2*, since we now have first-hand experience with this topic.

First of all, the example we implemented here is an example of what we called a stackful coroutine. Each coroutine (or thread, as we call it in the example implementation) has its own stack. This also means that we can interrupt and resume execution at any point in time. It doesn't matter if we're in the middle of a stack frame (in the middle of executing a function); we can simply tell the CPU to save the state we need to the stack, return to a different stack and restore the state it needs there, and resume as if nothing has happened.

You can also see that we have to manage our stacks in some way. In our example, we just create a static stack (much like the OS does when we ask it for a thread, but smaller), but for this to be more efficient than using OS threads, we need to select a strategy to solve that potential problem.

If you look at our slightly expanded example in ch05/d-fibers-closure, you'll notice that we can make the API pretty easy to use, much like the API used for std::thread::spawn in the standard library. The flipside is of course the complexity of implementing this correctly on all combinations of ISA/ABIs that we want to support, and while specific to Rust, it's challenging to create a great and *safe* API over these kinds of stackful coroutines without any native language support for it.

To tie this into *Chapter 3*, where we discuss event queues and non-blocking calls, I want to point out that if you use fibers to handle concurrency, you would call yield after you've made a read interest in your non-blocking call. Typically, a runtime would supply these non-blocking calls, and the fact that we yield would be opaque to the user, but the fiber is suspended at that point. We would probably add one more state to our State enum called Pending or something else that signifies that the thread is waiting for some external event.

When the OS signals that the data is ready, we would mark the thread as `State::Ready` to resume and the scheduler would resume execution just like in this example.

While it requires a more sophisticated scheduler and infrastructure, I hope that you have gotten a good idea of how such a system would work in practice.

Summary

First of all, congratulations! You have now implemented a super simple but working example of fibers. You've set up your own stack and learned about ISAs, ABIs, calling conventions, and inline assembly in Rust.

It was quite the ride we had to take, but if you came this far and read through everything, you should give yourself a big pat on the back. This is not for the faint of heart, but you pulled through.

This example (and chapter) might take a little time to fully digest, but there is no rush for that. You can always go back to this example and read the code again to fully understand it. I really do recommend that you play around with the code yourself and get to know it. Change the scheduling algorithm around, add more context to the threads you create, and use your imagination.

You will probably experience that debugging problems in low-level code like this can be pretty hard, but that's part of the learning process and you can always revert back to a working version.

Now that we have covered one of the largest and most difficult examples in this book, we'll go on to learn about another popular way of handling concurrency by looking into how futures and async/await works in Rust. The rest of this book is in fact dedicated solely to learning about futures and async/await in Rust, and since we've gained so much fundamental knowledge at this point, it will be much easier for us to get a good and deep understanding of how they work. You've done a great job so far!

Part 3: Futures and async/await in Rust

This part will explain Futures and async/await in Rust from the ground up. Building upon the knowledge acquired thus far, we will construct a central example that will serve as a recurring theme in the subsequent chapters, eventually leading to the creation of a runtime capable of executing futures in Rust. Throughout this exploration, we will delve into concepts such as coroutines, runtimes, reactors, executors, wakers, and much more.

This part comprises the following chapters:

- *Chapter 6, Futures in Rust*
- *Chapter 7, Coroutines and async/await*
- *Chapter 8, Runtimes, Wakers, and the Reactor-Executor Pattern*
- *Chapter 9, Coroutines, Self-referential Structs, and Pinning*
- *Chapter 10, Create Your Own Runtime*

6
Futures in Rust

In *Chapter 5*, we covered one of the most popular ways of modeling concurrency in a programming language: fibers/green threads. Fibers/green threads are an example of stackful coroutines. The other popular way of modeling asynchronous program flow is by using what we call stackless coroutines, and combining Rust's futures with `async/await` is an example of that. We will cover this in detail in the next chapters.

This first chapter will introduce Rust's futures to you, and the main goals of this chapter are to do the following:

- Give you a high-level introduction to concurrency in Rust
- Explain what Rust provides and not in the language and standard library when working with async code
- Get to know why we need a runtime library in Rust
- Understand the difference between a leaf future and a non-leaf future
- Get insight into how to handle CPU-intensive tasks

To accomplish this, we'll divide this chapter into the following sections:

- What is a future?
- Leaf futures
- Non-leaf futures
- Runtimes
- A mental model of an async runtime
- What the Rust language and standard library take care of
- I/O vs CPU-intensive tasks
- Advantages and disadvantages of Rust's async model

What is a future?

A future is a representation of some operation that will be completed in the future.

Async in Rust uses a poll-based approach in which an asynchronous task will have three phases:

1. **The poll phase**: A future is polled, which results in the task progressing until a point where it can no longer make progress. We often refer to the part of the runtime that polls a future as an executor.
2. **The wait phase**: An event source, most often referred to as a reactor, registers that a future is waiting for an event to happen and makes sure that it will wake the future when that event is ready.
3. **The wake phase**: The event happens and the future is woken up. It's now up to the executor that polled the future in *step 1* to schedule the future to be polled again and make further progress until it completes or reaches a new point where it can't make further progress and the cycle repeats.

Now, when we talk about futures, I find it useful to make a distinction between **non-leaf** futures and **leaf** futures early on because, in practice, they're pretty different from one another.

Leaf futures

Runtimes create leaf futures, which represent a resource such as a socket.

This is an example of a leaf future:

```
let mut stream = tokio::net::TcpStream::connect("127.0.0.1:3000");
```

Operations on these resources, such as a reading from a socket, will be non-blocking and return a future, which we call a leaf future since it's the future that we're actually waiting on.

It's unlikely that you'll implement a leaf future yourself unless you're writing a runtime, but we'll go through how they're constructed in this book as well.

It's also unlikely that you'll pass a leaf future to a runtime and run it to completion alone, as you'll understand by reading the next paragraph.

Non-leaf futures

Non-leaf futures are the kind of futures we as users of a runtime write ourselves using the `async` keyword to create a task that can be run on the executor.

The bulk of an async program will consist of non-leaf futures, which are a kind of pause-able computation. This is an important distinction since these futures represent a set of operations. Often, such a task will `await` a leaf future as one of many operations to complete the task.

This is an example of a non-leaf future:

```
let non_leaf = async {
    let mut stream = TcpStream::connect("127.0.0.1:3000").await.unwrap();
    println!("connected!");
    let result = stream.write(b"hello world\n").await;
    println!("message sent!");
    ...
};
```

The two highlighted lines indicate points where we pause the execution, yield control to a runtime, and eventually resume. In contrast to leaf futures, these kinds of futures do not themselves represent an I/O resource. When we poll them, they will run until they get to a leaf future that returns `Pending` and then yields control to the scheduler (which is a part of what we call the runtime).

> Runtimes
>
> Languages such as C#, JavaScript, Java, Go, and many others come with a runtime for handling concurrency. So, if you're used to one of those languages, this will seem a bit strange to you. Rust is different from these languages in the sense that Rust doesn't come with a runtime for handling concurrency, so you need to use a library that provides this for you.
>
> Quite a bit of complexity attributed to futures is actually complexity rooted in runtimes; creating an efficient runtime is hard.
>
> Learning how to use one correctly requires quite a bit of effort as well, but you'll see that there are several similarities between this kind of runtime, so learning one makes learning the next much easier.
>
> The difference between Rust and other languages is that you have to make an active choice when it comes to picking a runtime. Most often, in other languages, you'll just use the one provided for you.

A mental model of an async runtime

I find it easier to reason about how futures work by creating a high-level mental model we can use. To do that, I have to introduce the concept of a runtime that will drive our futures to completion.

> Note
>
> The mental model I create here is not the only way to drive futures to completion, and Rust's futures do not impose any restrictions on how you actually accomplish this task.

A fully working async system in Rust can be divided into three parts:

- Reactor (responsible for notifying about I/O events)
- Executor (scheduler)
- Future (a task that can stop and resume at specific points)

So, how do these three parts work together?

Let's take a look at a diagram that shows a simplified overview of an async runtime:

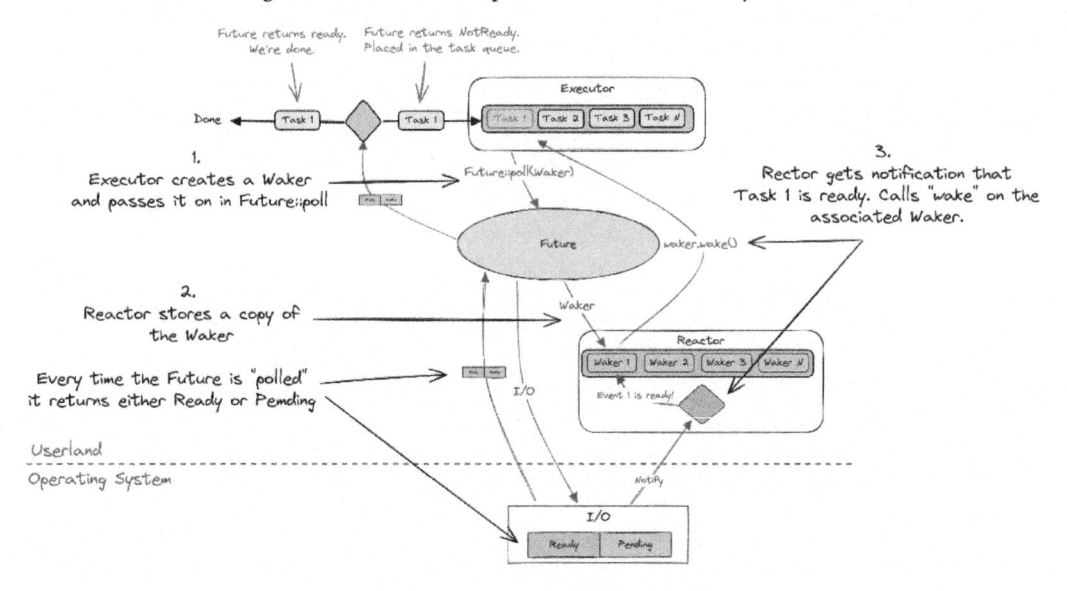

Figure 6.1 – Reactor, executor, and waker

In *step 1* of the figure, an executor holds a list of futures. It will try to run the future by polling it (the poll phase), and when it does, it hands it a `Waker`. The future either returns `Poll:Ready` (which means it's finished) or `Poll::Pending` (which means it's not done but can't get further at the moment). When the executor receives one of these results, it knows it can start polling a different future. We call these points where control is shifted back to the executor *yield points*.

In *step 2*, the reactor stores a copy of the `Waker` that the executor passed to the future when it polled it. The reactor tracks events on that I/O source, usually through the same type of event queue that we learned about in *Chapter 4*.

In *step 3*, when the reactor gets a notification that an event has happened on one of the tracked sources, it locates the `Waker` associated with that source and calls `Waker::wake` on it. This will in turn inform the executor that the future is ready to make progress so it can poll it once more.

If we write a short async program using pseudocode, it will look like this:

```
async fn foo() {
    println!("Start!");
    let txt = io::read_to_string().await.unwrap();
    println!("{txt}");
}
```

The line where we write `await` is the one that will return control back to the scheduler. This is often called a *yield point* since it will return either `Poll::Pending` or `Poll::Ready` (most likely it will return `Poll::Pending` the first time the future is polled).

Since the `Waker` is the same across all executors, reactors can, in theory, be completely oblivious to the type of executor, and vice-versa. *Executors and reactors never need to communicate with one another directly.*

This design is what gives the futures framework its power and flexibility and allows the Rust standard library to provide an ergonomic, zero-cost abstraction for us to use.

> **Note**
> I introduced the concept of reactors and executors here like it's something everyone knows about. I know that's not the case, and don't worry, we'll go through this in detail in the next chapter.

What the Rust language and standard library take care of

Rust only provides what's necessary to model asynchronous operations in the language. Basically, it provides the following:

- A common interface that represents an operation, which will be completed in the future through the `Future` trait
- An ergonomic way of creating tasks (stackless coroutines to be precise) that can be suspended and resumed through the `async` and `await` keywords
- A defined interface to wake up a suspended task through the `Waker` type

That's really what Rust's standard library does. As you see there is no definition of non-blocking I/O, how these tasks are created, or how they're run. There is no non-blocking version of the standard library, so to actually run an asynchronous program, you have to either create or decide on a runtime to use.

I/O vs CPU-intensive tasks

As you know now, what you normally write are called non-leaf futures. Let's take a look at this `async` block using pseudo-Rust as an example:

```
let non_leaf = async {
    let mut stream = TcpStream::connect("127.0.0.1:3000").await.unwrap();

    // request a large dataset
    let result = stream.write(get_dataset_request).await.unwrap();

    // wait for the dataset
    let mut response = vec![];
    stream.read(&mut response).await.unwrap();

    // do some CPU-intensive analysis on the dataset
    let report = analyzer::analyze_data(response).unwrap();

    // send the results back
    stream.write(report).await.unwrap();
};
```

I've highlighted the points where we yield control to the runtime executor. It's important to be aware that the code we write between the yield points runs on the *same thread* as our executor.

That means that while our `analyzer` is working on the dataset, the executor is busy doing calculations instead of handling new requests.

Fortunately, there are a few ways to handle this, and it's not difficult, but it's something you must be aware of:

1. We could create a new leaf future, which sends our task to another thread and resolves when the task is finished. We could `await` this leaf-future like any other future.

2. The runtime could have some kind of supervisor that monitors how much time different tasks take and moves the executor itself to a different thread so it can continue to run even though our `analyzer` task is blocking the original executor thread.

3. You can create a reactor yourself that is compatible with the runtime, which does the analysis any way you see fit and returns a future that can be awaited.

Now, the first way is the usual way of handling this, but some executors implement the second method as well. The problem with #2 is that if you switch runtime, you need to make sure that it supports this kind of supervision as well or else you will end up blocking the executor.

The third method is more of theoretical importance; normally, you'd be happy to send the task to the thread pool that most runtimes provide.

Most executors have a way to accomplish #1 using methods such as `spawn_blocking`.

These methods send the task to a thread pool created by the runtime where you can either perform CPU-intensive tasks or blocking tasks that are not supported by the runtime.

Summary

So, in this short chapter, we introduced Rust's futures to you. You should now have a basic idea of what Rust's async design looks like, what the language provides for you, and what you need to get elsewhere. You should also have an idea of what a leaf future and a non-leaf future are.

These aspects are important as they're design decisions built into the language. You know by now that Rust uses stackless coroutines to model asynchronous operations, but since a coroutine doesn't do anything in and of itself, it's important to know that the choice of how to schedule and run these coroutines is left up to you.

We'll get a much better understanding as we start to explain how this all works in detail as we move forward.

Now that we've seen a high-level overview of Rust's futures, we'll start explaining how they work from the ground up. The next chapter will cover the concept of futures and how they're connected with coroutines and the `async/await` keywords in Rust. We'll see for ourselves how they represent tasks that can pause and resume their execution, which is a prerequisite to having multiple tasks be *in progress* concurrently, and how they differ from the pausable/resumable tasks we implemented as fibers/green threads in *Chapter 5*.

7
Coroutines and async/await

Now that you've gotten a brief introduction to Rust's async model, it's time to take a look at how this fits in the context of everything else we've covered in this book so far.

Rust's futures are an example of an asynchronous model based on stackless coroutines, and in this chapter, we'll take a look at what that really means and how it differs from stackful coroutines (fibers/green threads).

We'll center everything around an example based on a simplified model of futures and `async/await` and see how we can use that to create suspendable and resumable tasks just like we did when creating our own fibers.

The good news is that this is a lot easier than implementing our own fibers/green threads since we can stay in Rust, which is safer. The flip side is that it's a little more abstract and ties into programming language theory as much as it does computer science.

In this chapter, we'll cover the following:

- Introduction to stackless coroutines
- An example of hand-written coroutines
- `async/await`

Technical requirements

The examples in this chapter will all be cross-platform, so the only thing you need is Rust installed and the repository that belongs to the book downloaded locally. All the code in this chapter will be found in the `ch07` folder.

We'll use `delayserver` in this example as well, so you need to open a terminal, enter the `delayserver` folder at the root of the repository, and write `cargo run` so it's ready and available for the examples going forward.

Remember to change the ports in the code if you for some reason have to change what port `delayserver` listens on.

Introduction to stackless coroutines

So, we've finally arrived at the point where we introduce the last method of modeling asynchronous operations in this book. You probably remember that we gave a high-level overview of stackful and stackless coroutines in *Chapter 2*. In *Chapter 5*, we implemented an example of stackful coroutines when writing our own fibers/green threads, so now it's time to take a closer look at how stackless coroutines are implemented and used.

A stackless coroutine is a way of representing a task that can be interrupted and resumed. If you remember all the way back in *Chapter 1*, we mentioned that if we want tasks to run concurrently (be *in progress* at the same time) but not necessarily in parallel, we need to be able to **pause and resume** the task.

In its simplest form, a coroutine is just a task that can stop and resume by yielding control to either its caller, another coroutine, or a scheduler.

Many languages will have a coroutine implementation that also provides a runtime that handles scheduling and non-blocking I/O for you, but it's helpful to make a distinction between what a coroutine is and the rest of the machinery involved in creating an asynchronous system.

This is especially true in Rust, since Rust doesn't come with a runtime and only provides the infrastructure you need to create coroutines that have native support in the language. Rust makes sure that everyone programming in Rust uses the same abstraction for tasks that can be paused and resumed, but it leaves all the other details of getting an asynchronous system up and running for the programmer.

> **Stackless coroutines or just coroutines?**
>
> Most often you'll see *stackless coroutines* simply referred to as *coroutines*. To try to keep some consistency (you remember I don't like to introduce terms that mean different things based on the context), I've consistently referred to coroutines as either *stackless* or *stackful*, but going forward, I'll simply refer to stackless coroutines as **coroutines**. This is also what you'll have to expect when reading about them in other sources.

Fibers/green threads represent this kind of resumable task in a very similar way to how an operating system does. A task has a stack where it stores/restores its current execution state, making it possible to pause and resume the task.

A state machine in its simplest form is a data structure that has a predetermined set of states it can be in. In the case of coroutines, each state represents a possible pause/resume point. We don't store the state needed to pause/resume the task in a separate stack. We save it in a data structure instead.

This has some advantages, which I've covered before, but the most prominent ones are that they're very efficient and flexible. The downside is that you'd never want to write these state machines by hand (you'll see why in this chapter), so you need some kind of support from the compiler or another mechanism for rewriting your code to state machines instead of normal function calls.

The result is that you get something that looks very simple. It looks like a function/subroutine that you can easily map to something that you can run using a simple `call` instruction in assembly, but what you actually get is something pretty complex and different from this, and it doesn't look anything like what you'd expect.

> **Generators vs coroutines**
>
> Generators are state machines as well, exactly the kind we'll cover in this chapter. They're usually implemented in a language to create state machines that yield values to the calling function.
>
> Theoretically, you could make a distinction between coroutines and generators based on what they yield to. Generators are usually limited to yielding to the calling function. Coroutines can yield to another coroutine, a scheduler, or simply the caller, in which case they're just like generators.
>
> In my eyes, there is really no point in making a distinction between them. They represent the same underlying mechanism for creating tasks that can pause and resume their executions, so in this book, we'll treat them as basically the same thing.

Now that we've covered what coroutines are in text, we can start looking at what they look like in code.

An example of hand-written coroutines

The example we'll use going forward is a simplified version of Rust's asynchronous model. We'll create and implement the following:

- Our own simplified `Future` trait
- A simple HTTP client that can only make GET requests
- A task we can pause and resume implemented as a state machine
- Our own simplified `async`/`await` syntax called `coroutine`/`wait`
- A homemade preprocessor to transform our `coroutine`/`wait` functions into state machines the same way `async`/`await` is transformed

So, to actually demystify coroutines, futures, and `async`/`await`, we will have to make some compromises. If we didn't, we'd end up re-implementing everything that is `async`/`await` and futures in Rust today, which is too much for just understanding the underlying techniques and concepts.

Therefore, our example will do the following:

- Avoid error handling. If anything fails, we panic.
- Be specific and not generic. Creating generic solutions introduces a lot of complexity and makes the underlying concepts harder to reason about since we consequently have to create extra abstraction levels. Our solution will have some generic aspects where needed, though.
- Be limited in what it can do. You are of course free to expand, change, and play with all the examples (I encourage you to do so), but in the example, we only cover what we need and not anything more.
- Avoid macros.

So, with that out of the way, let's get started on our example.

The first thing you need to do is to create a new folder. This first example can be found in ch07/a-coroutine in the repository, so I suggest you name the folder a-coroutine as well.

Then, initialize a new crate by entering the folder and write cargo init.

Now that we have a new project up and running, we can create the modules and folders we need:

First, in main.rs, declare two modules as follows:

ch07/a-coroutine/src/main.rs

```
mod http;
mod future;
```

Next, create two new files in the src folder:

- future.rs, which will hold our future-related code
- http.rs, which will be the code related to our HTTP client

One last thing we need to do is to add a dependency on mio. We'll be using TcpStream from mio, as we'll build on this example in the following chapters and use mio as our non-blocking I/O library since we're already familiar with it:

ch07/a-coroutine/Cargo.toml

```
[dependencies]
mio = { version = "0.8", features = ["net", "os-poll"] }
```

Let's start in future.rs and implement our future-related code first.

Futures module

In `futures.rs`, the first thing we'll do is define a `Future` trait. It looks as follows:

ch07/a-coroutine/src/future.rs

```
pub trait Future {
    type Output;
    fn poll(&mut self) -> PollState<Self::Output>;
}
```

If we contrast this with the `Future` trait in Rust's standard library, you'll see it's very similar, except that we don't take `cx: &mut Context<'_>` as an argument and we return an enum with a slightly different name just to differentiate it so we don't mix them up:

```
pub trait Future {
    type Output;

    fn poll(self: Pin<&mut Self>, cx: &mut Context<'_>) -> Poll<Self::Output>;
}
```

The next thing we do is to define a `PollState<T>` enum:

ch07/a-coroutine/src/future.rs

```
pub enum PollState<T> {
    Ready(T),
    NotReady,
}
```

Again, if we compare this to the `Poll` enum in Rust's standard library, we see that they're practically the same:

```
pub enum Poll<T> {
    Ready(T),
    Pending,
}
```

For now, this is all we need to get the first iteration of our example up and running. Let's move on to the next file: `http.rs`.

HTTP module

In this module, we'll implement a very simple HTTP client. This client can only make GET requests to our `delayserver` since we just use this as a representation of a typical I/O operation and don't care specifically about being able to do more than we need.

The first thing we'll do is import some types and traits from the standard library as well as our `Futures` module:

ch07/a-coroutine/src/http.rs

```rust
use crate::future::{Future, PollState};
use std::io::{ErrorKind, Read, Write};
```

Next, we create a small helper function to write our HTTP requests. We've used this exact bit of code before in this book, so I'll not spend time explaining it again here:

ch07/a-coroutine/src/http.rs

```rust
fn get_req(path: &str) -> String {
    format!(
        "GET {path} HTTP/1.1\r\n\
            Host: localhost\r\n\
            Connection: close\r\n\
            \r\n"
    )
}
```

So, now we can start writing our HTTP client. The implementation is very short and simple:

```rust
pub struct Http;

impl Http {
    pub fn get(path: &str) -> impl Future<Output = String> {
        HttpGetFuture::new(path)
    }
}
```

We don't really need a struct here, but we add one since we might want to add some state at a later point. It's also a good way to group functions belonging to the HTTP client together.

Our HTTP client only has one function, `get`, which, eventually, will send a GET request to our `delayserver` with the path we specify (remember that the path is everything in bold in this example URL: http://127.0.0.1:8080/**1000/HelloWorld**),

The first thing you'll notice in the function body is that there is not much happening here. We only return `HttpGetFuture` and that's it.

In the function signature, you see that it returns an object implementing the `Future` trait that outputs a `String` when it's resolved. The string we return from this function will be the response we get from the server.

Now, we could have implemented the future trait directly on the `Http` struct, but I think it's a better design to allow one `Http` instance to give out multiple `Futures` instead of making the `Http` implement `Future` itself.

Let's take a closer look at `HttpGetFuture` since there is much more happening there.

Just to point this out so that there is no doubt going forward, `HttpGetFuture` is an example of a **leaf future**, and it will be the only leaf future we'll use in this example.

Let's add the struct declaration to the file:

ch07/a-coroutine/src/http.rs

```
struct HttpGetFuture {
    stream: Option<mio::net::TcpStream>,
    buffer: Vec<u8>,
    path: String,
}
```

This data structure will hold onto some data for us:

- `stream`: This holds an `Option<mio::net::TcpStream>`. This will be an `Option` since we won't connect to the stream at the same point as we create this structure.
- `buffer`: We'll read the data from the `TcpStream` and put it all in this buffer until we've read all the data returned from the server.
- `path`: This simply stores the path for our GET request so we can use it later.

The next thing we'll take a look at is the `impl` block for our `HttpGetFuture`:

ch07/a-coroutine/src/http.rs

```
impl HttpGetFuture {
    fn new(path: &'static str) -> Self {
        Self {
            stream: None,
            buffer: vec![],
            Path: path.to_string(),
        }
    }
}
```

```rust
    fn write_request(&mut self) {
        let stream = std::net::TcpStream::connect("127.0.0.1:8080").unwrap();
        stream.set_nonblocking(true).unwrap();
        let mut stream = mio::net::TcpStream::from_std(stream);
        stream.write_all(get_req(&self.path).as_bytes()).unwrap();
        self.stream = Some(stream);
    }
}
```

The `impl` block defines two functions. The first is `new`, which simply sets the initial state.

The next function is `write_requst`, which sends the GET request to the server. You've seen this code before in the example in *Chapter 4*, so this should look familiar.

> **Note**
> When *creating* `HttpGetFuture`, we don't actually *do* anything related to the GET request, which means that the call to `Http::get` returns immediately with just a simple data structure.

In contrast to earlier examples, we pass in the *IP address* for `localhost` instead of the DNS name. We take the same shortcut as before and let `connect` be blocking and everything else be non-blocking.

The next step is to write the GET request to the server. This will be non-blocking, and we don't have to wait for it to finish since we'll be waiting for the response anyway.

The last part of this file is the most important one—the implementation of the `Future` trait we defined:

ch07/a-coroutine/src/http.rs

```rust
impl Future for HttpGetFuture {
    type Output = String;

    fn poll(&mut self) -> PollState<Self::Output> {
        if self.stream.is_none() {
            println!("FIRST POLL - START OPERATION");
            self.write_request();
            return PollState::NotReady;
        }

        let mut buff = vec![0u8; 4096];
        loop {
            match self.stream.as_mut().unwrap().read(&mut buff) {
                Ok(0) => {
```

```
                    let s = String::from_utf8_lossy(&self.buffer);
                    break PollState::Ready(s.to_string());
                }
                Ok(n) => {
                    self.buffer.extend(&buff[0..n]);
                    continue;
                }
                Err(e) if e.kind() == ErrorKind::WouldBlock => {
                    break PollState::NotReady;
                }
                Err(e) if e.kind() == ErrorKind::Interrupted => {
                    continue;
                }
                Err(e) => panic!("{e:?}"),
            }
        }
    }
}
```

Okay, so this is where everything happens. The first thing we do is set the associated type called `Output` to `String`.

The next thing we do is to check whether this is the first time `poll` was called or not. We do this by checking if `self.stream` is `None`.

If it's the first time we call `poll`, we print a message (just so we can see the first time this future was polled), and then we write the GET request to the server.

On the first poll, we return `PollState::NotReady`, so `HttpGetFuture` will have to be polled at least once more to actually return any results.

The next part of the function is trying to read data from our `TcpStream`.

We've covered this before, so I'll make this brief, but there are basically five things that can happen:

1. The call successfully returns with 0 bytes read. We've read all the data from the stream and have received the entire GET response. We create a `String` from the data we've read and wrap it in `PollState::Ready` before we return.
2. The call successfully returns with `n > 0` bytes read. If that's the case, we read the data into our buffer, append the data into `self.buffer`, and immediately try to read more data from the stream.

3. We get an error of kind `WouldBlock`. If that's the case, we know that since we set the stream to non-blocking, the data isn't ready yet or there is more data but we haven't received it yet. In that case, we return `PollState::NotReady` to communicate that more calls to the poll are needed to finish the operation.

4. We get an error of kind `Interrupted`. This is a bit of a special case since reads can be interrupted by a signal. If it does, the usual way to handle the error is to simply try reading once more.

5. We get an error that we can't handle, and since our example does no error handling, we simply `panic!`

There is one subtle thing I want to point out. We can view this as a very simple state machine with three states:

- Not started, indicated by `self.stream` being `None`
- Pending, indicated by `self.stream` being `Some` and a read to `stream.read` returning `WouldBlock`
- Resolved, indicated by `self.stream` being `Some` and a call to `stream.read` returning 0 bytes

As you see, this model maps nicely to the states reported by the OS when trying to read our `TcpStream`.

Most leaf futures such as this will be quite simple, and although we didn't make the states explicit here, it still fits in the state machine model that we're basing our coroutines around.

Do all futures have to be lazy?

A lazy future is one where no work happens before it's polled the first time.

This will come up a lot if you read about futures in Rust, and since our own `Future` trait is based on that exact same model, the same question will arise here. The simple answer to this question is no!

There is nothing that forces leaf futures, such as the one we wrote here, to be lazy. We could have sent the HTTP request when we called the `Http::get` function if we wanted to. If you think about it, if we did just that, it would have caused a potentially big change that would impact how we achieve concurrency in our program.

The way it works now is that someone has to call `poll` at least one time to actually send the request. The consequence is that whoever calls `poll` on this future will have to call `poll` on many futures to kick off the operation if they want them to run concurrently.

If we kicked off the operation immediately when the future was created, you could create many futures and they would all run concurrently even though you polled them to completion one by one. If you poll them to completion one by one in the current design, the futures would *not* progress concurrently. Let that sink in for a moment.

Languages such as JavaScript start the operation when the coroutine is created, so there is no "one way" to do this. Every time you encounter a coroutine implementation, you should find out whether they're lazy or eager since this impacts how you program with them.

Even though we could make our future eager in this case, we really shouldn't. Since programmers in Rust expect futures to be lazy, they might depend on nothing happening before you call `poll` on them, and there may be unexpected side effects if the futures you write behave differently.

Now, when you read that Rust's futures are always lazy, a claim that I see very often, it refers to the compiler-generated state machines resulting from using `async/await`. As we'll see later, when your async functions are rewritten by the compiler, they're constructed in a way so that nothing you write in the body of an `async` function will execute before the first call to `Future::poll`.

Okay, so we've covered the `Future` trait and the leaf future we named `HttpGetFuture`. The next step is to create a task that we can stop and resume at predefined points.

Creating coroutines

We'll continue to build our knowledge and understanding from the ground up. The first thing we'll do is create a task that we can stop and resume by modeling it as a state machine by hand.

Once we've done that, we'll take a look at how this way of modeling pausable tasks enables us to write a syntax much like `async/await` and rely on code transformations to create these state machines instead of writing them by hand.

We'll create a simple program that does the following:

1. Prints a message when our pausable task is starting.
2. Makes a GET request to our `delayserver`.
3. Waits for the GET request.
4. Prints the response from the server.
5. Makes a second GET request to our `delayserver`.
6. Waits for the second response from the server.
7. Prints the response from the server.
8. Exits the program.

In addition, we'll execute our program by calling `Future::poll` on our hand-crafted coroutine as many times as required to run it to completion. There's no runtime, reactor, or executor yet since we'll cover those in the next chapter.

If we wrote our program as an async function, it would look as follows:

```
async fn async_main() {
    println!("Program starting")
    let txt = Http::get("/1000/HelloWorld").await;
    println!("{txt}");
    let txt2 = Http::("500/HelloWorld2").await;
    println!("{txt2}");
}
```

In main.rs, start by making the necessary imports and module declarations:

ch07/a-coroutine/src/main.rs

```
use std::time::Instant;

mod future;
mod http;

use crate::http::Http;
use future::{Future, PollState};
```

The next thing we write is our stoppable/resumable task called Coroutine:

ch07/a-coroutine/src/main.rs

```
struct Coroutine {
    state: State,
}
```

Once that's done, we write the different states this task could be in:

ch07/a-coroutine/src/main.rs

```
enum State {
    Start,
    Wait1(Box<dyn Future<Output = String>>),
    Wait2(Box<dyn Future<Output = String>>),
    Resolved,
}
```

This specific coroutine can be in four states:

- **Start**: The Coroutine has been created but it hasn't been polled yet

- **Wait1**: When we call `Http::get`, we get a `HttpGetFuture` returned that we store in the `State` enum. At this point, we return control back to the calling function so it can do other things if needed. We chose to make this generic over all `Future` functions that output a `String`, but since we only have one kind of future right now, we could have made it simply hold a `HttpGetFuture` and it would work the same way.
- **Wait2**: The second call to `Http::get` is the second place where we'll pass control back to the calling function.
- **Resolved**: The future is resolved and there is no more work to do.

> **Note**
>
> We could have simply defined `Coroutine` as an enum since the only state it holds is an enum indicating its state. But, we'll set up this example so we can add some state to `Coroutine` later on in this book.

Next is the implementation of `Coroutine`:

ch07/a-coroutine/src/main.rs

```
impl Coroutine {
    fn new() -> Self {
        Self {
            state: State::Start,
        }
    }
}
```

So far, this is pretty simple. When creating a new `Coroutine`, we simply set it to `State::Start` and that's it.

Now we come to the part where the work is actually done in the `Future` implementation for `Coroutine`. I'll walk you through the code:

ch07/a-coroutine/src/main.rs

```
impl Future for Coroutine {
    type Output = ();

    fn poll(&mut self) -> PollState<Self::Output> {
        loop {
            match self.state {
                State::Start => {
                    println!("Program starting");
                    let fut = Box::new(Http::get("/600/HelloWorld1"));
```

```rust
                    self.state = State::Wait1(fut);
                }
                State::Wait1(ref mut fut) => match fut.poll() {
                    PollState::Ready(txt) => {
                        println!("{txt}");
                        let fut2 = Box::new(Http::get("/400/HelloWorld2"));
                        self.state = State::Wait2(fut2);
                    }
                    PollState::NotReady => break PollState::NotReady,
                },
                State::Wait2(ref mut fut2) => match fut2.poll() {
                    PollState::Ready(txt2) => {
                        println!("{txt2}");
                        self.state = State::Resolved;
                        break PollState::Ready(());
                    }
                    PollState::NotReady => break PollState::NotReady,
                },

                State::Resolved => panic!("Polled a resolved future"),
            }
        }
    }
}
```

Let's start from the top:

1. The first thing we do is set the `Output` type to `()`. Since we won't be returning anything, it just makes our example simpler.

2. Next up is the implementation of the `poll` method. The first thing you notice is that we write a `loop` instance that matches `self.state`. We do this so we can drive the state machine forward until we reach a point where we can't progress any further without getting `PollState::NotReady` from one of our child futures.

3. If the state is `State::Start`, we know that this is the first time it was polled, so we run whatever instructions we need until we reach the point where we get a new future that we need to resolve.

4. When we call `Http::get`, we receive a future in return that we need to poll to completion before we progress any further.

5. At this point, we change the state to `State::Wait1` and we store the future we want to resolve so we can access it in the next state.
6. Our state machine has now changed its state from `Start` to `Wait1`. Since we're looping on the `match` statement, we immediately progress to the next state and will reach the match arm in `State::Wait1` on the next iteration.
7. The first thing we do in `Wait1` to call `poll` on the `Future` instance we're waiting on.
8. If the future returns `PollState::NotReady`, we simply bubble that up to the caller by breaking out of the loop and returning `NotReady`.
9. If the future returns `PollState::Ready` together with our data, we know that we can execute the instructions that rely on the data from the first future and advance to the next state. In our case, we only print out the returned data, so that's only one line of code.
10. Next, we get to the point where we get a new future by calling `Http::get`. We set the state to `Wait2`, just like we did when going from `State::Start` to `State::Wait1`.
11. Like we did the first time we got a future that we needed to resolve before we continue, we save it so we can access it in `State::Wait2`.
12. Since we're in a loop, the next thing that happens is that we reach the matching arm for `Wait2`, and here, we repeat the same steps as we did for `State::Wait1` but on a different future.
13. If it returns `Ready` with our data, we act on it and we set the final state of our `Coroutine` to `State::Resolved`. There is one more important change: this time, we want to communicate to the caller that this future is done, so we break out of the loop and return `PollState::Ready`.

If anyone tries to call `poll` on our `Coroutine` again, we will panic, so the caller must make sure to keep track of when the future returns `PollState::Ready` and make sure to not call `poll` on it ever again. The last thing we do before we get to our `main` function is create a new `Coroutine` in a function we call `async_main`. This way, we can keep the changes to a minimum when we start talking about `async/await` in the last part of this chapter:

ch07/a-coroutine/src/main.rs

```
fn async_main() -> impl Future<Output = ()> {
    Coroutine::new()
}
```

So, at this point, we're finished writing our coroutine and the only thing left is to write some logic to drive our state machine through its different stages of the `main` function.

One thing to note here is that our main function is just a regular main function. The loop in our main function is what drives the asynchronous operations to completion:

ch07/a-coroutine/src/main.rs

```
fn main() {
    let mut future = async_main();
    loop {
        match future.poll() {
            PollState::NotReady => {
                println!("Schedule other tasks");
            },
            PollState::Ready(_) => break,
        }
        thread::sleep(Duration::from_millis(100));
    }
}
```

This function is very simple. We first get the future returned from `async_main` and then we call `poll` on it in a loop until it returns `PollState::Ready`.

Every time we receive a `PollState::NotReady` in return, the control is yielded back to us. we could do other work here, such as scheduling another task, if we want to, but in our case, we just print `Schedule other tasks`.

We also limit how often the loop is run by sleeping for 100 milliseconds on every call. This way we won't be overwhelmed with printouts and we can assume that there are roughly 100 milliseconds between every time we see `"Schedule other tasks"` printed to the console.

If we run the example, we get this output:

```
Program starting
FIRST POLL - START OPERATION
Schedule other tasks
Schedule other tasks
Schedule other tasks
Schedule other tasks
Schedule other tasks
Schedule other tasks
HTTP/1.1 200 OK
content-length: 11
connection: close
content-type: text/plain; charset=utf-8
date: Tue, 24 Oct 2023 20:39:13 GMT

HelloWorld1
FIRST POLL - START OPERATION
```

```
Schedule other tasks
Schedule other tasks
Schedule other tasks
Schedule other tasks
HTTP/1.1 200 OK
content-length: 11
connection: close
content-type: text/plain; charset=utf-8
date: Tue, 24 Oct 2023 20:39:13 GMT

HelloWorld2
```

By looking at the printouts, you can get an idea of the program flow.

1. First, we see `Program starting`, which executes at the start of our coroutine.
2. We then see that we immediately move on to the `FIRST POLL - START OPERATION` message that we only print when the future returned from our HTTP client is polled the first time.
3. Next, we can see that we're back in our `main` function, and at this point, we could theoretically go ahead and run other tasks if we had any
4. Every 100 ms, we check if the task is finished and get the same message telling us that we can schedule other tasks
5. Then, after roughly 600 milliseconds, we receive a response that's printed out
6. We repeat the process once more until we receive and print out the second response from the server

Congratulations, you've now created a task that can be paused and resumed at different points, allowing it to be in progress.

Who on earth wants to write code like this to accomplish a simple task?

The answer is no one!

Yes, it's a bit bombastic, but I dare guess that very few programmers prefer writing a 55-line state machine when you compare it to the 7 lines of normal sequential code you'd have to write to accomplish the same thing.

If we recall the goals of most userland abstractions over concurrent operations, we'll see that this way of doing it only checks one of the three boxes that we're aiming for:

- Efficient
- Expressive
- Easy to use and hard to misuse

Our state machine will be efficient, but that's pretty much it.

However, you might also notice that there is a system to the craziness. This might not come as a surprise, but the code we wrote could be much simpler if we tagged the start of each function and each point we wanted to yield control back to the caller with a few keywords and had our state machine generated for us. And that's the basic idea behind `async/await`.

Let's go and see how this would work in our example.

async/await

The previous example could simply be written as the following using `async/await` keywords:

```
async fn async_main() {
    println!("Program starting")
    let txt = Http::get("/1000/HelloWorld").await;
    println!("{txt}");
    let txt2 = Http::("500/HelloWorld2").await;
    println!("{txt2}");
}
```

That's seven lines of code, and it looks very familiar to code you'd write in a normal subroutine/function.

It turns out that we can let the compiler write these state machines for us instead of writing them ourselves. Not only that, we could get very far just using simple macros to help us, which is exactly how the current `async/await` syntax was prototyped before it became a part of the language. You can see an example of that at `https://github.com/alexcrichton/futures-await`.

The downside is of course that these functions look like normal subroutines but are in fact very different in nature. With a strongly typed language such as Rust, which borrow semantics instead of using a garbage collector, it's impossible to hide the fact that these functions are different. This can cause a bit of confusion for programmers, who expect everything to behave the same way.

> **Coroutine bonus example**
>
> To show how close our example is to the behavior we get using the `std::future::Future` trait and `async/await` in Rust, I created the exact same example as we just did in `a-coroutines` using "proper" futures and the `async/await` syntax instead. The first thing you'll notice is that it only required very minor changes to the code. Secondly, you can see for yourself that the output shows the exact same program flow as it did in the example where we hand-wrote the state machine ourselves. You will find this example in the `ch07/a-coroutines-bonus` folder in the repository.

So, let's take this a step further. To avoid confusion, and since our coroutines only yield to the calling function right now (there is no scheduler, event loop, or anything like that yet), we use a slightly different syntax called `coroutine/wait` and create a way to have these state machines generated for us.

coroutine/wait

The `coroutine/wait` syntax will have clear similarities to the `async/await` syntax, although it's a lot more limited.

The basic rules are as follows:

- Every function prefixed with `coroutine` will be rewritten to a state machine like the one we wrote.
- The return type of functions marked with `coroutine` will be rewritten so they return `-> impl Future<Output = String>` (yes, our syntax will only deal with futures that output a `String`).
- Only objects implementing the `Future` trait can be postfixed with `.wait`. These points will be represented as separate stages in our state machine.
- Functions prefixed with `coroutine` can call normal functions, but normal functions can't call `coroutine` functions and expect anything to happen unless they call `poll` on them repeatedly until they return `PollState::Ready`.

Our implementation will make sure that if we write the following code, it will compile to the same state machine we wrote at the start of this chapter(with the exception that all coroutines will return a String):

```
coroutine fn async_main() {
    println!("Program starting")
    let txt = Http::get("/1000/HelloWorld").wait;
    println!("{txt}");
    let txt2 = Http::("500/HelloWorld2").wait;
    println!("{txt2}");
}
```

But wait. `coroutine/wait` aren't valid keywords in Rust. I would get a compilation error if I wrote that!

You're right. So, I created a small program called `corofy` that rewrites the `coroutine/wait` functions into these state machines for us. Let's explain that quickly.

corofy—the coroutine preprocessor

The best way of rewriting code in Rust is using the macro system. The downside is that it's not clear exactly what it compiles down to, and expanding the macros is not optimal for our use case since one of the main goals is to take a look at the differences between the code we write and what it transforms into. In addition to that, macros can get quite complex to read and understand unless you work a lot with them on a regular basis.

Instead, corofy is a normal Rust program you can find in the repository under ch07/corofy.

If you enter that folder, you can install the tool globally by writing the following:

```
cargo install --path .
```

Now you can use the tool from anywhere. It works by providing it with an input file containing the coroutine/wait syntax, such as corofy ./src/main.rs [optional output file]. If you don't specify an output file, it will create a file in the same folder postfixed with _corofied.

> **Note**
>
> The tool is extremely limited. The honest reason why is that I want to finish this example before we reach the year 2300, and I finished rewriting the entire Rust compiler from scratch just to give a robust experience using the coroutine/wait keywords.
>
> It turns out that writing transformations like this without access to Rust's type system is very difficult. The main use case for this tool will be to transform the examples we write here, but it would probably work for slight variations of the same examples as well (like adding more wait points or doing more interesting tasks in between each wait point). Take a look at the README for corofy for more information about its limitations.
>
> One more thing: I assume that you specified no explicit output file going forward so the output file will have the same name as the input file postfixed with _corofied.

The program reads the file you give it and searches for usages of the coroutine keyword. It takes these functions, comments them out (so they're still in the file), puts them last in the file, and writes out the state machine implementation directly below, indicating what parts of the state machine are the code you actually wrote between the wait points.

Now that I've introduced our new tool, it's time to put it to use.

b-async-await—an example of a coroutine/wait transformation

Let's start by expanding our example slightly. Now that we have a program that writes out our state machines, it's easier for us to create some examples and cover some more complex parts of our coroutine implementation.

We'll base the following examples on the exact same code as we did in the first one. In the repository, you'll find this example under `ch07/b-async-await`.

If you write every example from the book and don't rely on the existing code in the repository, you can do one of two things:

- Keep changing the code in the first example
- Create a new cargo project called `b-async-await` and copy everything in the `src` folder and the `dependencies` section from `Cargo.toml` from the previous example over to the new one.

No matter what you choose, you should have the same code in front of you.

Let's simply change the code in `main.rs` to this:

ch07/b-async-await/src/main.rs

```rust
use std::time::Instant;

mod http;
mod future;

use future::*;
use crate::http::Http;

fn get_path(i: usize) -> String {
    format!("/{}/HelloWorld{i}", i * 1000)
}

coroutine fn async_main() {
    println!("Program starting");

    let txt = Http::get(&get_path(0)).wait;
    println!("{txt}");
    let txt = Http::get(&get_path(1)).wait;
    println!("{txt}");
    let txt = Http::get(&get_path(2)).wait;
    println!("{txt}");
    let txt = Http::get(&get_path(3)).wait;
    println!("{txt}");
    let txt = Http::get(&get_path(4)).wait;
    println!("{txt}");
}
```

```
fn main() {
    let start = Instant::now();
    let mut future = async_main();

    loop {
        match future.poll() {
            PollState::NotReady => (),
            PollState::Ready(_) => break,
        }
    }
    println!("\nELAPSED TIME: {}", start.elapsed().as_secs_f32());
}
```

This code contains a few changes. First, we add a convenience function for creating new paths for our GET request called `get_path` to create a path we can use in our GET request with a delay and a message based on the integer we pass in.

Next, in our `async_main` function, we create five requests with delays varying from 0 to 4 seconds.

The last change we've made is in our `main` function. We no longer print out a message on every call to poll, and therefore, we don't use `thread::sleep` to limit the number of calls. Instead, we measure the time from when we enter the `main` function to when we exit it because we can use that as a way to prove whether our code runs concurrently or not.

Now that our `main.rs` looks like the preceding example, we can use `corofy` to rewrite it into a state machine, so assuming we're in the root folder of `ch07/b-async-await`, we can write the following:

```
corofy ./src/main.rs
```

That should output a file called `main_corofied.rs` in the `src` folder that you can open and inspect.

Now, you can copy all the contents of `main_corofied.rs` in this file and paste it into `main.rs`.

> **Note**
>
> For convenience, there is a file called `original_main.rs` in the root of the project that contains the code for `main.rs` that we presented, so you don't need to save the original content of `main.rs`. If you write out every example yourself by copying it from the book in your own project, it would be smart to store the original contents of `main.rs` somewhere before you overwrite it.

I won't show the entire state machine here since the 39 lines of code using `coroutine/wait` end up being 170 lines of code when written as a state machine, but our `State` enum now looks like this:

```
enum State0 {
    Start,
    Wait1(Box<dyn Future<Output = String>>),
```

```
    Wait2(Box<dyn Future<Output = String>>),
    Wait3(Box<dyn Future<Output = String>>),
    Wait4(Box<dyn Future<Output = String>>),
    Wait5(Box<dyn Future<Output = String>>),
    Resolved,
}
```

If you run the program using `cargo run`, you now get the following output:

```
Program starting
FIRST POLL - START OPERATION
HTTP/1.1 200 OK
content-length: 11
connection: close
content-type: text/plain; charset=utf-8
date: Tue, xx xxx xxxx 21:05:55 GMT

HelloWorld0
FIRST POLL - START OPERATION
HTTP/1.1 200 OK
content-length: 11
connection: close
content-type: text/plain; charset=utf-8
date: Tue, xx xxx xxxx 21:05:56 GMT

HelloWorld1
FIRST POLL - START OPERATION
HTTP/1.1 200 OK
content-length: 11
connection: close
content-type: text/plain; charset=utf-8
date: Tue, xx xxx xxxx 21:05:58 GMT

HelloWorld2
FIRST POLL - START OPERATION
HTTP/1.1 200 OK
content-length: 11
connection: close
content-type: text/plain; charset=utf-8
date: Tue, xx xxx xxxx 21:06:01 GMT

HelloWorld3
FIRST POLL - START OPERATION
HTTP/1.1 200 OK
content-length: 11
connection: close
content-type: text/plain; charset=utf-8
```

```
date: Tue, xx xxx xxxx 21:06:05 GMT

HelloWorld4


ELAPSED TIME: 10.043025
```

So, you see that our code runs as expected.

Since we called `wait` on every call to `Http::get`, the code ran sequentially, which is evident when we look at the elapsed time of 10 seconds.

That makes sense since the delays we asked for were 0 + 1 + 2 + 3 + 4, which equals 10 seconds.

What if we want our futures to run concurrently?

Do you remember we talked about these futures being *lazy*? Good. So, you know that we won't get concurrency just by creating a future. We need to poll them to start the operation.

To solve this, we take some inspiration from **Tokio** and create a function that does just that called `join_all`. It takes a collection of futures and drives them all to completion concurrently.

Let's create the last example for this chapter where we do just this.

c-async-await—concurrent futures

Okay, so we'll build on the last example and do just the same thing. Create a new project called `c-async-await` and copy `Cargo.toml` and everything in the `src` folder over.

The first thing we'll do is go to `future.rs` and add a `join_all` function below our existing code:

ch07/c-async-await/src/future.rs

```
pub fn join_all<F: Future>(futures: Vec<F>) -> JoinAll<F> {
    let futures = futures.into_iter().map(|f| (false, f)).collect();
    JoinAll {
        futures,
        finished_count: 0,
    }
}
```

This function takes a collection of futures as an argument and returns a `JoinAll<F>` future.

The function simply creates a new collection. In this collection, we will have tuples consisting of the original futures we received and a `bool` value indicating whether the future is resolved or not.

Next, we have the definition of our `JoinAll` struct:

ch07/c-async-await/src/future.rs

```
pub struct JoinAll<F: Future> {
    futures: Vec<(bool, F)>,
    finished_count: usize,
}
```

This struct will simply store the collection we created and a `finished_count`. The last field will make it a little bit easier to keep track of how many futures have been resolved.

As we're getting used to by now, most of the interesting parts happen in the `Future` implementation for `JoinAll`:

```
impl<F: Future> Future for JoinAll<F> {
    type Output = String;

    fn poll(&mut self) -> PollState<Self::Output> {
        for (finished, fut) in self.futures.iter_mut() {
            if *finished {
                continue;
            }

            match fut.poll() {
                PollState::Ready(_) => {
                    *finished = true;
                    self.finished_count += 1;
                }
                PollState::NotReady => continue,
            }
        }

        if self.finished_count == self.futures.len() {
            PollState::Ready(String::new())
        } else {
            PollState::NotReady
        }
    }
}
```

We set `Output` to `String`. This might strike you as strange since we don't actually return anything from this implementation. The reason is that `corofy` will only work with futures that return a `String` (it's one of its many, many shortcomings), so we just accept that and return an empty string on completion.

Next up is our `poll` implementation. The first thing we do is to loop over each (flag, future) tuple:

```
for (finished, fut) in self.futures.iter_mut()
```

Inside the loop, we first check if the flag for this future is set to `finished`. If it is, we simply go to the next item in the collection.

If it's not finished, we `poll` the future.

If we get `PollState::Ready` back, we set the flag for this future to `true` so that we won't poll it again and we increase the finished count.

> **Note**
>
> It's worth noting that the `join_all` implementation we create here will not work in any meaningful way with futures that return a value. In our case, we simply throw the value away, but remember, we're trying to keep this as simple as possible for now and the only thing we want to show is the concurrency aspect of calling `join_all`.
>
> Tokio's `join_all` implementation puts all the returned values in a `Vec<T>` and returns them when the `JoinAll` future resolves.

If we get `PollState::NotReady`, we simply continue to the next future in the collection.

After iterating through the entire collection, we check if we've resolved all the futures we originally received in `if self.finished_count == self.futures.len()`.

If all our futures have been resolved, we return `PollState::Ready` with an empty string (to make `corofy` happy). If there are still unresolved futures, we return `PollState::NotReady`.

> **Important**
>
> There is one subtle point to make a note of here. The first time `JoinAll::poll` is called, it will call `poll` on each future in the collection. Polling each future will kick off whatever operation they represent and allow them to *progress concurrently*. This is one way to achieve concurrency with lazy coroutines, such as the ones we're dealing with here.

Next up are the changes we'll make in `main.rs`.

The `main` function will be the same, as well as the imports and declarations at the start of the file, so I'll only present the `coroutine/await` functions that we've changed:

```
coroutine fn request(i: usize) {
    let path = format!("/{}/HelloWorld{i}", i * 1000);
    let txt = Http::get(&path).wait;
    println!("{txt}");
}

coroutine fn async_main() {
    println!("Program starting");
    let mut futures = vec![];

    for i in 0..5 {
        futures.push(request(i));
    }
    future::join_all(futures).wait;
}
```

> **Note**
> In the repository, you'll find the correct code to put in `main.rs` in `ch07/c-async-await/original_main.rs` if you ever lose track of it with all the copy/pasting we're doing.

Now we have two `coroutine/wait` functions. `async_main` stores a set of coroutines created by `read_request` in a `Vec<T: Future>`.

Then it creates a `JoinAll` future and calls `wait` on it.

The next `coroutine/wait` function is `read_requests`, which takes an integer as input and uses that to create GET requests. This coroutine will in turn wait for the response and print out the result once it arrives.

Since we create the requests with delays of 0, 1, 2, 3, 4 seconds, we should expect the entire program to finish in just over four seconds because all the tasks will be in progress *concurrently*. The ones with short delays will be finished by the time the task with a four-second delay finishes.

We can now transform our `coroutine/await` functions into state machines by making sure we're in the folder `ch07/c-async-await` and writing `corofy ./src/main.rs`.

You should now see a file called `main_corofied.rs` in the `src` folder. Copy its contents and replace what's in `main.rs` with it.

If you run the program by writing `cargo run`, you should get the following output:

```
Program starting
FIRST POLL - START OPERATION
FIRST POLL - START OPERATION
FIRST POLL - START OPERATION
FIRST POLL - START OPERATION
FIRST POLL - START OPERATION
HTTP/1.1 200 OK
content-length: 11
connection: close
content-type: text/plain; charset=utf-8
date: Tue, xx xxx xxxx 21:11:36 GMT

HelloWorld0
HTTP/1.1 200 OK
content-length: 11
connection: close
content-type: text/plain; charset=utf-8
date: Tue, xx xxx xxxx 21:11:37 GMT

HelloWorld1
HTTP/1.1 200 OK
content-length: 11
connection: close
content-type: text/plain; charset=utf-8
date: Tue, xx xxx xxxx 21:11:38 GMT

HelloWorld2
HTTP/1.1 200 OK
content-length: 11
connection: close
content-type: text/plain; charset=utf-8
date: Tue, xx xxx xxxx 21:11:39 GMT

HelloWorld3
HTTP/1.1 200 OK
content-length: 11
connection: close
content-type: text/plain; charset=utf-8
date: Tue, xx xxx xxxx 21:11:40 GMT

HelloWorld4

ELAPSED TIME: 4.0084987
```

The thing to make a note of here is the elapsed time. It's now just over four seconds, just like we expected it would be when our futures run concurrently.

If we take a look at how `coroutine/await` changed the experience of writing coroutines from a programmer's perspective, we'll see that we're much closer to our goal now:

- **Efficient**: State machines require no context switches and only save/restore the data associated with that specific task. We have no growing vs segmented stack issues, as they all use the same OS-provided stack.
- **Expressive**: We can write code the same way as we do in "normal" Rust, and with compiler support, we can get the same error messages and use the same tooling
- **Easy to use and hard to misuse**: This is a point where we probably fall slightly short of a typical fiber/green threads implementation due to the fact that our programs are heavily transformed "behind our backs" by the compiler, which can result in some rough edges. Specifically, you can't call an `async` function from a normal function and expect anything meaningful to happen; you have to actively poll it to completion somehow, which gets more complex as we start adding runtimes into the mix. However, for the most part, we can write programs just the way we're used to.

Final thoughts

Before we round off this chapter, I want to point out that it should now be clear to us why coroutines aren't really **pre-emptable**. If you remember back in *Chapter 2*, we said that a *stackful* coroutine (such as our fibers/green threads example) could be *pre-empted* and its execution could be paused at any point. That's because they have a stack, and pausing a task is as simple as storing the current execution state to the stack and jumping to another task.

That's not possible here. The only places we can stop and resume execution are at the pre-defined suspension points that we manually tagged with `wait`.

In theory, if you have a tightly integrated system where you control the compiler, the coroutine definition, the scheduler, and the I/O primitives, you could add additional states to the state machine and create additional points where the task could be suspended/resumed. These suspension points could be opaque to the user and treated differently than normal wait/suspension points.

For example, every time you encounter a normal function call, you could add a suspension point (a new state to our state machine) where you check in with the scheduler if the current task has used up its time budget or something like that. If it has, you could schedule another task to run and resume the task at a later point even though this didn't happen in a cooperative manner.

However, even though this would be invisible to the user, it's not the same as being able to stop/resume execution from any point in your code. It would also go against the usually implied cooperative nature of coroutines.

Summary

Good job! In this chapter, we introduced quite a bit of code and set up an example that we'll continue using in the following chapters.

So far, we've focused on futures and `async`/`await` to model and create tasks that can be paused and resumed at specific points. We know this is a prerequisite to having tasks that are in progress at the same time. We did this by introducing our own simplified `Future` trait and our own `coroutine`/`wait` syntax that's way more limited than Rust's futures and `async`/`await` syntax, but it's easier to understand and get a mental idea of how this works in contrast to fibers/green threads (at least I hope so).

We have also discussed the difference between eager and lazy coroutines and how they impact how you achieve concurrency. We took inspiration from Tokio's `join_all` function and implemented our own version of it.

In this chapter, we simply created tasks that could be paused and resumed. There are no event loops, scheduling, or anything like that yet, but don't worry. They're exactly what we'll go through in the next chapter. The good news is that getting a clear idea of coroutines, like we did in this chapter, is one of the most difficult things to do.

8
Runtimes, Wakers, and the Reactor-Executor Pattern

In the previous chapter, we created our own pausable tasks (coroutines) by writing them as state machines. We created a common API for these tasks by requiring them to implement the Future trait. We also showed how we can create these coroutines using some keywords and programmatically rewrite them so that we don't have to implement these state machines by hand, and instead write our programs pretty much the same way we normally would.

If we stop for a moment and take a bird's eye view over what we got so far, it's conceptually pretty simple: we have an interface for pausable tasks (the Future trait), and we have two keywords (coroutine/wait) to indicate code segments we want rewritten as a state machine that divides our code into segments we can pause between.

However, we have no event loop, and we have no scheduler yet. In this chapter, we'll expand on our example and add a runtime that allows us to run our program efficiently and opens up the possibility to schedule tasks concurrently much more efficiently than what we do now.

This chapter will take you on a journey where we implement our runtime in two stages, gradually making it more useful, efficient, and capable. We'll start with a brief overview of what runtimes are and why we want to understand some of their characteristics. We'll build on what we just learned in *Chapter 7*, and show how we can make it much more efficient and avoid continuously polling the future to make it progress by leveraging the knowledge we gained in *Chapter 4*.

Next, we'll show how we can get a more flexible and loosely coupled design by dividing the runtime into two parts: an **executor** and a **reactor**.

In this chapter, you will learn about basic runtime design, reactors, executors, wakers, and spawning, and we'll build on a lot of the knowledge we've gained throughout the book.

This will be one of the big chapters in this book, not because the topic is too complex or difficult, but because we have quite a bit of code to write. In addition to that, I try to give you a good mental model of what's happening by providing quite a few diagrams and explaining everything very thoroughly. It's not one of those chapters you typically blaze through before going to bed, though, but I do promise it's absolutely worth it in the end.

The chapter will be divided into the following segments:

- Introduction to runtimes and why we need them
- Improving our base example
- Creating a proper runtime
- Step 1 – Improving our runtime design by adding a Reactor and a Waker
- Step 2 – Implementing a proper Executor
- Step 3 – Implementing a proper Reactor
- Experimenting with our new runtime

So, let's dive right in!

Technical requirements

The examples in this chapter will build on the code from our last chapter, so the requirements are the same. The examples will all be cross-platform and work on all platforms that Rust (https://doc.rust-lang.org/beta/rustc/platform-support.html#tier-1-with-host-tools) and mio (https://github.com/tokio-rs/mio#platforms) supports. The only thing you need is Rust installed and the repository that belongs to the book downloaded locally. All the code in this chapter will be found in the `ch08` folder.

To follow the examples step by step, you'll also need `corofy` installed on your machine. If you didn't install it in *Chapter 7*, install it now by going into the `ch08/corofy` folder in the repository and running this command:

```
cargo install --force --path .
```

Alternatively, you can just copy the relevant files in the repository when we come to the points where we use `corofy` to rewrite our `coroutine/wait` syntax. Both versions will be available to you there as well.

We'll also use `delayserver` in this example, so you need to open a separate terminal, enter the `delayserver` folder at the root of the repository, and write `cargo run` so that it's ready and available for the examples going forward.

Remember to change the ports in the code if you for some reason have to change the port `delayserver` listens on.

Introduction to runtimes and why we need them

As you know by now, you need to bring your own runtime for driving and scheduling asynchronous tasks in Rust.

Runtimes come in many flavors, from the popular **Embassy** embedded runtime (`https://github.com/embassy-rs/embassy`), which centers more on general multitasking and can replace the need for a **real-time operating system (RTOS)** on many platforms, to **Tokio** (`https://github.com/tokio-rs/tokio`), which centers on non-blocking I/O on popular server and desktop operating systems.

All runtimes in Rust need to do at least two things: schedule and drive objects implementing Rust's `Future` trait to completion. Going forward in this chapter, we'll mostly focus on runtimes for doing non-blocking I/O on popular desktop and server operating systems such as Windows, Linux, and macOS. This is also by far the most common type of runtime most programmers will encounter in Rust.

Taking control over how tasks are scheduled is *very* invasive, and it's pretty much a one-way street. If you rely on a userland scheduler to run your tasks, you cannot, at the same time, use the OS scheduler (without jumping through several hoops), since mixing them in your code will wreak havoc and might end up defeating the whole purpose of writing an asynchronous program.

The following diagram illustrates the different schedulers:

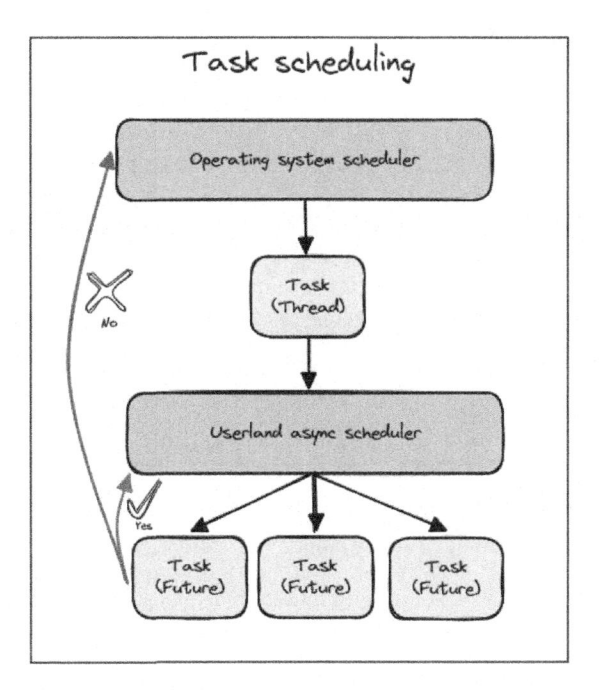

Figure 8.1 – Task scheduling in a single-threaded asynchronous system

An example of yielding to the OS scheduler is making a blocking call using the default `std::net::TcpStream` or `std::thread::sleep` methods. Even *potentially* blocking calls using primitives such as `Mutex` provided by the standard library might yield to the OS scheduler.

That's why you'll often find that asynchronous programming tends to color everything it touches, and it's tough to only run a part of your program using `async`/`await`.

The consequence is that runtimes must use a non-blocking version of the standard library. In theory, you could make one non-blocking version of the standard library that all runtimes use, and that was one of the goals of the `async_std` initiative (https://book.async.rs/introduction). However, having the community agree upon one way to solve this task was a tall order and one that hasn't really come to fruition yet.

Before we start implementing our examples, we'll discuss the overall design of a typical async runtime in Rust. Most runtimes such as Tokio, Smol, or async-std will divide their runtime into two parts.

The part that tracks events we're waiting on and makes sure to wait on notifications from the OS in an efficient manner is often called the *reactor* or *driver*.

The part that schedules tasks and polls them to completion is called the *executor*.

Let's take a high-level look at this design so that we know what we'll be implementing in our example.

Reactors and executors

Dividing the runtime into two distinct parts makes a lot of sense when we take a look at how Rust models asynchronous tasks. If you read the documentation for `Future` (https://doc.rust-lang.org/std/future/trait.Future.html) and `Waker` (https://doc.rust-lang.org/std/task/struct.Waker.html), you'll see that Rust doesn't only define a `Future` trait and a `Waker` type but also comes with important information on how they're supposed to be used.

One example of this is that `Future` traits are *inert*, as we covered in *Chapter 6*. Another example is that a call to `Waker::wake` will guarantee *at least one call* to `Future::poll` on the corresponding task.

So, already by reading the documentation, you will see that there is at least some thought put into how runtimes should behave.

The reason for learning this pattern is that it's almost a glove-to-hand fit for Rust's asynchronous model.

Since many readers, including me, will not have English as a first language, I'll explain the names here at the start since, well, they seem to be easy to misunderstand.

If the name **reactor** gives you associations with *nuclear reactors*, and you start thinking of reactors as something that powers, or drives, a runtime, drop that thought right now. A reactor is simply something that reacts to a whole set of incoming events and dispatches them one by one to a handler. It's an event loop, and in our case, it dispatches events to an executor. Events that are handled by a reactor could be anything from a timer that expires, an interrupt if you write programs for embedded systems, or an I/O event such as a READABLE event on TcpStream.

You could have several kinds of reactors running in the same runtime.

If the name **executor** gives you associations to *executioners* (the medieval times kind) or *executables*, drop that thought as well. If you look up what an executor is, it's a person, often a lawyer, who administers a person's will. Most often, since that person is dead. Which is also the point where whatever mental model the naming suggests to you falls apart since nothing, and no one, needs to come in harm's way for the executor to have work to do in an asynchronous runtime, but I digress.

The important point is that an executor simply decides who gets time on the CPU to progress and when they get it. The executor must also call Future::poll and advance the state machines to their next state. It's a type of scheduler.

It can be frustrating to get the wrong idea from the start since the subject matter is already complex enough without thinking about how on earth nuclear reactors and executioners fit in the whole picture.

Since reactors will respond to events, they need some integration with the *source* of the event. If we continue using TcpStream as an example, something will call *read* or *write* on it, and at that point, the reactor needs to know that it should track certain events on that source.

For this reason, non-blocking I/O primitives and reactors need tight integration, and depending on how you look at it, the I/O primitives will either have to bring their own reactor or you'll have a reactor that provides I/O primitives such as sockets, ports, and streams.

Now that we've covered some of the overarching design, we can start writing some code.

Runtimes tend to get complex pretty quickly, so to keep this as simple as possible, we'll avoid any error handling in our code and use unwrap or expect for everything. We'll also choose simplicity over cleverness and readability over efficiency to the best of our abilities.

Our first task will be to take the first example we wrote in *Chapter 7* and improve it by avoiding having to actively poll it to make progress. Instead, we lean on what we learned about non-blocking I/O and epoll in the earlier chapters.

Improving our base example

We'll create a version of the first example in *Chapter 7* since it's the simplest one to start with. Our only focus is showing how to schedule and drive the runtimes more efficiently.

We start with the following steps:

1. Create a new project and name it a-runtime (alternatively, navigate to ch08/a-runtime in the book's repository).

2. Copy the `future.rs` and `http.rs` files in the `src` folder from the first project we created in *Chapter 7*, named `a-coroutine` (alternatively, copy the files from `ch07/a-coroutine` in the book's repository) to the `src` folder in our new project.

3. Make sure to add `mio` as a dependency by adding the following to `Cargo.toml`:

```
[dependencies]
mio = { version = "0.8", features = ["net", "os-poll"] }
```

4. Create a new file in the `src` folder called `runtime.rs`.

We'll use `corofy` to change the following `coroutine/wait` program into its state machine representation that we can run.

In `src/main.rs`, add the following code:

ch08/a-runtime/src/main.rs

```
mod future;
mod http;
mod runtime;

use future::{Future, PollState};
use runtime::Runtime;

fn main() {
    let future = async_main();
    let mut runtime = Runtime::new();
    runtime.block_on(future);
}

coroutine fn async_main() {
    println!("Program starting");
    let txt = http::Http::get("/600/HelloAsyncAwait").wait;
    println!("{txt}");
    let txt = http::Http::get("/400/HelloAsyncAwait").wait;
    println!("{txt}");
}
```

This program is basically the same one we created in *Chapter 7*, only this time, we create it from our `coroutine/wait` syntax instead of writing the state machine by hand. Next, we need to transform this into code by using `corofy` since the compiler doesn't recognize our own `coroutine/wait` syntax.

1. If you're in the root folder of `a-runtime`, run `corofy ./src/main.rs`.
2. You should now have a file that's called `main_corofied.rs`.
3. Delete the code in `main.rs` and copy the contents of `main_corofied.rs` into `main.rs`.
4. You can now delete `main_corofied.rs` since we won't need it going forward.

If everything is done right, the project structure should now look like this:

```
src
 |-- future.rs
 |-- http.rs
 |-- main.rs
 |-- runtime.rs
```

> **Tip**
> You can always refer to the book's repository to make sure everything is correct. The correct example is located in the `ch08/a-runtime` folder. In the repository, you'll also find a file called `main_orig.rs` in the root folder that contains the `coroutine/wait` program if you want to rerun it or have problems getting everything working correctly.

Design

Before we go any further, let's visualize how our system is currently working if we consider it with two futures created by `coroutine/wait` and two calls to `Http::get`. The loop that polls our `Future` trait to completion in the `main` function takes the role of the executor in our visualization, and as you see, we have a chain of futures consisting of:

1. Non-leaf futures created by `async/await` (or `coroutine/wait` in our example) that simply call `poll` on the next future until it reaches a leaf future
2. Leaf futures that poll an actual source that's either `Ready` or `NotReady`

The following diagram shows a simplified overview of our current design:

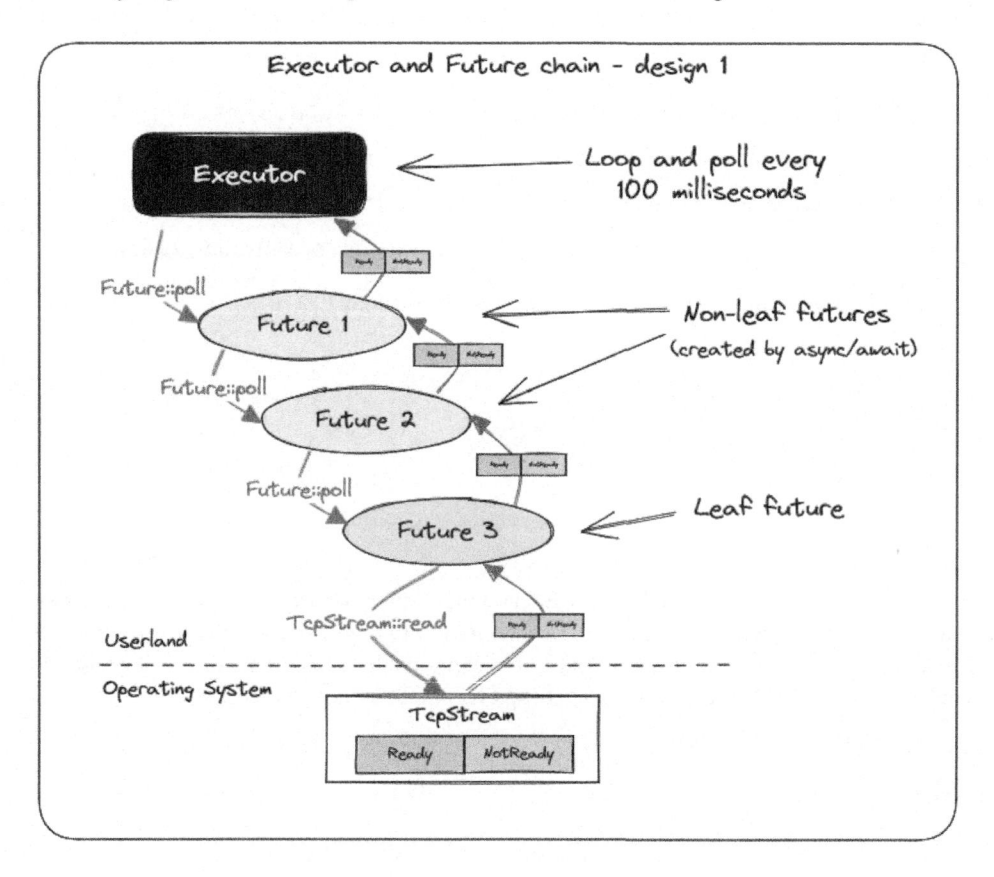

Figure 8.2 – Executor and Future chain: current design

If we take a closer look at the future chain, we can see that when a future is polled, it polls all its child futures until it reaches a leaf future that represents something we're actually waiting on. If that future returns `NotReady`, it will propagate that up the chain immediately. However, if it returns `Ready`, the state machine will advance all the way until the next time a future returns `NotReady`. The top-level future will not resolve until all child futures have returned `Ready`.

The next diagram takes a closer look at the future chain and gives a simplified overview of how it works:

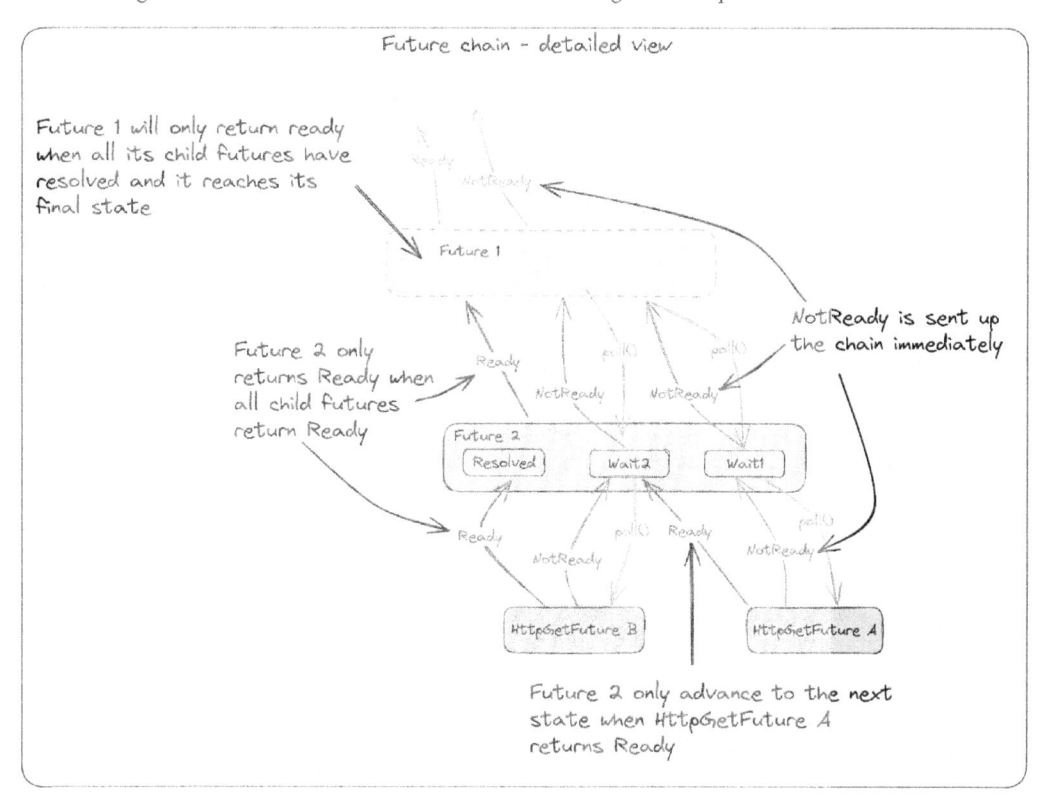

Figure 8.3 – Future chain: a detailed view

The first improvement we'll make is to avoid the need for continuous polling of our top-level future to drive it forward.

We'll change our design so that it looks more like this:

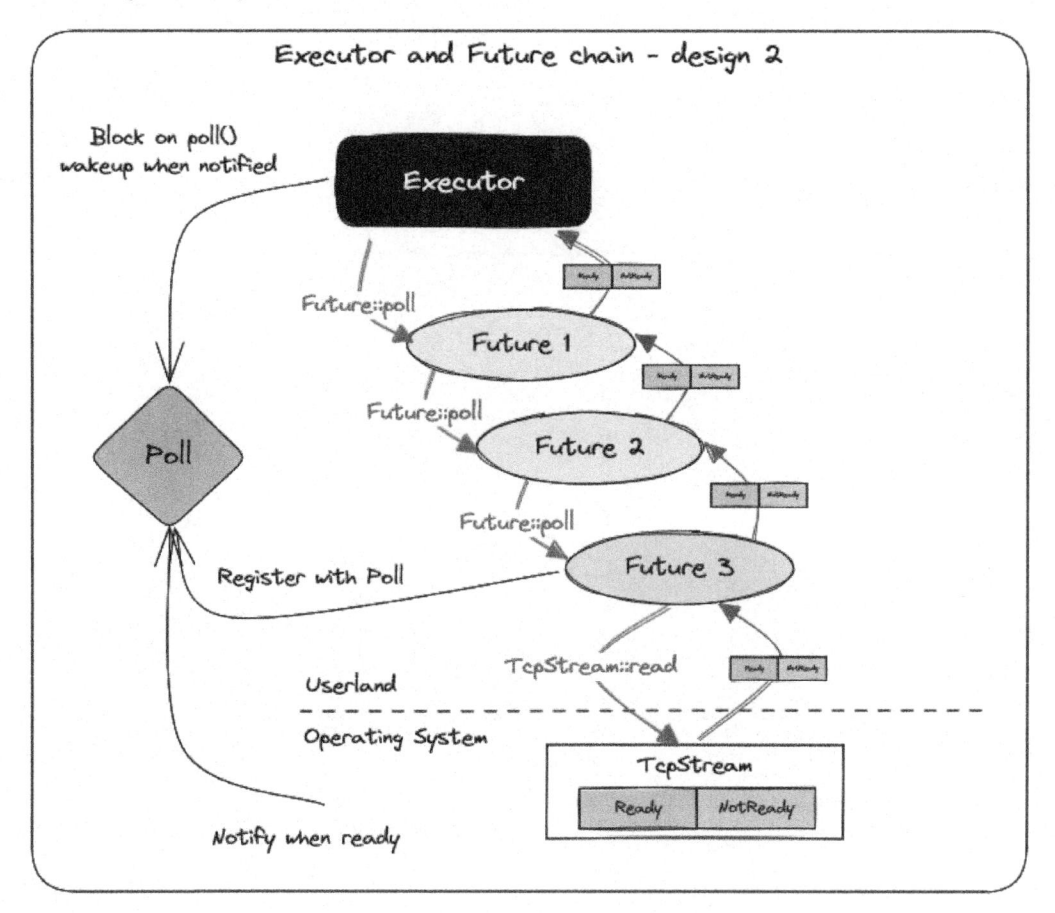

Figure 8.4 – Executor and Future chain: design 2

In this design, we use the knowledge we gained in *Chapter 4*, but instead of simply relying on `epoll`, we'll use `mio`'s cross-platform abstraction instead. The way it works should be well known to us by now since we already implemented a simplified version of it earlier.

Instead of continuously looping and polling our top-level future, we'll register interest with the `Poll` instance, and when we get a `NotReady` result returned, we wait on `Poll`. This will put the thread to sleep, and no work will be done until the OS wakes us up again to notify us that an event we're waiting on is ready.

This design will be much more efficient and scalable.

Changing the current implementation

Now that we have an overview of our design and know what to do, we can go on and make the necessary changes to our program, so let's go through each file we need to change. We'll start with `main.rs`.

main.rs

We already made some changes to `main.rs` when we ran `corofy` on our updated `coroutine/wait` example. I'll just point out the change here so that you don't miss it since there is really nothing more we need to change here.

Instead of polling the future in the `main` function, we created a new `Runtime` struct and passed the future as an argument to the `Runtime::block_on` method. There are no more changes that we need to in this file. Our `main` function changed to this:

ch08/a-runtime/src/main.rs

```rust
fn main() {
    let future = async_main();
    let mut runtime = Runtime::new();
    runtime.block_on(future);
}
```

The logic we had in the `main` function has now moved into the `runtime` module, and that's also where we need to change the code that polls the future to completion from what we had earlier.

The next step will, therefore, be to open `runtime.rs`.

runtime.rs

The first thing we do in `runtime.rs` is pull in the dependencies we need:

ch08/a-runtime/src/runtime.rs

```rust
use crate::future::{Future, PollState};
use mio::{Events, Poll, Registry};
use std::sync::OnceLock;
```

The next step is to create a static variable called `REGISTRY`. If you remember, `Registry` is the way we register interest in events with our `Poll` instance. We want to register interest in events on our `TcpStream` when making the actual HTTP GET request. We could have `Http::get` accept a `Registry` struct that it stored for later use, but we want to keep the API clean, and instead, we want to access `Registry` inside `HttpGetFuture` without having to pass it around as a reference:

ch08/a-runtime/src/runtime.rs

```
static REGISTRY: OnceLock<Registry> = OnceLock::new();
pub fn registry() -> &'static Registry {
    REGISTRY.get().expect("Called outside a runtime context")
}
```

We use `std::sync::OnceLock` so that we can initialize `REGISTRY` when the runtime starts, thereby preventing anyone (including ourselves) from calling `Http::get` without having a `Runtime` instance running. If we did call `Http::get` without having our runtime initialized, it would panic since the only public way to access it outside the `runtime` module is through the `pub fn registry() {...}` function, and that call would fail.

> **Note**
>
> We might as well have used a thread-local static variable using the `thread_local!` macro from the standard library, but we'll need to access this from multiple threads when we expand the example later in this chapter, so we start the design with this in mind.

The next thing we add is a `Runtime` struct:

ch08/a-runtime/src/runtime.rs

```
pub struct Runtime {
    poll: Poll,
}
```

For now, our runtime will only store a `Poll` instance. The interesting part is in the implementation of `Runtime`. Since it's not too long, I'll present the whole implementation here and explain it next:

ch08/a-runtime/src/runtime.rs

```
impl Runtime {
    pub fn new() -> Self {
        let poll = Poll::new().unwrap();
        let registry = poll.registry().try_clone().unwrap();
        REGISTRY.set(registry).unwrap();
```

```
        Self { poll }
    }
}

pub fn block_on<F>(&mut self, future: F)
where
    F: Future<Output = String>,
{
    let mut future = future;
    loop {
        match future.poll() {
            PollState::NotReady => {
                println!("Schedule other tasks\n");
                let mut events = Events::with_capacity(100);
                self.poll.poll(&mut events, None).unwrap();
            }


            PollState::Ready(_) => break,
        }
    }
}
```

The first thing we do is create a new function. This will initialize our runtime and set everything we need up. We create a new `Poll` instance, and from the `Poll` instance, we get an owned version of `Registry`. If you remember from *Chapter 4*, this is one of the methods we mentioned but didn't implement in our example. However, here, we take advantage of the ability to split the two pieces up.

We store `Registry` in the `REGISTRY` global variable so that we can access it from the `http` module later on without having a reference to the runtime itself.

The next function is the `block_on` function. I'll go through it step by step:

1. First of all, this function takes a generic argument and will block on anything that implements our `Future` trait with an `Output` type of `String` (remember that this is currently the only kind of `Future` trait we support, so we'll just return an empty string if there is no data to return).

2. Instead of having to take `mut future` as an argument, we define a variable that we declare as `mut` in the function body. It's just to keep the API slightly cleaner and avoid us having to make minor changes later on.

3. Next, we create a loop. We'll loop until the top-level future we received returns `Ready`.

   If the future returns `NotReady`, we write out a message letting us know that at this point we could do other things, such as processing something unrelated to the future or, more likely, polling another top-level future if our runtime supported multiple top-level futures (don't worry – it will be explained later on).

Note that we need to pass in an `Events` collection to mio's `Poll::poll` method, but since there is only one top-level future to run, we don't really care which event happened; we only care that something happened and that it most likely means that data is ready (remember – we always have to account for false wakeups anyway).

That's all the changes we need to make to the `runtime` module for now.

The last thing we need to do is register *interest* for *read* events after we've written the request to the server in our `http` module.

Let's open `http.rs` and make some changes.

http.rs

First of all, let's adjust our dependencies so that we pull in everything we need:

ch08/a-runtime/src/http.rs

```rust
use crate::{future::PollState, runtime, Future};
use mio::{Interest, Token};
use std::io::{ErrorKind, Read, Write};
```

We need to add a dependency on our `runtime` module as well as a few types from `mio`.

We only need to make one more change in this file, and that's in our `Future::poll` implementation, so let's go ahead and locate that:

We made one important change here that I've highlighted for you. The implementation is exactly the same, with one important difference:

ch08/a-runtime/src/http.rs

```rust
impl Future for HttpGetFuture {
    type Output = String;

    fn poll(&mut self) -> PollState<Self::Output> {
        if self.stream.is_none() {
            println!("FIRST POLL - START OPERATION");
            self.write_request();

            runtime::registry()
                .register(self.stream.as_mut().unwrap(), Token(0), Interest::READABLE)
```

```
                    .unwrap();
            }

            let mut buff = vec![0u8; 4096];
            loop {
                match self.stream.as_mut().unwrap().read(&mut buff) {
                    Ok(0) => {
                        let s = String::from_utf8_lossy(&self.buffer);
                        break PollState::Ready(s.to_string());
                    }
                    Ok(n) => {
                        self.buffer.extend(&buff[0..n]);
                        continue;
                    }
                    Err(e) if e.kind() == ErrorKind::WouldBlock => {
                        break PollState::NotReady;
                    }

                    Err(e) => panic!("{e:?}"),
                }
            }
        }
    }
}
```

On the first poll, after we've written the request, we register interest in READABLE events on this TcpStream. We also removed the line:

```
return PollState::NotReady;
```

By removing his line, we'll poll TcpStream immediately, which makes sense since we don't really want to return control to our scheduler if we get the response immediately. You wouldn't go wrong either way here since we registered our TcpStream as an event source with our reactor and would get a wakeup in any case. These changes were the last piece we needed to get our example back up and running.

If you remember the version from *Chapter 7*, we got the following output:

```
Program starting
FIRST POLL - START OPERATION
Schedule other tasks
Schedule other tasks
Schedule other tasks
Schedule other tasks
Schedule other tasks
Schedule other tasks
```

```
Schedule other tasks
HTTP/1.1 200 OK
content-length: 11
connection: close
content-type: text/plain; charset=utf-8
date: Thu, 16 Nov xxxx xx:xx:xx GMT

HelloWorld1
FIRST POLL - START OPERATION
Schedule other tasks
Schedule other tasks
Schedule other tasks
Schedule other tasks
Schedule other tasks
HTTP/1.1 200 OK
content-length: 11
connection: close
content-type: text/plain; charset=utf-8
date: Thu, 16 Nov xxxx xx:xx:xx GMT

HelloWorld2
```

In our new and improved version, we get the following output if we run it with `cargo run`:

```
Program starting
FIRST POLL - START OPERATION
Schedule other tasks

HTTP/1.1 200 OK
content-length: 11
connection: close
content-type: text/plain; charset=utf-8
date: Thu, 16 Nov xxxx xx:xx:xx GMT

HelloAsyncAwait
FIRST POLL - START OPERATION
Schedule other tasks

HTTP/1.1 200 OK
content-length: 11
connection: close
content-type: text/plain; charset=utf-8
date: Thu, 16 Nov xxxx xx:xx:xx GMT
```

`HelloAsyncAwait`

> **Note**
> If you run the example on Windows, you'll see that you get two `Schedule other tasks` messages after each other. The reason for that is that Windows emits an extra event when the `TcpStream` is dropped on the server end. This doesn't happen on Linux. Filtering out these events is quite simple, but we won't focus on doing that in our example since it's more of an optimization that we don't really need for our example to work.

The thing to make a note of here is how many times we printed `Schedule other tasks`. We print this message every time we poll and get `NotReady`. In the first version, we printed this every 100 ms, but that's just because we had to delay on each sleep to not get overwhelmed with printouts. Without it, our CPU would work 100% on polling the future.

If we add a delay, we also add latency even if we make the delay much shorter than 100 ms since we won't be able to respond to events immediately.

Our new design makes sure that we respond to events as soon as they're ready, and we do no unnecessary work.

So, by making these minor changes, we have already created a much better and more scalable version than we had before.

This version is fully single-threaded, which keeps things simple and avoids the complexity and overhead synchronization. When you use Tokio's `current-thread` scheduler, you get a scheduler that is based on the same idea as we showed here.

However, there are also some drawbacks to our current implementation, and the most noticeable one is that it requires a very tight integration between the *reactor part* and the *executor part* of the runtime centered on `Poll`.

We want to yield to the OS scheduler *when there is no work to do* and have the OS wake us up when an event has happened so that we can progress. In our current design, this is done through blocking on `Poll::poll`.

Consequently, both the executor (scheduler) and the reactor must know about `Poll`. The downside is, then, that if you've created an executor that suits a specific use case perfectly and want to allow users to use a different reactor that doesn't rely on `Poll`, you can't.

More importantly, you might want to run multiple different reactors that wake up the executor for different reasons. You might find that there is something that `mio` doesn't support, so you create a different reactor for those tasks. How are they supposed to wake up the executor when it's blocking on `mio::Poll::poll(...)`?

To give you a few examples, you could use a separate reactor for handling timers (for example, when you want a task to sleep for a given time), or you might want to implement a thread pool for handling CPU-intensive or blocking tasks as a reactor that wakes up the corresponding future when the task is ready.

To solve these problems, we need a loose coupling between the reactor and executor part of the runtime by having a way to wake up the executor that's not tightly coupled to a single reactor implementation.

Let's look at how we can solve this problem by creating a better runtime design.

Creating a proper runtime

So, if we visualize the degree of dependency between the different parts of our runtime, our current design could be described this way:

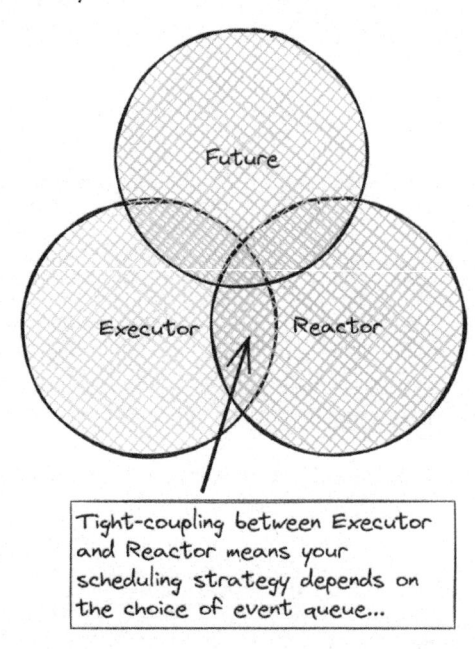

Figure 8.5 – Tight coupling between reactor and executor

If we want a loose coupling between the reactor and executor, we need an interface provided to signal the executor that it should wake up when an event that allows a future to progress has occurred. It's no coincidence that this type is called Waker (https://doc.rust-lang.org/stable/std/task/struct.Waker.html) in Rust's standard library. If we change our visualization to reflect this, it will look something like this:

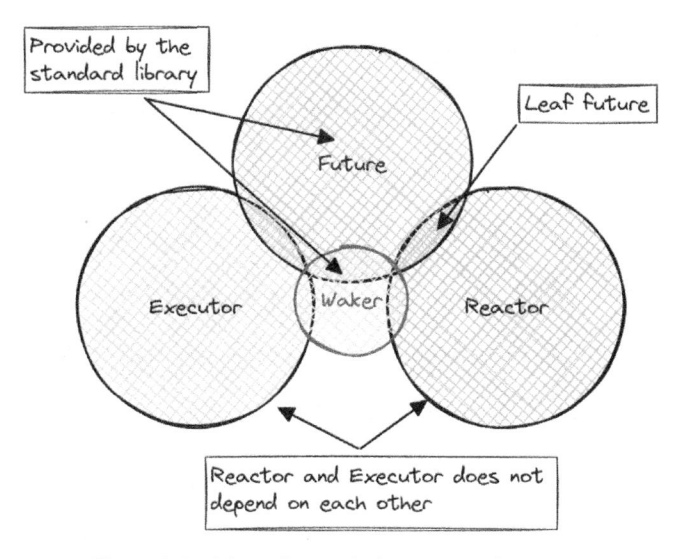

Figure 8.6 – A loosely coupled reactor and executor

It's no coincidence that we land on the same design as what we have in Rust today. It's a minimal design from Rust's point of view, but it allows for a wide variety of runtime designs without laying too many restrictions for the future.

> **Note**
>
> Even though the design is pretty minimal today from a language perspective, there are plans to stabilize more async-related traits and interfaces in the future.
>
> Rust has a working group tasked with including widely used traits and interfaces in the standard library, which you can find more information about here: https://rust-lang.github.io/wg-async/welcome.html. You can also get an overview of items they work on and track their progress here: https://github.com/orgs/rust-lang/projects/28/views/1.
>
> Maybe you even want to get involved (https://rust-lang.github.io/wg-async/welcome.html#-getting-involved) in making async Rust better for everyone after reading this book?

If we change our system diagram to reflect the changes we need to make to our runtime going forward, it will look like this:

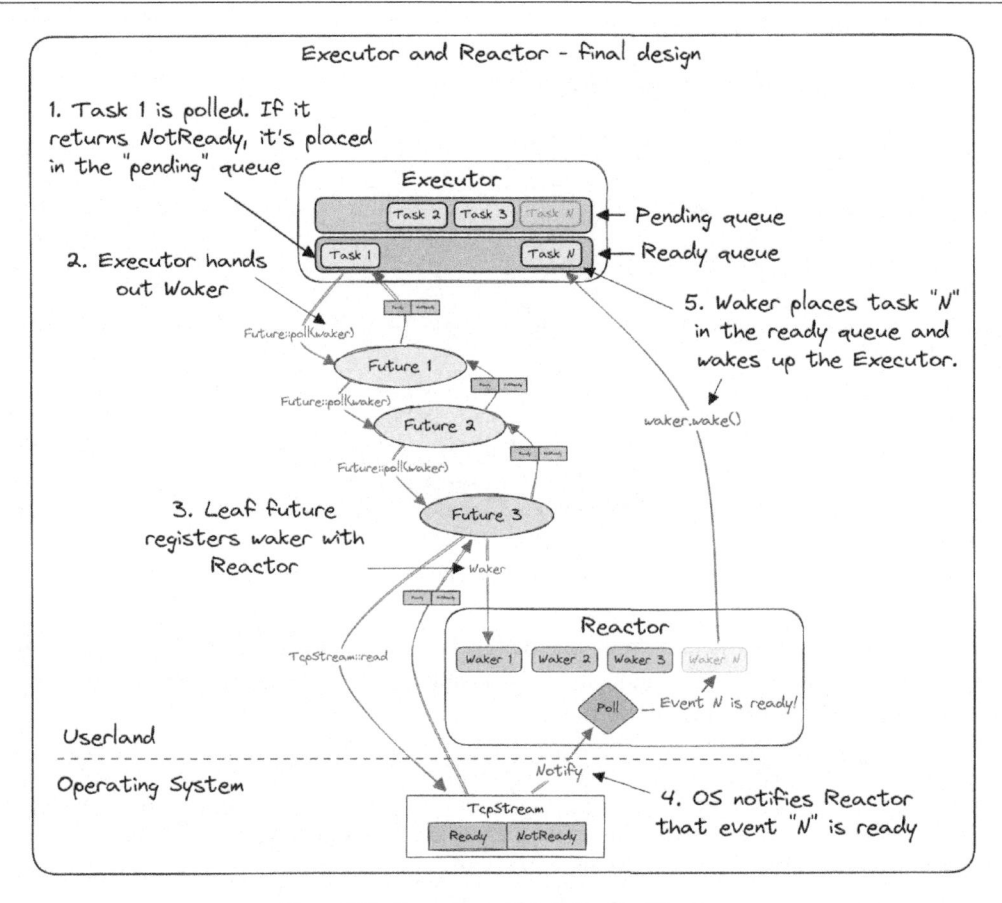

Figure 8.7 – Executor and reactor: final design

We have two parts that have no direct dependency on each other. We have an `Executor` that schedules tasks and passes on a `Waker` when polling a future that eventually will be caught and stored by the `Reactor`. When the `Reactor` receives a notification that an event is ready, it locates the `Waker` associated with that task and calls `Wake::wake` on it.

This enables us to:

- Run several OS threads that each have their own executor, but share the same reactor
- Have multiple reactors that handle different kinds of leaf futures and make sure to wake up the correct executor when it can progress

So, now that we have an idea of what to do, it's time to start writing it in code.

Step 1 – Improving our runtime design by adding a Reactor and a Waker

In this step, we'll make the following changes:

1. Change the project structure so that it reflects our new design.
2. Find a way for the executor to sleep and wake up that does not rely directly on `Poll` and create a `Waker` based on this that allows us to wake up the executor and identify which task is ready to progress.
3. Change the trait definition for `Future` so that poll takes a `&Waker` as an argument.

> **Tip**
>
> You'll find this example in the `ch08/b-reactor-executor` folder. If you follow along by writing the examples from the book, I suggest that you create a new project called `b-reactor-executor` for this example by following these steps:
>
> 1. Create a new folder called `b-reactor-executor`.
>
> 2. Enter the newly created folder and write `cargo init`.
>
> 3. Copy everything in the `src` folder in the previous example, `a-runtime`, into the `src` folder of a new project.
>
> 4. Copy the `dependencies` section of the `Cargo.toml` file into the `Cargo.toml` file in the new project.

Let's start by making some changes to our project structure to set it up so that we can build on it going forward. The first thing we do is divide our `runtime` module into two submodules, `reactor` and `executor`:

1. Create a new subfolder in the `src` folder called `runtime`.
2. Create two new files in the `runtime` folder called `reactor.rs` and `executor.rs`.
3. Just below the imports in `runtime.rs`, declare the two new modules by adding these lines:

   ```
   mod executor;
   mod reactor;
   ```

You should now have a folder structure that looks like this:

```
src
 |-- runtime
        |-- executor.rs
        |-- reactor.rs
 |-- future.rs
```

```
|-- http.rs
|-- main.rs
|-- runtime.rs
```

To set everything up, we start by deleting everything in `runtime.rs` and replacing it with the following lines of code:

ch08/b-reactor-executor/src/runtime.rs

```
pub use executor::{spawn, Executor, Waker};
pub use reactor::reactor;

mod executor;
mod reactor;

pub fn init() -> Executor {
    reactor::start();
    Executor::new()
}
```

The new content of `runtime.rs` first declares two submodules called `executor` and `reactor`. We then declare one function called `init` that starts our `Reactor` and creates a new `Executor` that it returns to the caller.

The next point on our list is to find a way for our `Executor` to sleep and wake up when needed without relying on `Poll`.

Creating a Waker

So, we need to find a different way for our executor to sleep and get woken up that doesn't rely directly on `Poll`.

It turns out that this is quite easy. The standard library gives us what we need to get something working. By calling `std::thread::current()`, we can get a `Thread` object. This object is a handle to the current thread, and it gives us access to a few methods, one of which is `unpark`.

The standard library also gives us a method called `std::thread::park()`, which simply asks the OS scheduler to park our thread until we ask for it to get *unparked* later on.

It turns out that if we combine these, we have a way to both *park* and *unpark* the executor, which is exactly what we need.

Let's create a `Waker` type based on this. In our example, we'll define the `Waker` inside the `executor` module since that's where we create this exact type of `Waker`, but you could argue that it belongs to the `future` module since it's a part of the `Future` trait.

Step 1 – Improving our runtime design by adding a Reactor and a Waker

> **Important note**
>
> Our `Waker` relies on calling `park/unpark` on the `Thread` type from the standard library. This is OK for our example since it's easy to understand, but given that any part of the code (including any libraries you use) can get a handle to the same thread by calling `std::thread::current()` and call `park/unpark` on it, it's not a robust solution. If unrelated parts of the code call `park/unpark` on the same thread, we can miss wakeups or end up in deadlocks. Most production libraries create their own `Parker` type or rely on something such as `crossbeam::sync::Parker` (https://docs.rs/crossbeam/latest/crossbeam/sync/struct.Parker.html) instead.

We won't implement `Waker` as a trait since passing trait objects around will significantly increase the complexity of our example, and it's not in line with the current design of `Future` and `Waker` in Rust either.

Open the `executor.rs` file located inside the `runtime` folder, and let's add all the imports we're going to need right from the start:

ch08/b-reactor-executor/src/runtime/executor.rs

```rust
use crate::future::{Future, PollState};
use std::{
    cell::{Cell, RefCell},
    collections::HashMap,
    sync::{Arc, Mutex},
    thread::{self, Thread},
};
```

The next thing we add is our `Waker`:

ch08/b-reactor-executor/src/runtime/executor.rs

```rust
#[derive(Clone)]
pub struct Waker {
    thread: Thread,
    id: usize,
    ready_queue: Arc<Mutex<Vec<usize>>>,
}
```

The `Waker` will hold three things for us:

- `thread` – A handle to the `Thread` object we mentioned earlier.
- `id` – An `usize` that identifies which task this `Waker` is associated with.

- `ready_queue` – This is a reference that can be shared between threads to a `Vec<usize>`, where `usize` represents the ID of a task that's in the ready queue. We share this object with the executor so that we can push the task ID associated with the `Waker` onto that queue when it's ready.

The implementation of our `Waker` will be quite simple:

ch08/b-reactor-executor/src/runtime/executor.rs

```
impl Waker {
    pub fn wake(&self) {
        self.ready_queue
            .lock()
            .map(|mut q| q.push(self.id))
            .unwrap();
        self.thread.unpark();
    }
}
```

When `Waker::wake` is called, we first take a lock on the `Mutex` that protects the ready queue we share with the executor. We then push the `id` value that identifies the task that this `Waker` is associated with onto the ready queue.

After that's done, we call `unpark` on the executor thread and wake it up. It will now find the task associated with this `Waker` in the ready queue and call `poll` on it.

It's worth mentioning that many designs take a *shared reference (for example, an Arc<…>)* to the *future/task itself*, and push that onto the queue. By doing so, they skip a level of indirection that we get here by representing the task as a `usize` instead of passing in a reference to it.

However, I personally think this way of doing it is easier to understand and reason about, and the end result will be the same.

> **How does this Waker compare to the one in the standard library?**
>
> The `Waker` we create here will take the same role as the `Waker` type from the standard library. The biggest difference is that the `std::task::Waker` method is wrapped in a `Context` struct and requires us to jump through a few hoops when we create it ourselves. Don't worry – we'll do all this at the end of this book, but neither of these differences is important for understanding the role it plays, so that's why we stick to our own simplified version of asynchronous Rust for now.

The last thing we need to do is to change the definition of the `Future` trait so that it takes `&Waker` as an argument.

Changing the Future definition

Since our Future definition is in the `future.rs` file, we start by opening that file.

The first thing we need to change is to pull in the Waker so that we can use it. At the top of the file, add the following code:

ch08/b-reactor-executor/src/future.rs

```
use crate::runtime::Waker;
```

The next thing we do is to change our Future trait so that it takes &Waker as an argument:

ch08/b-reactor-executor/src/future.rs

```
pub trait Future {
    type Output;

    fn poll(&mut self, waker: &Waker) -> PollState<Self::Output>;
}
```

At this point, you have a choice. We won't be using the `join_all` function or the `JoinAll<F: Future>` struct going forward.

If you don't want to keep them, you can just delete everything related to `join_all`, and that's all you need to do in `future.rs`.

If you want to keep them for further experimentation, you need to change the Future implementation for JoinAll so that it accepts a `waker: &Waker` argument, and remember to pass the Waker when polling the joined futures in `match fut.poll(waker)`.

The remaining things to do in *step 1* are to make some minor changes where we implement the Future trait.

Let's start in `http.rs`. The first thing we do is adjust our dependencies a little to reflect the changes we made to our runtime module, and we add a dependency on our new Waker. Replace the dependencies section at the top of the file with this:

ch08/b-reactor-executor/src/http.rs

```
use crate::{future::PollState, runtime::{self, reactor, Waker}, Future};
use mio::Interest;
use std::io::{ErrorKind, Read, Write};
```

The compiler will complain about not finding the reactor yet, but we'll get to that shortly.

Next, we have to navigate to the `impl Future for HttpGetFuture` block, where we need to change the `poll` method so that it accepts a `&Waker` argument:

ch08/b-reactor-executor/src/http.rs

```
impl Future for HttpGetFuture {
    type Output = String;

    fn poll(&mut self, waker: &Waker) -> PollState<Self::Output> {
...
```

The last file we need to change is `main.rs`. Since `corofy` doesn't know about `Waker` types, we need to change a few lines in the coroutines it generated for us in `main.rs`.

First of all, we have to add a dependency on our new `Waker`, so add this at the start of the file:

ch08/b-reactor-executor/src/main.rs

```
use runtime::Waker;
```

In the `impl Future for Coroutine` block, change the following three lines of code that I've highlighted:

ch08/b-reactor-executor/src/main.rs

```
fn poll(&mut self, waker: &Waker)
match f1.poll(waker)
match f2.poll(waker)
```

And that's all we need to do in *step 1*. We'll get back to fixing the errors in this file as the last step we do; for now, we just focus on everything concerning the `Waker`.

The next step will be to create a proper `Executor`.

Step 2 – Implementing a proper Executor

In this step, we'll create an executor that will:

- Hold many top-level futures and switch between them
- Enable us to spawn new top-level futures from anywhere in our asynchronous program

- Hand out `Waker` types so that they can sleep when there is nothing to do and wake up when one of the top-level futures can progress
- Enable us to run several executors by having each run on its dedicated OS thread

> **Note**
>
> It's worth mentioning that our executor won't be fully multithreaded in the sense that tasks/futures can't be sent from one thread to another, and the different `Executor` instances will not know of each other. Therefore, executors can't steal work from each other (no work-stealing), and we can't rely on executors picking tasks from a global task queue.
>
> The reason is that the `Executor` design will be much more complex if we go down that route, not only because of the added logic but also because we have to add constraints, such as requiring everything to be `Send + Sync`.
>
> Some of the complexity in asynchronous Rust today can be attributed to the fact that many runtimes in Rust are multithreaded by default, which makes asynchronous Rust deviate more from "normal" Rust than it actually needs to.
>
> It's worth mentioning that since most production runtimes in Rust are multithreaded by default, most of them also have a work-stealing executor. This will be similar to the last version of our bartender example in *Chapter 1*, where we achieved a slightly increased efficiency by letting the bartenders "steal" tasks that are *in progress* from each other.
>
> However, this example should still give you an idea of how we can leverage all the cores on a machine to run asynchronous tasks, giving us both concurrency and parallelism, even though it will have limited capabilities.

Let's start by opening up `executor.rs` located in the `runtime` subfolder.

This file should already contain our `Waker` and the dependencies we need, so let's start by adding the following lines of code just below our dependencies:

ch08/b-reactor-executor/src/runtime/executor.rs

```rust
type Task = Box<dyn Future<Output = String>>;

thread_local! {
    static CURRENT_EXEC: ExecutorCore = ExecutorCore::default();
}
```

The first line is a *type alias*; it simply lets us create an alias called `Task` that refers to the type: `Box<dyn Future<Output = String>>`. This will help keep our code a little bit cleaner.

The next line might be new to some readers. We define a thread-local static variable by using the `thread_local!` macro.

The `thread_local!` macro lets us define a static variable that's unique to the thread it's first called from. This means that all threads we create will have their own instance, and it's impossible for one thread to access another thread's CURRENT_EXEC variable.

We call the variable CURRENT_EXEC since it holds the `Executor` that's currently running on this thread.

The next lines we add to this file is the definition of `ExecutorCore`:

ch08/b-reactor-executor/src/runtime/executor.rs

```
#[derive(Default)]
struct ExecutorCore {
    tasks: RefCell<HashMap<usize, Task>>,
    ready_queue: Arc<Mutex<Vec<usize>>>,
    next_id: Cell<usize>,
}
```

ExecutorCore holds all the state for our `Executor`:

- `tasks` – This is a `HashMap` with a `usize` as the *key* and a `Task` (remember the alias we created previously) as *data*. This will hold all the top-level futures associated with the executor on this thread and allow us to give each an `id` property to identify them. We can't simply mutate a static variable, so we need internal mutability here. Since this will only be callable from one thread, a `RefCell` will do so since there is no need for synchronization.

- `ready_queue` – This is a simple `Vec<usize>` that stores the IDs of tasks that should be polled by the executor. If we refer back to *Figure 8.7*, you'll see how this fits into the design we outlined there. As mentioned earlier, we could store something such as an `Arc<dyn Future<...>>` here instead, but that adds quite a bit of complexity to our example. The only downside with the current design is that instead of getting a reference to the task directly, we have to look it up in our `tasks` collection, which takes time. An `Arc<...>` (shared reference) to this collection will be given to each `Waker` that this executor creates. Since the `Waker` can (and will) be sent to a different thread and signal that a specific task is ready by adding the task's ID to `ready_queue`, we need to wrap it in an `Arc<Mutex<...>>`.

- `next_id` – This is a counter that gives out the next available I, which means that it should never hand out the same ID twice for this executor instance. We'll use this to give each top-level future a unique ID. Since the executor instance will only be accessible on the same thread it was created, a simple `Cell` will suffice in giving us the internal mutability we need.

ExecutorCore derives the `Default` trait since there is no special initial state we need here, and it keeps the code short and concise.

The next function is an important one. The spawn function allows us to register new top-level futures with our executor from anywhere in our program:

ch08/b-reactor-executor/src/runtime/executor.rs

```rust
pub fn spawn<F>(future: F)
where
    F: Future<Output = String> + 'static,
{
    CURRENT_EXEC.with(|e| {
        let id = e.next_id.get();
        e.tasks.borrow_mut().insert(id, Box::new(future));
        e.ready_queue.lock().map(|mut q| q.push(id)).unwrap();
        e.next_id.set(id + 1);
    });
}
```

The spawn function does a few things:

- It gets the next available ID.
- It assigns the ID to the future it receives and stores it in a HashMap.
- It adds the ID that represents this task to ready_queue so that it's polled at least once (remember that Future traits in Rust don't do anything unless they're polled at least once).
- It increases the ID counter by one.

The unfamiliar syntax accessing CURRENT_EXEC by calling with and passing in a closure is just a consequence of how thread local statics is implemented in Rust. You'll also notice that we must use a few special methods because we use RefCell and Cell for internal mutability for tasks and next_id, but there is really nothing inherently complex about this except being a bit unfamiliar.

> **A quick note about static lifetimes**
>
> When a 'static lifetime is used as a trait bound as we do here, it doesn't actually mean that the lifetime of the Future trait we pass in *must be* static (meaning it will have to live until the end of the program). It means that it *must be able to* last until the end of the program, or, put another way, the lifetime can't be constrained in any way.
>
> Most often, when you encounter something that requires a 'static bound, it simply means that you'll have to give ownership over the thing you pass in. If you pass in any references, they need to have a 'static lifetime. It's less difficult to satisfy this constraint than you might expect.

The final part of *step 2* will be to define and implement the Executor struct itself.

The `Executor` struct is very simple, and there is only one line of code to add:

ch08/b-reactor-executor/src/runtime/executor.rs

```rust
pub struct Executor;
```

Since all the state we need for our example is held in `ExecutorCore`, which is a static thread-local variable, our `Executor` struct doesn't need any state. This also means that we don't strictly need a struct at all, but to keep the API somewhat familiar, we do it anyway.

Most of the executor implementation is a handful of simple helper methods that end up in a `block_on` function, which is where the interesting parts really happen.

Since these helper methods are short and easy to understand, I'll present them all here and just briefly go over what they do:

> **Note**
> We open the `impl Executor` block here but will not close it until we've finished implementing the `block_on` function.

ch08/b-reactor-executor/src/runtime/executor.rs

```rust
impl Executor {
    pub fn new() -> Self {
        Self {}
    }

    fn pop_ready(&self) -> Option<usize> {
        CURRENT_EXEC.with(|q| q.ready_queue.lock().map(|mut q| q.pop()).unwrap())
    }

    fn get_future(&self, id: usize) -> Option<Task> {
        CURRENT_EXEC.with(|q| q.tasks.borrow_mut().remove(&id))
    }

    fn get_waker(&self, id: usize) -> Waker {
        Waker {
            id,
            thread: thread::current(),
            ready_queue: CURRENT_EXEC.with(|q| q.ready_queue.clone()),
        }
    }
}
```

```rust
fn insert_task(&self, id: usize, task: Task) {
    CURRENT_EXEC.with(|q| q.tasks.borrow_mut().insert(id, task));
}

fn task_count(&self) -> usize {
    CURRENT_EXEC.with(|q| q.tasks.borrow().len())
}
```

So, we have six methods here:

- `new` – Creates a new `Executor` instance. For simplicity, we have no initialization here, and everything is done lazily by design in the `thread_local!` macro.
- `pop_ready` – This function takes a lock on `read_queue` and pops off an ID that's ready from the back of `Vec`. Calling `pop` here means that we also remove the item from the collection. As a side note, since `Waker` pushes its ID to the *back* of `ready_queue` and we pop off from the *back* as well, we essentially get a **Last In First Out** (**LIFO**) queue. Using something such as `VecDeque` from the standard library would easily allow us to choose the order in which we remove items from the queue if we wish to change that behavior.
- `get_future` – This function takes the ID of a top-level future as an argument, removes the future from the `tasks` collection, and returns it (if the task is found). This means that if the task returns `NotReady` (signaling that we're not done with it), we need to remember to add it back to the collection again.
- `get_waker` – This function creates a new `Waker` instance.
- `insert_task` – This function takes an `id` property and a `Task` property and inserts them into our `tasks` collection.
- `task_count` – This function simply returns a count of how many tasks we have in the queue.

The final and last part of the `Executor` implementation is the `block_on` function. This is also where we close the `impl Executor` block:

ch08/b-reactor-executor/src/runtime/executor.rs

```rust
pub fn block_on<F>(&mut self, future: F)
where
    F: Future<Output = String> + 'static,
{
    spawn(future);

    loop {
        while let Some(id) = self.pop_ready() {
```

```rust
            let mut future = match self.get_future(id) {
                Some(f) => f,
                // guard against false wakeups
                None => continue,
            };
            let waker = self.get_waker(id);

            match future.poll(&waker) {
                PollState::NotReady => self.insert_task(id, future),
                PollState::Ready(_) => continue,
            }
        }

        let task_count = self.task_count();
        let name = thread::current().name().unwrap_or_default().to_string();

        if task_count > 0 {
            println!("{name}: {task_count} pending tasks. Sleep until notified.");
            thread::park();
        } else {
            println!("{name}: All tasks are finished");
            break;
        }
    }
  }
}
```

`block_on` will be the entry point to our `Executor`. Often, you will pass in one top-level future first, and when the top-level future progresses, it will spawn new top-level futures onto our executor. Each new future can, of course, spawn new futures onto the `Executor` too, and that's how an asynchronous program basically works.

In many ways, you can view this first top-level future in the same way you view the `main` function in a normal Rust program. `spawn` is similar to `thread::spawn`, with the exception that the tasks stay on the same OS thread in this example. This means the tasks won't be able to run in parallel, which in turn allows us to avoid any need for synchronization between tasks to avoid data races.

Let's go through the function step by step:

1. The first thing we do is spawn the future we received onto ourselves. There are many ways this could be implemented, but this is the easiest way to do it.
2. Then, we have a loop that will run as long as our asynchronous program is running.

3. Every time we loop, we create an inner `while let Some(...)` loop that runs as long as there are tasks in `ready_queue`.
4. If there is a task in `ready_queue`, we take ownership of the `Future` object by removing it from the collection. We guard against false wakeups by just continuing if there is no future there anymore (meaning that we're done with it but still get a wakeup). This will, for example, happen on Windows since we get a READABLE event when the connection closes, but even though we could filter those events out, mio doesn't guarantee that false wakeups won't happen, so we have to handle that possibility anyway.
5. Next, we create a new `Waker` instance that we can pass into `Future::poll()`. Remember that this `Waker` instance now holds the `id` property that identifies this specific `Future` trait and a handle to the thread we're currently running on.
6. The next step is to call `Future::poll`.
7. If we get `NotReady` in return, we insert the task back into our `tasks` collection. I want to emphasize that when a `Future` trait returns `NotReady`, we know it will arrange it so that `Waker::wake` is called at a later point in time. It's not the executor's responsibility to track the readiness of this future.
8. If the `Future` trait returns `Ready`, we simply continue to the next item in the ready queue. Since we took ownership over the `Future` trait, this will drop the object before we enter the next iteration of the `while let` loop.
9. Now that we've polled all the tasks in our ready queue, the first thing we do is get a task count to see how many tasks we have left.
10. We also get the name of the current thread for future logging purposes (it has nothing to do with how our executor works).
11. If the task count is larger than 0, we print a message to the terminal and call `thread::park()`. Parking the thread will yield control to the OS scheduler, and our `Executor` does nothing until it's woken up again.
12. If the task count is 0, we're done with our asynchronous program and exit the main loop.

That's pretty much all there is to it. By this point, we've covered all our goals for *step 2*, so we can continue to the last and final step and implement a `Reactor` for our runtime that will wake up our executor when something happens.

Step 3 – Implementing a proper Reactor

The final part of our example is the `Reactor`. Our `Reactor` will:

- Efficiently wait and handle events that our runtime is interested in
- Store a collection of `Waker` types and make sure to wake the correct `Waker` when it gets a notification on a source it's tracking

- Provide the necessary mechanisms for leaf futures such as `HttpGetFuture`, to register and deregister interests in events
- Provide a way for leaf futures to store the last received `Waker`

When we're done with this step, we should have everything we need for our runtime, so let's get to it.

Start by opening the `reactor.rs` file.

The first thing we do is add the dependencies we need:

ch08/b-reactor-executor/src/runtime/reactor.rs

```
use crate::runtime::Waker;
use mio::{net::TcpStream, Events, Interest, Poll, Registry, Token};
use std::{
    collections::HashMap,
    sync::{
        atomic::{AtomicUsize, Ordering},
        Arc, Mutex, OnceLock,
    },
    thread,
};
```

After we've added our dependencies, we create a *type alias* called `Wakers` that aliases the type for our `wakers` collection:

ch08/b-reactor-executor/src/runtime/reactor.rs

```
type Wakers = Arc<Mutex<HashMap<usize, Waker>>>;
```

The next line will declare a static variable called REACTOR:

ch08/b-reactor-executor/src/runtime/reactor.rs

```
static REACTOR: OnceLock<Reactor> = OnceLock::new();
```

This variable will hold a `OnceLock<Reactor>`. In contrast to our CURRENT_EXEC static variable, this will be possible to access from different threads. OnceLock allows us to define a static variable that we can write to once so that we can initialize it when we start our `Reactor`. By doing so, we also make sure that there can only be a single instance of this specific reactor running in our program.

The variable will be private to this module, so we create a public function allowing other parts of our program to access it:

ch08/b-reactor-executor/src/runtime/reactor.rs

```
pub fn reactor() -> &'static Reactor {
    REACTOR.get().expect("Called outside an runtime context")
}
```

The next thing we do is define our `Reactor` struct:

ch08/b-reactor-executor/src/runtime/reactor.rs

```
pub struct Reactor {
    wakers: Wakers,
    registry: Registry,
    next_id: AtomicUsize,
}
```

This will be all the state our `Reactor` struct needs to hold:

- `wakers` – A HashMap of `Waker` objects, each identified by an integer
- `registry` – Holds a `Registry` instance so that we can interact with the event queue in `mio`
- `next_id` – Stores the next available ID so that we can track which event occurred and which `Waker` should be woken

The implementation of `Reactor` is actually quite simple. It's only four short methods for interacting with the `Reactor` instance, so I'll present them all here and give a brief explanation next:

ch08/b-reactor-executor/src/runtime/reactor.rs

```
impl Reactor {
    pub fn register(&self, stream: &mut TcpStream, interest: Interest, id: usize) {
        self.registry.register(stream, Token(id), interest).unwrap();
    }

    pub fn set_waker(&self, waker: &Waker, id: usize) {
        let _ = self
            .wakers
            .lock()
            .map(|mut w| w.insert(id, waker.clone()).is_none())
            .unwrap();
    }

    pub fn deregister(&self, stream: &mut TcpStream, id: usize) {
        self.wakers.lock().map(|mut w| w.remove(&id)).unwrap();
```

```rust
            self.registry.deregister(stream).unwrap();
        }

        pub fn next_id(&self) -> usize {
            self.next_id.fetch_add(1, Ordering::Relaxed)
        }
    }
}
```

Let's briefly explain what these four methods do:

- `register` – This method is a thin wrapper around `Registry::register`, which we know from *Chapter 4*. The one thing to make a note of here is that we pass in an `id` property so that we can identify which event has occurred when we receive a notification later on.

- `set_waker` – This method adds a `Waker` to our `HashMap` using the provided `id` property as a key to identify it. If there is a `Waker` there already, we replace it and drop the old one. An important point to remember is that **we should always store the most recent Waker** so that this function can be called multiple times, even though there is already a `Waker` associated with the `TcpStream`.

- `deregister` – This function does two things. First, it removes the `Waker` from our `wakers` collection. Then, it deregisters the `TcpStream` from our `Poll` instance.

- I want to remind you at this point that while we only work with `TcpStream` in our examples, this could, in theory, be done with anything that implements mio's `Source` trait, so the same thought process is valid in a much broader context than what we deal with here.

- `next_id` – This simply gets the current `next_id` value and increments the counter atomically. We don't care about any happens before/after relationships happening here; we only care about not handing out the same value twice, so `Ordering::Relaxed` will suffice here. Memory ordering in atomic operations is a complex topic that we won't be able to dive into in this book, but if you want to know more about the different memory orderings in Rust and what they mean, the official documentation is the right place to start: https://doc.rust-lang.org/stable/std/sync/atomic/enum.Ordering.html.

Now that our `Reactor` is set up, we only have two short functions left. The first one is `event_loop`, which will hold the logic for our event loop that waits and reacts to new events:

ch08/b-reactor-executor/src/runtime/reactor.rs

```rust
fn event_loop(mut poll: Poll, wakers: Wakers) {
    let mut events = Events::with_capacity(100);
    loop {
        poll.poll(&mut events, None).unwrap();
        for e in events.iter() {
```

```
            let Token(id) = e.token();
            let wakers = wakers.lock().unwrap();

            if let Some(waker) = wakers.get(&id) {
                waker.wake();
            }
        }
    }
}
```

This function takes a `Poll` instance and a `Wakers` collection as arguments. Let's go through it step by step:

- The first thing we do is create an `events` collection. This should be familiar since we did the exact same thing in *Chapter 4*.
- The next thing we do is create a `loop` that in our case will continue to loop for eternity. This makes our example short and simple, but it has the downside that we have no way of shutting our event loop down once it's started. Fixing that is not especially difficult, but since it won't be necessary for our example, we don't cover this here.
- Inside the loop, we call `Poll::poll` with a timeout of `None`, which means it will never time out and block until it receives an event notification.
- When the call returns, we loop through every event we receive.
- If we receive an event, it means that something we registered interest in happened, so we get the `id` we passed in when we first registered an interest in events on this `TcpStream`.
- Lastly, we try to get the associated `Waker` and call `Waker::wake` on it. We guard ourselves from the fact that the `Waker` may have been removed from our collection already, in which case we do nothing.

It's worth noting that we can filter events if we want to here. Tokio provides some methods on the `Event` object to check several things about the event it reported. For our use in this example, we don't need to filter events.

Finally, the last function is the second public function in this module and the one that initializes and starts the runtime:

ch08/b-reactor-executor/src/runtime/runtime.rs

```
pub fn start() {
    use thread::spawn;

    let wakers = Arc::new(Mutex::new(HashMap::new()));
```

```
        let poll = Poll::new().unwrap();
        let registry = poll.registry().try_clone().unwrap();
        let next_id = AtomicUsize::new(1);
        let reactor = Reactor {
            wakers: wakers.clone(),
            registry,
            next_id,
        };

        REACTOR.set(reactor).ok().expect("Reactor already running");
        spawn(move || event_loop(poll, wakers));
    }
```

The `start` method should be fairly easy to understand. The first thing we do is create our `Wakers` collection and our `Poll` instance. From the `Poll` instance, we get an owned version of `Registry`. We initialize `next_id` to 1 (for debugging purposes, I wanted to initialize it to a different start value than our `Executor`) and create our `Reactor` object.

Then, we set the static variable we named REACTOR by giving it our `Reactor` instance.

The last thing is probably the *most important one to pay attention to*. We spawn a new OS thread and start our `event_loop` function on that one. This also means that we pass on our `Poll` instance to the event loop thread for good.

Now, the best practice would be to store the `JoinHandle` returned from `spawn` so that we can join the thread later on, but our thread has no way to shut down the event loop anyway, so joining it later makes little sense, and we simply discard the handle.

I don't know if you agree with me, but the logic here is not that complex when we break it down into smaller pieces. Since we know how `epoll` and `mio` work already, the rest is pretty easy to understand.

Now, we're not done yet. We still have some small changes to make to our `HttpGetFuture` leaf future since it doesn't register with the reactor at the moment. Let's fix that.

Start by opening the `http.rs` file.

Since we already added the correct imports when we opened the file to adapt everything to the new `Future` interface, there are only a few places we need to change that so this leaf future integrates nicely with our reactor.

The first thing we do is give `HttpGetFuture` an identity. It's the source of events we want to track with our `Reactor`, so we want it to have the same ID until we're done with it:

ch08/b-reactor-executor/src/http.rs

```
struct HttpGetFuture {
    stream: Option<mio::net::TcpStream>,
```

```
    buffer: Vec<u8>,
    path: String,
    id: usize,
}
```

We also need to retrieve a new ID from the reactor when the future is created:

ch08/b-reactor-executor/src/http.rs

```
impl HttpGetFuture {
    fn new(path: String) -> Self {
        let id = reactor().next_id();
        Self {
            stream: None,
            buffer: vec![],
            path,
            id,
        }
    }
}
```

Next, we have to locate the `poll` implementation for `HttpGetFuture`.

The first thing we need to do is make sure that we register interest with our `Poll` instance and register the `Waker` we receive with the `Reactor` the first time the future gets polled. Since we don't register directly with `Registry` anymore, we remove that line of code and add these new lines instead:

ch08/b-reactor-executor/src/http.rs

```
if self.stream.is_none() {
        println!("FIRST POLL - START OPERATION");
        self.write_request();
        let stream = self.stream.as_mut().unwrap();
          runtime::reactor().register(stream, Interest::READABLE, self.id);
        runtime::reactor().set_waker(waker, self.id);
    }
```

Lastly, we need to make some minor changes to how we handle the different conditions when reading from `TcpStream`:

ch08/b-reactor-executor/src/http.rs

```
match self.stream.as_mut().unwrap().read(&mut buff) {
                Ok(0) => {
```

```
                    let s = String::from_utf8_lossy(&self.buffer);
                    runtime::reactor().deregister(self.stream.as_mut().
    unwrap(), self.id);
                    break PollState::Ready(s.to_string());
                }
                Ok(n) => {
                    self.buffer.extend(&buff[0..n]);
                    continue;
                }
                Err(e) if e.kind() == ErrorKind::WouldBlock => {
                    runtime::reactor().set_waker(waker, self.id);
                    break PollState::NotReady;
                }

                Err(e) => panic!("{e:?}"),
            }
```

The first change is to deregister the stream from our `Poll` instance when we're done.

The second change is a little more subtle. If you read the documentation for `Future::poll` in Rust (https://doc.rust-lang.org/stable/std/future/trait.Future.html#tymethod.poll) carefully, you'll see that it's expected that the `Waker` from the *most recent call* should be scheduled to wake up. That means that every time we get a `WouldBlock` error, we need to make sure we store the most recent `Waker`.

The reason is that the future could have moved to a different executor in between calls, and we need to wake up the correct one (it won't be possible to move futures like those in our example, but let's play by the same rules).

And that's it!

Congratulations! You've now created a fully working runtime based on the reactor-executor pattern. Well done!

Now, it's time to test it and run a few experiments with it.

Let's go back to `main.rs` and change the `main` function so that we get our program running correctly with our new runtime.

First of all, let's remove the dependency on the `Runtime` struct and make sure our imports look like this:

ch08/b-reactor-executor/src/main.rs

```
mod future;
mod http;
mod runtime;
```

```
use future::{Future, PollState};
use runtime::Waker;
```

Next, we need to make sure that we initialize our runtime and pass in our future to `executor.block_on`. Our `main` function should look like this:

ch08/b-reactor-executor/src/main.rs

```
fn main() {
    let mut executor = runtime::init();
    executor.block_on(async_main());
}
```

And finally, let's try it out by running it:

`cargo run.`

You should get the following output:

```
Program starting
FIRST POLL - START OPERATION
main: 1 pending tasks. Sleep until notified.
HTTP/1.1 200 OK
content-length: 15
connection: close
content-type: text/plain; charset=utf-8
date: Thu, xx xxx xxxx 15:38:08 GMT

HelloAsyncAwait
FIRST POLL - START OPERATION
main: 1 pending tasks. Sleep until notified.
HTTP/1.1 200 OK
content-length: 15
connection: close
content-type: text/plain; charset=utf-8
date: Thu, xx xxx xxxx 15:38:08 GMT

HelloAsyncAwait
main: All tasks are finished
```

Great – it's working just as expected!!!

However, we're not really using any of the new capabilities of our runtime yet so before we leave this chapter, let's have some fun and see what it can do.

Experimenting with our new runtime

If you remember from *Chapter 7*, we implemented a `join_all` method to get our futures running concurrently. In libraries such as Tokio, you'll find a `join_all` function too, and the slightly more versatile `FuturesUnordered` API that allows you to join a set of predefined futures and run them concurrently.

These are convenient methods to have, but it does force you to know which futures you want to run concurrently in advance. If the futures you run using `join_all` want to spawn new futures that run concurrently with their "parent" future, there is no way to do that using only these methods.

However, our newly created spawn functionality does exactly this. Let's put it to the test!

An example using concurrency

> **Note**
> The exact same version of this program can be found in the `ch08/c-runtime-executor` folder.

Let's try a new program that looks like this:

```
fn main() {
    let mut executor = runtime::init();
    executor.block_on(async_main());
}

coro fn request(i: usize) {
    let path = format!("/{}/HelloWorld{i}", i * 1000);
    let txt = Http::get(&path).wait;
    println!("{txt}");
}

coro fn async_main() {
    println!("Program starting");

    for i in 0..5 {
        let future = request(i);
        runtime::spawn(future);
    }
}
```

This is pretty much the same example we used to show how `join_all` works in *Chapter 7*, only this time, we spawn them as top-level futures instead.

To run this example, follow these steps:

1. Replace everything *below the imports* in `main.rs` with the preceding code.
2. Run `corofy ./src/main.rs`.
3. Copy everything from `main_corofied.rs` to `main.rs` and delete `main_corofied.rs`.
4. Fix the fact that `corofy` doesn't know we changed our futures to take `waker: &Waker` as an argument. The easiest way is to simply run `cargo check` and let the compiler guide you to the places we need to change.

Now, you can run the example and see that the tasks run concurrently, just as they did using `join_all` in *Chapter 7*. If you measured the time it takes to run the tasks, you'd find that it all takes around 4 seconds, which makes sense if you consider that you just spawned 5 futures, and ran them concurrently. The longest wait time for a single future was 4 seconds.

Now, let's finish off this chapter with another interesting example.

Running multiple futures concurrently and in parallel

This time, we spawn multiple threads and give each thread its own `Executor` so that we can run the previous example simultaneously in parallel using the same `Reactor` for all `Executor` instances.

We'll also make a small adjustment to the printout so that we don't get overwhelmed with data.

Our new program will look like this:

```rust
mod future;
mod http;
mod runtime;
use crate::http::Http;
use future::{Future, PollState};
use runtime::{Executor, Waker};
use std::thread::Builder;

fn main() {
    let mut executor = runtime::init();
    let mut handles = vec![];

    for i in 1..12 {
        let name = format!("exec-{i}");
        let h = Builder::new().name(name).spawn(move || {
            let mut executor = Executor::new();
            executor.block_on(async_main());
        }).unwrap();
        handles.push(h);
```

```
        }
        executor.block_on(async_main());
        handles.into_iter().for_each(|h| h.join().unwrap());
}

coroutine fn request(i: usize) {
    let path = format!("/{}/HelloWorld{i}", i * 1000);
    let txt = Http::get(&path).wait;
    let txt = txt.lines().last().unwrap_or_default();
    println!(«{txt}»);



}

coroutine fn async_main() {
    println!("Program starting");

    for i in 0..5 {
        let future = request(i);
        runtime::spawn(future);
    }
}
```

The machine I'm currently running has 12 cores, so when I create 11 new threads to run the same asynchronous tasks, I'll use all the cores on my machine. As you'll notice, we also give each thread a unique name that we'll use when logging so that it's easier to track what happens behind the scenes.

> **Note**
> While I use 12 cores, you should use the number of cores on your machine. If we increase this number too much, our OS will not be able to give us more cores to run our program in parallel on and instead start pausing/resuming the threads we create, which adds no value to us since we handle the concurrency aspect ourselves in an a^tsync runtime.

You'll have to do the same steps as we did in the last example:

1. Replace the code that's currently in `main.rs` with the preceding code.
2. Run `corofy ./src/main.rs`.
3. Copy everything from `main_corofied.rs` to `main.rs` and delete `main_corofied.rs`.
4. Fix the fact that `corofy` doesn't know we changed our futures to take `waker: &Waker` as an argument. The easiest way is to simply run `cargo check` and let the compiler guide you to the places we need to change.

Now, if you run the program, you'll see that it still only takes around 4 seconds to run, but this time we made **60 GET requests instead of 5**. This time, we ran our futures both concurrently and in parallel.

At this point, you can continue experimenting with shorter delays or more requests and see how many concurrent tasks you can have before the system breaks down.

Pretty quickly, printouts to `stdout` will be a bottleneck, but you can disable those. Create a blocking version using OS threads and see how many threads you can run concurrently before the system breaks down compared to this version.

Only imagination sets the limit, but do take the time to have some fun with what you've created before we continue with the next chapter.

The only thing to be careful about is testing the concurrency limit of your system by sending these kinds of requests to a random server you don't control yourself since you can potentially overwhelm it and cause problems for others.

Summary

So, what a ride! As I said in the introduction for this chapter, this is one of the biggest ones in this book, but even though you might not realize it, you've already got a better grasp of how asynchronous Rust works than most people do. **Great work!**

In this chapter, you learned a lot about runtimes and why Rust designed the `Future` trait and the `Waker` the way it did. You also learned about reactors and executors, `Waker` types, `Futures` traits, and different ways of achieving concurrency through the `join_all` function and spawning new top-level futures on the executor.

By now, you also have an idea of how we can achieve both concurrency and parallelism by combining our own runtime with OS threads.

Now, we've created our own async universe consisting of `coro/wait`, our own `Future` trait, our own `Waker` definition, and our own runtime. I've made sure that we don't stray away from the core ideas behind asynchronous programming in Rust so that everything is directly applicable to `async/await`, `Future` traits, `Waker` types, and runtimes in day-to-day programming.

By now, we're in the final stretch of this book. The last chapter will finally convert our example to use the real `Future` trait, `Waker`, `async/await`, and so on instead of our own versions of it. In that chapter, we'll also reserve some space to talk about the state of asynchronous Rust today, including some of the most popular runtimes, but before we get that far, there is one more topic I want to cover: pinning.

One of the topics that seems hardest to understand and most different from all other languages is the concept of pinning. When writing asynchronous Rust, you will at some point have to deal with the fact that `Future` traits in Rust must be pinned before they're polled.

So, the next chapter will explain pinning in Rust in a practical way so that you understand why we need it, what it does, and how to do it.

However, you absolutely deserve a break after this chapter, so take some fresh air, sleep, clear your mind, and grab some coffee before we enter the last parts of this book.

9
Coroutines, Self-Referential Structs, and Pinning

In this chapter, we'll start by improving our coroutines by adding the ability to store variables across state changes. We'll see how this leads to our coroutines needing to take references to themselves and the issues that arise as a result of that. The reason for dedicating a whole chapter to this topic is that it's an integral part of getting async/await to work in Rust, and also a topic that is somewhat difficult to get a good understanding of.

The reason for this is that the whole concept of pinning is foreign to many developers and just like the Rust ownership system, it takes some time to get a good and working mental model of it.

Fortunately, the concept of pinning is not that difficult to understand, but how it's implemented in the language and how it interacts with Rust's type system is abstract and hard to grasp.

While we won't cover absolutely everything about pinning in this chapter, we'll try to get a good and sound understanding of it. The major goal here is to feel confident with the topic and understand why we need it and how to use it.

As mentioned previously, this chapter is not only about pinning in Rust, so the first thing we'll do is make some important improvements where we left off by improving the final example in *Chapter 8*.

Then, we'll explain what self-referential structs are and how they're connected to futures before we explain how pinning can solve our problems.

This chapter will cover the following main topics

- Improving our example 1 – variables
- Improving our example 2 – references
- Improving our example 3 – this is… not… good…
- Discovering self-referential structs

- Pinning in Rust
- Improving our example 4 – pinning to the rescue

Technical requirements

The examples in this chapter will build on the code from the previous chapter, so the requirements are the same. The examples will all be cross-platform and work on all platforms that Rust (https://doc.rust-lang.org/stable/rustc/platform-support.html) and mio (https://github.com/tokio-rs/mio#platforms) support. The only thing you need is Rust installed and this book's GitHub repository downloaded locally. All the code in this chapter can be found in the `ch09` folder.

To follow the examples step by step, you'll also need `corofy` installed on your machine. If you didn't install it in *Chapter 7*, install it now by going into the `ch07/corofy` folder in the repository and running the following:

```
cargo install --force --path .
```

We'll also use `delayserver` in this example, so you need to open a separate terminal, enter the `delayserver` folder at the root of the repository, and write `cargo run` so that it's ready and available for the examples going forward.

Remember to change the port number in the code if you have to change what port `delayserver` listens on.

Improving our example 1 – variables

So, let's recap what we have at this point by continuing where we left off in the previous chapter. We have the following:

- A `Future` trait
- A coroutine implementation using coroutine/await syntax and a preprocessor
- A reactor based on `mio::Poll`
- An executor that allows us to spawn as many top-level tasks as we want and schedules the ones that are ready to run
- An HTTP client that only makes HTTP GET requests to our local delayserver instance

It's not that bad – we might argue that our HTTP client is a *little* bit limited, but that's not the focus of this book, so we can live with that. Our coroutine implementation, however, is severely limited. Let's take a look at how we can make our coroutines slightly more useful.

The biggest downside with our current implementation is that nothing – and I mean nothing – can live across wait points. It makes sense to tackle this problem first.

Let's start by setting up our example.

We'll use the "library" code from d-multiple-threads example in *Chapter 8* (our last version of the example), but we'll change the main.rs file by adding a shorter and simpler example.

Let's set up the base example that we'll iterate on and improve in this chapter.

Setting up the base example

> **Note**
> You can find this example in this book's GitHub repository under ch09/a-coroutines-variables.

Perform the following steps:

1. Create a folder called a-coroutines-variables.
2. Enter the folder and run cargo init.
3. Delete the default main.rs file and copy everything from the ch08/d-multiple-threads/src folder into the ch10/a-coroutines-variables/src folder.
4. Open Cargo.toml and add the dependency on mio to the dependencies section:

   ```
   mio = {version = "0.8", features = ["net", "os-poll"]}
   ```

You should now have a folder structure that looks like this:

```
src
 |-- runtime
      |-- executor.rs
      |-- reactor.rs
 |-- future.rs
 |-- http.rs
 |-- main.rs
 |-- runtime.rs
```

We'll use corofy one last time to generate our boilerplate state machine for us. Copy the following into main.rs:

ch09/a-coroutines-variables/src/main.rs

```
mod future;
mod http;
mod runtime;
use crate::http::Http;
use future::{Future, PollState};
```

```
use runtime::Waker;

fn main() {
    let mut executor = runtime::init();
    executor.block_on(async_main());
}

coroutine fn async_main() {
    println!("Program starting");
    let txt = Http::get("/600/HelloAsyncAwait").wait;
    println!("{txt}");
    let txt = Http::get("/400/HelloAsyncAwait").wait;
    println!("{txt}");
}
```

This time, let's take a shortcut and write our *corofied* file directly back to main.rs since we've compared the files side by side enough times at this point. Assuming you're in the base folder, a-coroutine-variables, write the following:

```
corofy ./src/main.rs ./src/main.rs
```

The last step is to fix the fact that corofy doesn't know about Waker. You can let the compiler guide you to where you need to make changes by writing cargo check, but to help you along the way, there are three minor changes to make (note that the line number is the one reported by re-writing the same code that we wrote previously):

```
64:  fn poll(&mut self, waker: &Waker)
82:      match f1.poll(waker)
102:     match f2.poll(waker)
```

Now, check that everything is working as expected by writing cargo run.

You should see the following output (the output has been abbreviated to save a little bit of space):

```
Program starting
FIRST POLL - START OPERATION
main: 1 pending tasks. Sleep until notified.
HTTP/1.1 200 OK
```

```
[==== ABBREVIATED ====]
```

```
HelloAsyncAwait
main: All tasks are finished
```

> **Note**
>
> Remember that we need `delayserver` running in a terminal window so that we get a response to our HTTP GET requests. See the *Technical requirements* section for more information.

Now that we've got the boilerplate out of the way, it's time to start making the improvements we talked about.

Improving our base example

We want to see how we can improve our state machine so that it allows us to hold variables across wait points. To do that, we need to store them somewhere and restore the variables that are needed when we enter each state in our state machine.

> **Tip**
>
> Pretend that these rewrites are done by `corofy` (or the compiler). Even though `corofy` can't do these rewrites, it's possible to automate this process as well.

Or coroutine/wait program looks like this:

```
coroutine fn async_main() {
    println!("Program starting");
    let txt = Http::get("/600/HelloAsyncAwait").wait;
    println!("{txt}");
    let txt = Http::get("/400/HelloAsyncAwait").wait;
    println!("{txt}");
}
```

We want to change it so that it looks like this:

```
coroutine fn async_main() {
    let mut counter = 0;
    println!("Program starting");
    let txt = http::Http::get("/600/HelloAsyncAwait").wait;
    println!("{txt}");
    counter += 1;
    let txt = http::Http::get("/400/HelloAsyncAwait").wait;
    println!("{txt}");
    counter += 1;

    println!("Received {} responses.", counter);
}
```

In this version, we simply create a `counter` variable at the top of our `async_main` function and increase the counter for each response we receive from the server. At the end, we print out how many responses we received.

> **Note**
> For brevity, I won't present the entire code base going forward; instead, I will only present the relevant additions and changes. Remember that you can always refer to the same example in this book's GitHub repository.

The way we implement this is to add a new field called `stack` to our `Coroutine0` struct:

ch09/a-coroutines-variables/src/main.rs

```
struct Coroutine0 {
    stack: Stack0,
    state: State0,
}
```

The stack fields hold a `Stack0` struct that we also need to define:

ch09/a-coroutines-variables/src/main.rs

```
#[derive(Default)]
struct Stack0 {
    counter: Option<usize>,
}
```

This struct will only hold one field since we only have one variable. The field will be of the `Option<usize>` type. We also derive the `Default` trait for this struct so that we can initialize it easily.

> **Note**
>
> Futures created by async/await in Rust store this data in a slightly more efficient manner. In our example, we store every variable in a separate struct since I think it's easier to reason about, but it also means that the more variables we need to store, the more space our coroutine will need. It will grow linearly with the number of different variables that need to be stored/restored between state changes. This could be a lot of data. For example, if we have 100 state changes that each need one distinct i64-sized variable to be stored to the next state, that would require a struct that takes up 100 * 8b = 800 bytes in memory.
>
> Rust optimizes this by implementing coroutines as enums, where each state only holds the data it needs to restore in the *next* state. This way, the size of a coroutine is not dependent on the *total number of variables*; it's only dependent on the *size of the largest state that needs to be saved/restored*. In the preceding example, the size would be reduced to 8 bytes since the largest space any single state change needed is enough to hold one i64-sized variable. The same space will be reused over and over.
>
> The fact that this design allows for this optimization is significant and it's an advantage that stackless coroutines have over stackful coroutines when it comes to memory efficiency.

The next thing we need to change is the new method on Coroutine0:

ch09/a-coroutines-variables/src/main.rs

```rust
impl Coroutine0 {
    fn new() -> Self {
        Self {
            state: State0::Start,
            stack: Stack0::default(),
        }
    }
}
```

The default value for stack is not relevant to us since we'll overwrite it anyway.

The next few steps are the ones of most interest to us. In the Future implementation for Coroutine0, we'll pretend that corofy added the following code to initialize, store, and restore the stack variables for us. Let's take a look at what happens on the first call to poll now:

ch09/a-coroutines-variables/src/main.rs

```rust
State0::Start => {
            // initialize stack (hoist variables)
            self.stack.counter = Some(0);
            // ---- Code you actually wrote ----
            println!("Program starting");
```

```rust
                // --------------------------------------
                let fut1 = Box::new( http::Http::get("/600/HelloAsyncAwait"));
                self.state = State0::Wait1(fut1);

                // save stack

            }
```

Okay, so there are some important changes here that I've highlighted. Let's go through them:

- The first thing we do when we're in the `Start` state is add a segment at the top where we initialize our stack. One of the things we do is *hoist* all variable declarations for the relevant code section (in this case, before the first `wait` point) to the top of the function.
- In our example, we also initialize the variables to their initial value, which in this case is 0.
- We also added a comment stating that we should save the stack, but since all that happens before the first wait point is the initialization of `counter`, there is nothing to store here.

Let's take a look at what happens after the first wait point:

---

ch09/a-coroutines-variables/src/main.rs

```rust
State0::Wait1(ref mut f1) => {
                match f1.poll(waker) {
                    PollState::Ready(txt) => {
                        // Restore stack
                        let mut counter = self.stack.counter.take().unwrap();

                        // ---- Code you actually wrote ----
                        println!("{txt}");
                        counter += 1;
                        // --------------------------------------
                        let fut2 = Box::new( http::Http::get("/400/HelloAsyncAwait"));
                        self.state = State0::Wait2(fut2);

                        // save stack
                        self.stack.counter = Some(counter);
                    }
                    PollState::NotReady => break PollState::NotReady,
                }
            }
```

Hmm, this is interesting. I've highlighted the changes we need to make.

The first thing we do is to *restore* the stack by taking ownership over the counter (`take()` replaces the value currently stored in `self.stack.counter` with `None` in this case) and writing it to a variable with the same name that we used in the code segment (`counter`). Taking ownership and placing the value back in later is not an issue in this case and it mimics the code we wrote in our coroutine/wait example.

The next change is simply the segment that takes all the code after the first wait point and pastes it in. In this case, the only change is that the `counter` variable is increased by 1.

Lastly, we save the stack state back so that we hold onto its updated state between the wait points.

> **Note**
>
> In *Chapter 5*, we saw how we needed to store/restore the register state in our fibers. Since *Chapter 5* showed an example of a *stackful coroutine* implementation, we didn't have to care about stack state at all since all the needed state was stored in the stacks we created.
>
> Since our coroutines are *stackless*, we don't store the entire call stack for each coroutine, but we do need to store/restore the parts of the stack that will be used *across wait points*. Stackless coroutines still need to save some information from the stack, as we've done here.

When we enter the `State0::Wait2` state, we start the same way:

ch09/a-coroutines-variables/src/main.rs

```
State0::Wait2(ref mut f2) => {
                match f2.poll(waker) {
                    PollState::Ready(txt) => {
                        // Restore stack
                        let mut counter = self.stack.counter.take().unwrap();

                        // ---- Code you actually wrote ----
                        println!("{txt}");
                        counter += 1;

                        println!(«Received {} responses.», counter);
                        // ---------------------------------
                        self.state = State0::Resolved;

                        // Save stack (all variables set to None already)

                        break PollState::Ready(String::new());
```

```
                    }
                    PollState::NotReady => break PollState::NotReady,
                }
            }
        }
```

Since there are no more wait points in our program, the rest of the code goes into this segment and since we're done with `counter` at this point, we can simply `drop` it by letting it go out of scope. If our variable held onto any resources, they would be released here as well.

With that, we've given our coroutines the power of saving variables across wait points. Let's try to run it by writing `cargo run`.

You should see the following output (I've removed the parts of the output that remain unchanged):

```
...
HelloAsyncAwait
Received 2 responses.
main: All tasks are finished
```

Okay, so our program works and does what's expected. Great!

Now, let's take a look at an example that needs to store *references* across wait points since that's an important aspect of having our coroutine/wait functions behave like "normal" functions.

Improving our example 2 – references

Let's set everything up for our next version of this example:

- Create a new folder called `b-coroutines-references` and copy everything from `a-coroutines-variables` over to it

- You can change the name of the project so that it corresponds with the folder by changing the name attribute in the `package` section in `Cargo.toml`, but it's not something you need to do for the example to work

> **Note**
>
> You can find this example in this book's GitHub repository in the `ch10/b-coroutines-references` folder.

This time, we'll learn how to store references to variables in our coroutines by using the following coroutine/wait example program:

```
use std::fmt::Write;
coroutine fn async_main() {
    let mut buffer = String::from("\nBUFFER:\n----\n");
```

```
        let writer = &mut buffer;
        println!("Program starting");
        let txt = http::Http::get("/600/HelloAsyncAwait").wait;
        writeln!(writer, "{txt}").unwrap();
        let txt = http::Http::get("/400/HelloAsyncAwait").wait;
        writeln!(writer, "{txt}").unwrap();

        println!("{}", buffer);
    }
```

So, in this example, we create a buffer variable of the String type that we initialize with some text, and we take a &mut reference to that and store it in a writer variable.

Every time we receive a response, we write the response to the buffer through the &mut reference we hold in writer before we print the buffer to the terminal at the end of the program.

Let's take a look at what we need to do to get this working.

The first thing we do is pull in the fmt::Write trait so that we can write to our buffer using the writeln! macro.

Add this to the top of main.rs:

ch09/b-coroutines-references/src/main.rs

```
use std::fmt::Write;
```

Next, we need to change our Stack0 struct so that it represents what we must store across wait points in our updated example:

ch09/b-coroutines-references/src/main.rs

```
#[derive(Default)]
struct Stack0 {
    buffer: Option<String>,
    writer: Option<*mut String>,
}
```

An important thing to note here is that writer can't be Option<&mut String> since we know it will be referencing the buffer field in the same struct. A struct where a field takes a reference on &self is called a **self-referential** struct and there is no way to represent that in Rust since the lifetime of the self-reference is impossible to express.

The solution is to cast the &mut self-reference to a pointer instead and ensure that we manage the lifetimes correctly ourselves.

The only other thing we need to change is the `Future::poll` implementation:

ch09/b-coroutines-references/src/main.rs

```
State0::Start => {
                    // initialize stack (hoist variables)
                    self.stack.buffer = Some(String::from("\nBUFFER:\n----\n"));
                    self.stack.writer = Some(self.stack.buffer.as_mut().unwrap());
                    // ---- Code you actually wrote ----
                    println!("Program starting");

                    // --------------------------------
                    let fut1 = Box::new(http::Http::get("/600/HelloAsyncAwait"));
                    self.state = State0::Wait1(fut1);

                    // save stack
                }
```

Okay, so this looks a bit odd. The first line we change is pretty straightforward. We initialize our buffer variable to a new String type, just like we did at the top of our coroutine/wait program.

The next line, however, looks a bit dangerous.

We cast the &mut reference to our buffer to a *mut pointer.

> **Important**
>
> Yes, I know we could have chosen another way of doing this since we can take a reference to buffer everywhere we need to instead of storing it in its variable, but that's only because our example is very simple. Imagine that we use a library that needs to borrow data that's local to the async function and we somehow have to manage the lifetimes manually like we do here but in a much more complex scenario.

The self.stack.buffer.as_mut().unwrap() line returns a &mut reference to the buffer field. Since self.stack.writer is of the Option<*mut String> type, the reference will be *coerced* to a pointer (meaning that Rust does this cast implicitly by inferring it from the context).

> **Note**
>
> We take *mut String here since we deliberately don't want a *string slice* (&str), which is often what we get (and want) when using a reference to a String type in Rust.

Let's take a look at what happens after the first wait point:

ch09/b-coroutines-references/src/main.rs

```
State0::Wait1(ref mut f1) => {
                match f1.poll(waker) {
                    PollState::Ready(txt) => {
                        // Restore stack
                        let writer = unsafe { &mut *self.stack.
writer.take().unwrap() };

                        // ---- Code you actually wrote ----
                        writeln!(writer, «{txt}»).unwrap();
                        // --------------------------------
                        let fut2 = Box::new(http::Http::get("/400/
HelloAsyncAwait"));
                        self.state = State0::Wait2(fut2);

                        // save stack
                        self.stack.writer = Some(writer);
                    }
                    PollState::NotReady => break PollState::NotReady,
                }
            }
        }
```

The first change we make is regarding how we restore our stack. We need to restore our `writer` variable so that it holds a `&mut String` type that points to our buffer. To do this, we have to write some `unsafe` code that dereferences our pointer and lets us take a `&mut` reference to our `buffer`.

> **Note**
> Casting a reference to a pointer is safe. The unsafe part is dereferencing the pointer.

Next, we add the line of code that writes the response. We can keep this the same as how we wrote it in our coroutine/wait function.

Lastly, we save the stack state back since we need both variables to live across the wait point.

> **Note**
> We don't have to take ownership over the pointer stored in the `writer` field to use it since we can simply copy it, but to be somewhat consistent, we take ownership over it, just like we did in the first example. It also makes sense since if there is no need to store the pointer for the next await point, we can simply let it go out of scope by not storing it back.

The last part is when we've reached `Wait2` and our future returns `PollState::Ready`:

```rust
State0::Wait2(ref mut f2) => {
                match f2.poll(waker) {
                    PollState::Ready(txt) => {
                        // Restore stack
                        let buffer = self.stack.buffer.as_ref().take().unwrap();
                        let writer = unsafe { &mut *self.stack.writer.take().unwrap() };

                        // ---- Code you actually wrote ----
                        writeln!(writer, «{txt}»).unwrap();

                        println!("{}", buffer);
                        // ---------------------------------
                        self.state = State0::Resolved;

                    // Save stack / free resources
                    let _ = self.stack.buffer.take();

                        break PollState::Ready(String::new());
                    }
                    PollState::NotReady => break PollState::NotReady,
                }
            }
        }
```

In this segment, we restore both variables since we write the last response through our writer variable, and then print everything that's stored in our `buffer` to the terminal.

I want to point out that the `println!("{}", buffer);` line takes a reference in the original coroutine/wait example, even though it might look like we pass in an owned `String`. Therefore, it makes sense that we restore the buffer to a `&String` type, and not the owned version. Transferring ownership would also invalidate the pointer in our `writer` variable.

The last thing we do is `drop` the data we don't need anymore. Our `self.stack.writer` field is already set to `None` since we took ownership over it when we restored the stack at the start, but we need to take ownership over the `String` type that `self.stack.buffer` holds as well so that it gets dropped at the end of this scope too. If we didn't do that, we would hold on to the memory that's been allocated to our `String` until the entire coroutine is dropped (which could be much later).

Now, we've made all our changes. If the rewrites we did previously were implemented in `corofy`, our coroutine/wait implementation could, in theory, support much more complex use cases.

Let's take a look at what happens when we run our program by writing `cargo run`:

```
Program starting
FIRST POLL - START OPERATION
main: 1 pending tasks. Sleep until notified.
FIRST POLL - START OPERATION
main: 1 pending tasks. Sleep until notified.

BUFFER:
----
HTTP/1.1 200 OK
content-length: 15
connection: close
content-type: text/plain; charset=utf-8
date: Thu, 30 Nov 2023 22:48:11 GMT

HelloAsyncAwait
HTTP/1.1 200 OK
content-length: 15
connection: close
content-type: text/plain; charset=utf-8
date: Thu, 30 Nov 2023 22:48:11 GMT

HelloAsyncAwait

main: All tasks are finished
```

Puh, great. All that dangerous `unsafe` turned out to work just fine, didn't it? Good job. Let's make one small improvement before we finish.

Improving our example 3 – this is… not… good…

Pretend you haven't read this section title and enjoy the fact that our previous example compiled and showed the correct result.

I think our coroutine implementation is so good now that we can look at some optimizations instead. There is one optimization in our executor in particular that I want to do immediately.

Before we get ahead of ourselves, let's set everything up:

- Create a new folder called `c-coroutines-problem` and copy everything from `b-coroutines-references` over to it
- You can change the name of the project so that it corresponds with the folder by changing the name attribute in the `package` section in `Cargo.toml`, but it's not something you need to do for the example to work

> **Tip**
>
> This example is located in this book's GitHub repository in the `ch09/c-coroutines-problem` folder.

With that, everything has been set up.

Back to the optimization. You see, new insights into the workload our runtime will handle in real life indicate that most futures will return `Ready` on the first poll. So, in theory, we can just poll the future we receive in `block_on` once and it will resolve immediately most of the time.

Let's navigate to `src/runtime/executor.rs` and take a look at how we can take advantage of this by adding a few lines of code.

If you navigate to our `Executor::block_on` function, you'll see that the first thing we do is `spawn` the future before we poll it. Spawning the future means that we allocate space for it in the heap and store the pointer to its location in a `HashMap` variable.

Since the future will most likely return `Ready` on the first `poll`, this is unnecessary work that could be avoided. Let's add this little optimization at the start of the `block_on` function to take advantage of this:

```
pub fn block_on<F>(&mut self, future: F)
    where
        F: Future<Output = String> + 'static,
{
    // ===== OPTIMIZATION, ASSUME READY
    let waker = self.get_waker(usize::MAX);
    let mut future = future;
    match future.poll(&waker) {
        PollState::NotReady => (),
        PollState::Ready(_) => return,
    }
    // ===== END

    spawn(future);

    loop {
        ...
```

Now, we simply poll the future immediately, and if the future resolves on the first poll, we return since we're all done. This way, we only spawn the future if it's something we need to wait on.

Yes, this assumes we never reach `usize::MAX` for our IDs, but let's pretend this is only a proof of concept. Our `Waker` will be discarded and replaced by a new one if the future is spawned and polled again anyway, so that shouldn't be a problem.

Let's try to run our program and see what we get:

```
Program starting
FIRST POLL - START OPERATION
main: 1 pending tasks. Sleep until notified.
FIRST POLL - START OPERATION
main: 1 pending tasks. Sleep until notified.
/400/HelloAsyn
free(): double free detected in tcache 2
Aborted
```

Wait, what?!?

That doesn't sound good! Okay, that's probably a kernel bug in Linux, so let's try it on Windows instead:

```
...
error: process didn't exit successfully: `target\release\c-coroutines-
problem.exe` (exit code: 0xc0000374, STATUS_HEAP_CORRUPTION)
```

That sounds even worse!! What happened here?

Let's take a closer look at exactly what happened with our async system when we made our small optimization.

Discovering self-referential structs

What happened is that we created a self-referential struct, initialized it so that it took a pointer to itself, and then moved it. Let's take a closer look:

1. First, we received a future object as an argument to `block_on`. This is not a problem since the future isn't self-referential yet, so we can move it around wherever we want to without issues (this is also why moving futures before they're polled is perfectly fine using proper async/await).

2. Then, we polled the future once. The optimization we did made one essential change. The future was located on the stack (inside the stack frame of our `block_on` function) when we polled it the first time.

3. When we polled the future the first time, we initialized the variables to their initial state. Our `writer` variable took a pointer to our `buffer` variable (stored as a part of our coroutine) and made it *self-referential* at this point.

4. The first time we polled the future, it returned `NotReady`

5. Since it returned `NotReady`, we spawned the future, which moves it into the tasks collection with the `HashMap<usize, Box<dyn Future<Output = String>>>` type in our `Executor`. The future is now placed in `Box`, which moves it to the heap.

6. The next time we poll the future, we restore the stack by dereferencing the pointer we hold for our `writer` variable. However, there's a big problem: the pointer is now pointing to the old location on the stack where the future was located at the first poll.

7. That can't end well, and it doesn't in our case.

You've now seen firsthand the problem with self-referential structs, how this applies to futures, and why we need something that prevents this from happening.

A **self-referential struct** is a struct that takes a reference to *self* and stores it in a field. Now, the term *reference* here is a little bit unprecise since there is no way to take a reference to *self* in Rust and store that reference in *self*. To do this in safe Rust, you have to cast the reference to a *pointer* (remember that references are just pointers with a special meaning in the programming language).

> **Note**
>
> When we create visualizations in this chapter, we'll disregard *padding*, even though we know structs will likely have some padding between fields, as we discussed in *Chapter 4*.

When this value is moved to another location in memory, the pointer is not updated and points to the "old" location.

If we take a look at a move from one location on the stack to another one, it looks something like this:

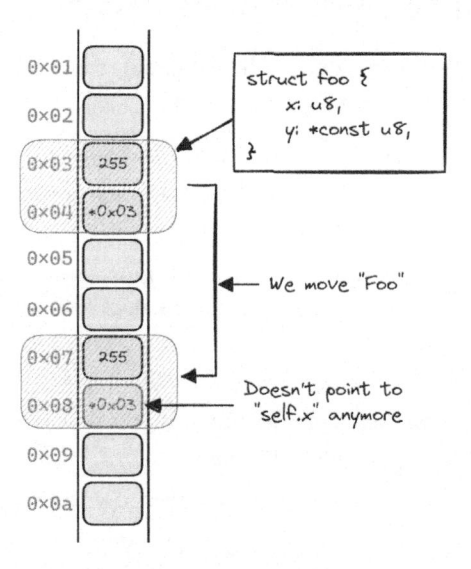

Figure 9.1 – Moving a self-referential struct

In the preceding figure, we can see the memory addresses to the left with a representation of the stack next to it. Since the pointer was not updated when the value was moved, it now points to the old location, which can cause serious problems.

> Note
>
> It can be very hard to detect these issues, and creating simple examples where a move like this causes serious issues is surprisingly difficult. The reason for this is that even though we move everything, the old values are not zeroed or overwritten immediately. Often, they're still there, so dereferencing the preceding pointer would *probably* produce the correct value. The problem only arises when you change the value of x in the new location, and expect y to point to it. Dereferencing y still produces a valid value in this case, but it's the *wrong* value.
>
> Optimized builds often optimize away needless moves, which can make bugs even harder to detect since most of the program will seem to work just fine, even though it contains a serious bug.

What is a move?

A *move* in Rust is one of those concepts that's unfamiliar to many programmers coming from C#, Javascript, and similar garbage-collected languages, and different from what you're used to for C and C++ programmers. The definition of *move* in Rust is closely related to its ownership system.

Moving means transferring ownership. In Rust, a *move* is the default way of passing values around and it happens every time you change ownership over an object. If the object you move only consists of copy types (types that implement the Copy trait), this is as simple as copying the data over to a new location on the stack.

For non-copy types, a move will copy all copy types that it contains over just like in the first example, but now, it will also copy pointers to resources such as heap allocations. The moved-from object is left inaccessible to us (for example, if you try to use the moved-from object, the compilation will fail and let you know that the object has moved), so there is only one owner over the allocation at any point in time.

In contrast to *cloning*, it does not recreate any resources and make a clone of them.

One more important thing is that the compiler makes sure that drop is never called on the moved-from object so that the only thing that can free the resources is the new object that took ownership over everything.

Figure 9.2 provides a simplified visual overview of the difference between move, clone, and copy (we've excluded any internal padding of the struct in this visualization). Here, we assume that we have a struct that holds two fields – a copy type, a, which is an i64 type, and a non-copy type, b, which is a Vec<u8> type:

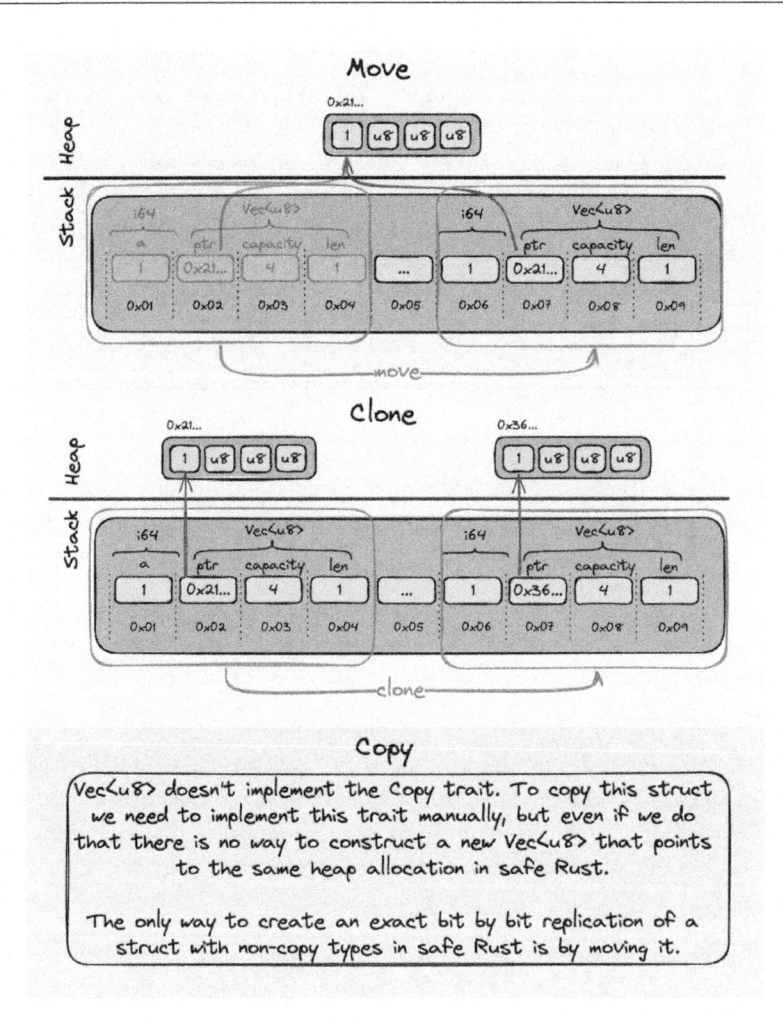

Figure 9.2 – Move, clone, and copy

A move will in many ways be like a deep copy of everything in our struct that's located on the stack. This is problematic when you have a pointer that points to `self`, like we have with self-referential structs, since `self` will start at a new memory address after the move but the pointer to `self` won't be adjusted to reflect that change.

Most of the time, when programming Rust, you probably won't think a lot about moves since it's part of the language you never explicitly use, but it's important to know what it is and what it does.

Now that we've got a good understanding of what the problem is, let's take a closer look at how Rust solves this by using its type system to prevent us from moving structs that rely on a stable place in memory to function correctly.

Pinning in Rust

The following diagram shows a slightly more complex self-referential struct so that we have something visual to help us understand:

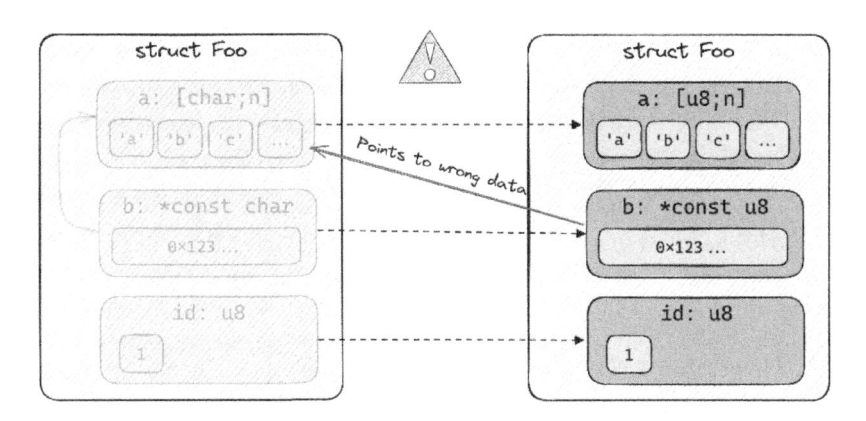

Figure 9.3 – Moving a self-referential struct with three fields

At a very high level, pinning makes it possible to rely on data that has a stable memory address by disallowing any operation that might move it:

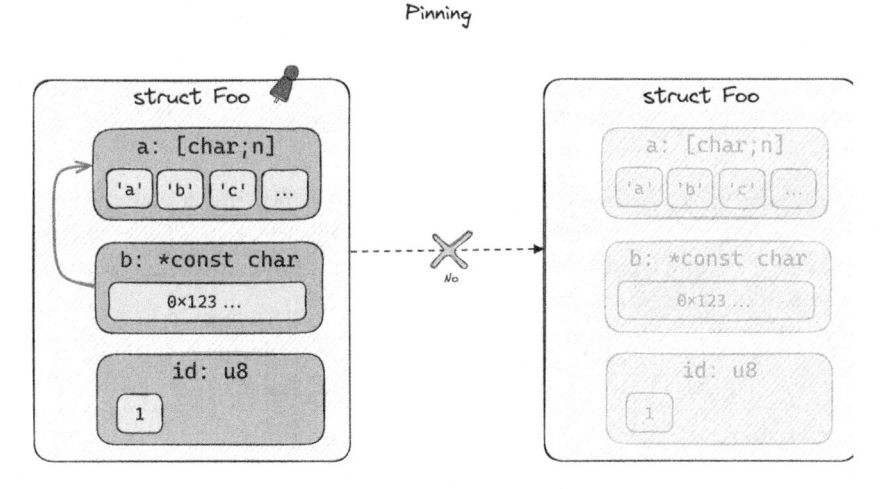

Figure 9.4 – Moving a pinned struct

The concept of pinning is pretty simple. The complex part is how it's implemented in the language and how it's used.

Pinning in theory

Pinning is a part of Rust's standard library and consists of two parts: the type, **Pin**, and the marker-trait, **Unpin**. Pinning is only a language construct. There is no special kind of location or memory that you move values to so they get pinned. There is no syscall to ask the operating system to ensure a value stays the same place in memory. It's only a part of the type system that's designed to prevent us from being able to move a value.

`Pin` does not remove the need for `unsafe` – it just gives the user of `unsafe` a guarantee that the value has a stable location in memory, so long as the user that pinned the value only uses *safe* Rust. This allows us to write self-referential types that are safe. It makes sure that all operations that can lead to problems must use `unsafe`.

Back to our coroutine example, if we were to move the struct, we'd have to write `unsafe` Rust. That is how Rust upholds its safety guarantee. If you somehow know that the future you created never takes a self-reference, you could choose to move it using `unsafe`, but the blame now falls on you if you get it wrong.

Before we dive a bit deeper into pinning, we need to define several terms that we'll need going forward.

Definitions

Here are the definitions we must understand:

- **Pin<T>** is the type it's all about. You'll find this as a part of Rust's standard library under the `std::pin` module. `Pin` wrap types that implement the `Deref` trait, which in practical terms means that it wraps *references and smart pointers*.

- **Unpin** is a *marker trait*. If a type implements `Unpin`, *pinning will have no effect on that type*. You read that right – no effect. The type will still be wrapped in `Pin` but you can simply take it out again.

    The impressive thing is that almost everything implements `Unpin` by default, and if you manually want to mark a type as `!Unpin`, you have to add a marker trait called `PhantomPinned` to your type. Having a type, T, implement `!Unpin` is the only way for something such as `Pin<&mut T>` to have any effect.

- **Pinning a type that's !Unpin** will guarantee that the value remains at the same location in memory until it gets dropped, so long as you stay in safe Rust.

- **Pin projections** are helper methods on a type that's pinned. The syntax often gets a little weird since they're only valid on pinned instances of `self`. For example, they often look like `fn foo(self: Pin<&mut self>)`.

- **Structural pinning** is connected to *pin projections* in the sense that, if you have Pin<&mut T> where T has one field, a, that can be moved freely and one that can't be moved, b, you can do the following:
  - Write a *pin projection* for a with the fn a(self: Pin<&mut self>) -> &A signature. In this case, we say that pinning is *not structural*.
  - Write a projection for b that looks like fn b(self: Pin<&mut self>) -> Pin<&mut B>, in which case we say that pinning is *structural* for b since it's pinned when the struct, T, is pinned.

With the most important definitions out of the way, let's look at the two ways we can pin a value.

Pinning to the heap

> **Note**
> The small code snippets we'll present here can be found in this book's GitHub repository in the ch09/d-pin folder. The different examples are implemented as different methods that you comment/uncomment in the main function.

Let's write a small example to illustrate the different ways of pinning a value:

ch09/d-pin/src/main.rs

```
use std::{marker::PhantomPinned, pin::Pin};

    #[derive(Default)]
    struct Foo {
    a: MaybeSelfRef,
    b: String,
}
```

So, we want to be able to create an instance using MaybeSelfRef::default() that we can move around as we wish, but then at some point *initialize* it to a state where it references itself; moving it would cause problems.

This is very much like futures that are not self-referential until they're polled, as we saw in our previous example. Let's write the `impl` block for `MaybeSelfRef` and take a look at the code::

ch09/d-pin/src/main.rs

```
impl MaybeSelfRef {
    fn init(self: Pin<&mut Self>) {
        unsafe {
            let Self { a, b, .. } = self.get_unchecked_mut();
            *b = Some(a);
        }
    }

    fn b(self: Pin<&mut Self>) -> Option<&mut usize> {
        unsafe { self.get_unchecked_mut().b.map(|b| &mut *b) }
    }
}
```

As you can see, `MaybeStelfRef` will only be self-referential after we call `init` on it.

We also define one more method that casts the pointer stored in b to `Option<&mut usize>`, which is a mutable reference to a.

One thing to note is that both our functions require `unsafe`. Without `Pin`, the only method requiring unsafe would be b since we dereference a pointer there. Acquiring a mutable reference to a pinned value always require `unsafe`, since there is nothing preventing us from moving the pinned value at that point.

Pinning to the heap is usually done by pinning a `Box`. There is even a convenient method on `Box` that allows us to get `Pin<Box<...>>`. Let's look at a short example:

ch09/d-pin/src/main.rs

```
fn main() {
    let mut x = Box::pin(MaybeSelfRef::default());
    x.as_mut().init();
    println!("{}", x.as_ref().a);
    *x.as_mut().b().unwrap() = 2;
    println!("{}", x.as_ref().a);
}
```

Here, we pin `MaybeSelfRef` to the heap and initialize it. We print out the value of a and then mutate the data through the self-reference in b, and set its value to 2. If we look at the output, we'll see that everything looks as expected:

```
    Finished dev [unoptimized + debuginfo] target(s) in 0.56s
     Running `target\debug\x-pin-experiments.exe`
0
2
```

The pinned value can never move and as *users* of `MaybeSelfRef`, we didn't have to write any `unsafe` code. Rust can guarantee that we never (in safe Rust) get a mutable reference to `MaybeSelfRef` since `Box` took ownership of it.

Heap pinning being safe is not so surprising since, in contrast to the stack, a heap allocation will be stable throughout the program, regardless of where we create it.

> **Important**
> This is the preferred way to pin values in Rust. Stack pinning is for those cases where you don't have a heap to work with or can't accept the cost of that extra allocation.

Let's take a look at stack pinning while we're at it.

Pinning to the stack

Pinning to the stack can be somewhat difficult. In *Chapter 5*, we saw how the stack worked and we know that it grows and shrinks as values are popped and pushed to the stack.

So, if we're going to pin to the stack, we have to pin it somewhere "high" on the stack. This means that if we pin a value to the stack inside a function call, we can't return from that function, and expect the value to still be pinned there. That would be impossible.

Pinning to the stack is hard since we pin by taking `&mut T`, and we have to guarantee that we won't move T until it's dropped. If we're not careful, this is easy to get wrong. Rust can't help us here, so it's up to us to uphold that guarantee. This is why stack pinning is `unsafe`.

Let's look at the same example using stack pinning:

ch09/d-pin/src/main.rs

```
fn stack_pinning_manual() {
    let mut x = MaybeSelfRef::default();
    let mut x = unsafe { Pin::new_unchecked(&mut x) };
    x.as_mut().init();
    println!("{}", x.as_ref().a);
    *x.as_mut().b().unwrap() = 2;
```

```
        println!("{}", x.as_ref().a);
}
```

The noticeable difference here is that it's `unsafe` to pin to the stack, so now, we need `unsafe` both as users of `MaybeSelfRef` and as implementors.

If we run the example with `cargo run`, the output will be the same as in our first example:

```
        Finished dev [unoptimized + debuginfo] target(s) in 0.58s
        Running `target\debug\x-pin-experiments.exe`
0
2
```

The reason stack pinning requires `unsafe` is that it's rather easy to accidentally break the guarantees that `Pin` is supposed to provide. Let's take a look at this example:

ch09/d-pin/src/main.rs

```
use std::mem::swap;
fn stack_pinning_manual_problem() {
    let mut x = MaybeSelfRef::default();
    let mut y = MaybeSelfRef::default();

    {
        let mut x = unsafe { Pin::new_unchecked(&mut x) };
        x.as_mut().init();
        *x.as_mut().b().unwrap() = 2;
    }
    swap(&mut x, &mut y);
    println!("
    x: {{
+------>a: {:p},
|       b: {:?},
|   }}
|
|   y: {{
|       a: {:p},
+------|b: {:?},
    }}",
        &x.a,
        x.b,
        &y.a,
        y.b,
    );
}
```

In this example, we create two instances of MaybeSelfRef called x and y. Then, we create a scope where we pin x and set the value of x.a to 2 by dereferencing the self-reference in b, as we did previously.

Now, when we exit the scope, x isn't pinned anymore, which means we can take a mutable reference to it without needing unsafe.

Since this is safe Rust and we should be able to do what we want, we swap x and y.

The output prints out the pointer address of the a field of both structs and the value of the pointer stored in b.

When we look at the output, we should see the problem immediately:

```
Finished dev [unoptimized + debuginfo] target(s) in 0.58s
    Running `target\debug\x-pin-experiments.exe`

    x: {
+----->a: 0xe45fcff558,
|       b: None,
|   }
|
|   y: {
|       a: 0xe45fcff570,
+-----|b: Some(0xe45fcff558),
    }
```

Although the pointer values will differ from run to run, it's pretty evident that y doesn't hold a pointer to self anymore.

Right now, it points somewhere in x. This is very bad and will cause the exact memory safety issues Rust is supposed to prevent.

> **Note**
>
> For this reason, the standard library has a pin! macro that helps us with safe stack pinning. The macro uses unsafe under the hood but makes it impossible for us to reach the pinned value again.

Now that we've seen all the pitfalls of stack pinning, my clear recommendation is to avoid it unless you need to use it. If you have to use it, then use the pin! macro so that you avoid the issues we've described here.

> **Tip**
>
> In this book's GitHub repository, you'll find a function called `stack_pinning_macro()` in the `ch09/d-pin/src/main.rs` file. This function shows the preceding example but using Rust's `pin!` macro.

Pin projections and structural pinning

Before we leave the topic of pinning, we'll quickly explain what pin projections and structural pinning are. Both sound complex, but they are very simple in practice. The following diagram shows how these terms are connected:

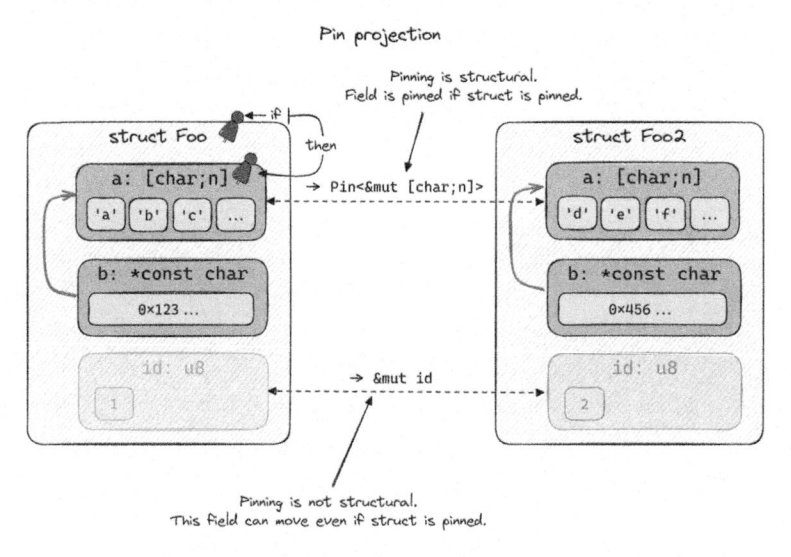

Figure 9.5 – Pin projection and structural pinning

Structural pinning means that if a struct is pinned, so is the field. We expose this through pin projections, as we'll see in the following code example.

If we continue with our example and create a struct called `Foo` that holds both `MaybeSelfRef` (field a) and a `String` type (field b), we could write two projections that return a pinned version of a and a regular mutable reference to b:

ch09/d-pin/src/main.rs

```
#[derive(Default)]
struct Foo {
    a: MaybeSelfRef,
    b: String,
}
```

```
impl Foo {
    fn a(self: Pin<&mut Self>) -> Pin<&mut MaybeSelfRef> {
        unsafe {
            self.map_unchecked_mut(|s| &mut s.a)
        }
    }

    fn b(self: Pin<&mut Self>) -> &mut String {
        unsafe {
            &mut self.get_unchecked_mut().b
        }
    }
}
```

Note that these methods will only be callable when Foo is pinned. You won't be able to call either of these methods on a regular instance of Foo.

Pin projections do have a few subtleties that you should be aware of, but they're explained in quite some detail in the official documentation (https://doc.rust-lang.org/stable/std/pin/index.html), so I'll refer you there for more information about the precautions you must take when writing projections.

> **Note**
> Since pin projections can be a bit error-prone to create yourself, there is a popular create for making pin projections called **pin_project** (https://docs.rs/pin-project/latest/pin_project/). If you ever end up having to make pin projections, it's worth checking out.

With that, we've pretty much covered all the advanced topics in async Rust. However, before we go on to our last chapter, let's see how pinning will prevent us from making the big mistake we made in the last iteration of our coroutine example.

Improving our example 4 – pinning to the rescue

Fortunately, the changes we need to make are small, but before we continue and make the changes, let's create a new folder and copy everything we had in our previous example over to that folder:

- Copy the entire c-coroutines-problem folder and name the new copy e-coroutines-pin
- Open Cargo.toml and rename the name of the package e-coroutines-pin

Coroutines, Self-Referential Structs, and Pinning

> **Tip**
> You'll find the example code we'll go through here in this book's GitHub repository under the `ch09/e-coroutines-pin` folder.

Now that we have a new folder set up, let's start making the necessary changes. The logical place to start is our `Future` definition in `future.rs`.

future.rs

The first thing we'll do is pull in `Pin` from the standard library at the very top:

ch09/e-coroutines-pin/src/future.rs

```rust
use std::pin::Pin;
```

The only other change we need to make is in the definition of `poll` in our `Future` trait:

```rust
fn poll(self: Pin<&mut Self>, waker: &Waker) -> PollState<Self::Output>;
```

That's pretty much it.

However, the implications of this change are noticeable pretty much everywhere poll is called, so we need to fix that as well.

Let's start with `http.rs`.

http.rs

The first thing we need to do is pull in `Pin` from the standard library. The start of the file should look like this:

ch09/e-coroutines-pin/src/http.rs

```rust
use crate::{future::PollState, runtime::{self, reactor, Waker}, Future};
use mio::Interest;
use std::{io::{ErrorKind, Read, Write}, pin::Pin};
```

The only other place we need to make some changes is in the `Future` implementation for `HttpGetFuture`, so let's locate that. We'll start by changing the arguments in `poll`:

ch09/e-coroutines-pin/src/http.rs

```rust
fn poll(mut self: Pin<&mut Self>, waker: &Waker) -> PollState<Self::Output>
```

Improving our example 4 – pinning to the rescue

Since `self` is now `Pin<&mut Self>`, there are several small changes we need to make so that the borrow checker stays happy. Let's start from the top:

ch09/e-coroutines-pin/src/http.rs

```
let id = self.id;
        if self.stream.is_none() {
            println!("FIRST POLL - START OPERATION");
            self.write_request();
            let stream = (&mut self).stream.as_mut().unwrap();
            runtime::reactor().register(stream, Interest::READABLE, id);
            runtime::reactor().set_waker(waker, self.id);
        }
```

The reason for assigning `id` to a variable at the top is that the borrow checker gives us some minor trouble when trying to pass in both `&mut self` and `&self` as arguments to the register/deregister functions, so we just assign `id` to a variable at the top and everyone is happy.

There are only two more lines to change, and that is where we create a `String` type from our internal buffer and deregister interest with the reactor:

ch09/e-coroutines-pin/src/http.rs

```
let s = String::from_utf8_lossy(&self.buffer).to_string();
runtime::reactor().deregister(self.stream.as_mut().unwrap(), id);
break PollState::Ready(s);
```

> **Important**
> Notice that this future is `Unpin`. There is nothing that makes it `unsafe` to move `HttpGetFuture` around, and this is indeed the case for most futures like this. Only the ones created by async/await are self-referential by design. That means there is no need for any `unsafe` here.

Next, let's move on to `main.rs` since there are some important changes we need to make there.

Main.rs

Let's start from the top and make sure we have the correct imports:

ch09/e-coroutines-pin/src/main.rs

```
mod future;
mod http;
mod runtime;
use future::{Future, PollState};
use runtime::Waker;
use std::{fmt::Write, marker::PhantomPinned, pin::Pin};
```

This time, we need both the `PhantomPinned` marker and `Pin`.

The next thing we need to change is in our `State0` enum. The futures we hold between states are now pinned:

ch09/e-coroutines-pin/src/main.rs

```
Wait1(Pin<Box<dyn Future<Output = String>>>),
Wait2(Pin<Box<dyn Future<Output = String>>>),
```

Next up is an important change. We need to make our coroutines `!Unpin` so that they can't be moved once they have been pinned. We can do this by adding a marker trait to our `Coroutine0` struct:

ch09/e-coroutines-pin/src/main.rs

```
struct Coroutine0 {
    stack: Stack0,
    state: State0,
    _pin: PhantomPinned,
}
```

We also need to add the `PhantomPinned` marker to our new function:

ch09/e-coroutines-pin/src/main.rs

```
impl Coroutine0 {
    fn new() -> Self {
        Self {
            state: State0::Start,
            stack: Stack0::default(),
            _pin: PhantomPinned,
        }
    }
}
```

}

The last thing we need to change is the `poll` method. Let's start with the function signature:

ch09/e-coroutines-pin/src/main.rs

```
fn poll(self: Pin<&mut Self>, waker: &Waker) -> PollState<Self::Output>
```

The easiest way I found to change our code was to simply define a new variable at the very top of the function called `this`, which replaces `self` everywhere in the function body.

I won't go through every line since the change is so trivial, but after the first line, it's a simple search and replace everywhere `self` was used earlier, and change it to `this`:

ch09/e-coroutines-pin/src/main.rs

```
let this = unsafe { self.get_unchecked_mut() };
        loop {
            match this.state {
                State0::Start => {
                    // initialize stack (hoist declarations - no stack yet)
                    this.stack.buffer = Some(String::from("\nBUFFER:\n----\n"));
                    this.stack.writer = Some(this.stack.buffer.as_mut().unwrap());
                    // ---- Code you actually wrote ----
                    println!("Program starting");
...
```

The important line here was `let this = unsafe { self.get_unchecked_mut() };`. Here, we had to use `unsafe` since the pinned value is `!Unpin` because of the marker trait we added.

Getting to the pinned value is `unsafe` since there is no way for Rust to guarantee that we won't move the pinned value.

The nice thing about this is that if we encounter any such problems later, we know we can search for the places where we used `unsafe` and that the problem must be there.

The next thing we need to change is to have the futures we store in our wait states pinned. We can do this by calling `Box::pin` instead of `Box::new`:

ch09/e-coroutines-pin/src/main.rs

```
let fut1 = Box::pin(http::Http::get("/600/HelloAsyncAwait"));
let fut2 = Box::pin(http::Http::get("/400/HelloAsyncAwait"));
```

The last place in `main.rs` where we need to make changes is in the locations where we poll our child futures since we now have to go through the `Pin` type to get a mutable reference:

ch09/e-coroutines-pin/src/main.rs

```
match f1.as_mut().poll(waker)
match f2.as_mut().poll(waker)
```

Note that we don't need `unsafe` here since these futures are `!Unpin`.

The last place we need to change a few lines of code is in `executor.rs`, so let's head over there as our last stop.

executor.rs

The first thing we must do is make sure our dependencies are correct. The only change we're making here is adding `Pin` from the standard library:

ch09/e-coroutines-pin/src/runtime/executor.rs

```
...
    thread::{self, Thread}, pin::Pin,
};
```

The next line we'll change is our `Task` type alias so that it now refers to `Pin<Box<...>>`:

```
type Task = Pin<Box<dyn Future<Output = String>>>;
```

The last line we'll change for now is in our spawn function. We have to pin the futures to the heap:

```
e.tasks.borrow_mut().insert(id, Box::pin(future));
```

If we try to run our example now, it won't even compile and give us the following error:

```
error[E0599]: no method named `poll` found for struct `Pin<Box<dyn
future::Future<Output = String>>>` in the current scope
  --> src\runtime\executor.rs:89:30
```

It won't even let us poll the future anymore without us pinning it first since `poll` is only callable for `Pin<&mut Self>` types and not `&mut self` anymore.

So, we have to decide whether we pin the value to the stack or the heap before we even try to poll it. In our case, our whole executor works by heap allocating futures, so that's the only thing that makes sense to do.

Let's remove our optimization entirely and change one line of code to make our executor work again:

ch09/e-coroutines-pin/src/runtime/executor.rs

```
match future.as_mut().poll(&waker) {
```

If you try to run the program again by writing `cargo run`, you should get the expected output back and not have to worry about the coroutine/wait generated futures being moved again (the output has been abbreviated slightly):

```
Finished dev [unoptimized + debuginfo] target(s) in 0.02s
     Running `target\debug\e-coroutines-pin.exe`
Program starting
FIRST POLL - START OPERATION
main: 1 pending tasks. Sleep until notified.
FIRST POLL - START OPERATION
main: 1 pending tasks. Sleep until notified.

BUFFER:
----
HTTP/1.1 200 OK
content-length: 15
[=== ABBREVIATED ===]
date: Sun, 03 Dec 2023 23:18:12 GMT

HelloAsyncAwait

main: All tasks are finished
```

You now have self-referential coroutines that can safely store both data and references across wait points. Congratulations!

Even though making these changes took up quite a few pages, the changes themselves were part pretty trivial for the most part. Most of the changes were due to `Pin` having a different API than what we had when using references before.

The good thing is that this sets us up nicely for migrating our whole runtime over to futures created by async/await instead of our own futures created by coroutine/wait with very few changes.

Summary

What a ride, huh? If you've got to the end of this chapter, you've done a fantastic job, and I have good news for you: you pretty much know everything about how Rust's futures work and what makes them special already. All the complicated topics are covered.

In the next, and last, chapter, we'll switch over from our hand-made coroutines to proper async/await. This will seem like a breeze compared to what you've gone through so far.

Before we continue, let's stop for a moment and take a look at what we've learned in this chapter.

First, we expanded our coroutine implementation so that we could store variables across wait points. This is pretty important if our coroutine/wait syntax is going to rival regular synchronous code in readability and ergonomics.

After that, we learned how we could store and restore variables that held references, which is just as important as being able to store data.

Next, we saw firsthand something that we'll *never* see in Rust unless we implement an asynchronous system, as we did in this chapter (which is quite the task just to prove a single point). We saw how moving coroutines that hold self-references caused serious memory safety issues, and exactly why we need something to prevent them.

That brought us to pinning and self-referential structs, and if you didn't know about these things already, you do now. In addition to that, you should at least know what a pin projection is and what we mean by structural pinning.

Then, we looked at the differences between pinning a value to the stack and pinning a value to the heap. You even saw how easy it was to break the `Pin` guarantee when pinning something to the stack and why you should be very careful when doing just that.

You also know about some tools that are widely used to tackle both pin projections and stack pinning and make both much safer and easier to use.

Next, we got firsthand experience with how we could use pinning to prevent the issues we had with our coroutine implementation.

If we take a look at what we've built so far, that's pretty impressive as well. We have the following:

- A coroutine implementation we've created ourselves
- Coroutine/wait syntax and a preprocessor that helps us with the boilerplate for our coroutines
- Coroutines that can safely store both data and references across wait points
- An efficient runtime that stores, schedules, and polls the tasks to completion

- The ability to spawn new tasks onto the runtime so that one task can spawn hundreds of new tasks that will run concurrently
- A reactor that uses `epoll/kqueue/IOCP` under the hood to efficiently wait for and respond to new events reported by the operating system

I think this is pretty cool.

We're not quite done with this book yet. In the next chapter, you'll see how we can have our runtime run futures created by async/await instead of our own coroutine implementation with just a few changes. This enables us to leverage all the advantages of async Rust. We'll also take some time to discuss the state of async Rust today, the different runtimes you'll encounter, and what we might expect in the future.

All the heavy lifting is done now. Well done!

10
Creating Your Own Runtime

In the last few chapters, we covered a lot of aspects that are relevant to asynchronous programming in Rust, but we did that by implementing alternative and simpler abstractions than what we have in Rust today.

This last chapter will focus on bridging that gap by changing our runtime so that it works with Rust futures and async/await instead of our own futures and coroutine/wait. Since we've pretty much covered everything there is to know about coroutines, state machines, futures, wakers, runtimes, and pinning, adapting what we have now will be a relatively easy task.

When we get everything working, we'll do some experiments with our runtime to showcase and discuss some of the aspects that make asynchronous Rust somewhat difficult for newcomers today.

We'll also take some time to discuss what we might expect in the future with asynchronous Rust before we summarize what we've done and learned in this book.

We'll cover the following main topics:

- Creating our own runtime with futures and async/await
- Experimenting with our runtime
- Challenges with asynchronous Rust
- The future of asynchronous Rust

Technical requirements

The examples in this chapter will build on the code from the last chapter, so the requirements are the same. The example is cross-platform and will work on all platforms that Rust (https://doc.rust-lang.org/beta/rustc/platform-support.html#tier-1-with-host-tools) and mio (https://github.com/tokio-rs/mio#platforms) support.

The only thing you need is Rust installed and the book's repository downloaded locally. All the code in this chapter can be found in the `ch10` folder.

We'll use `delayserver` in this example as well, so you need to open a separate terminal, enter the `delayserver` folder at the root of the repository, and type `cargo run` so it's ready and available for the examples going forward.

Remember to change the ports in the code if for some reason you have to change what port `delayserver` listens on.

```
Creating our own runtime with futures and async/await
```

Okay, so we're in the home stretch; the last thing we'll do is change our runtime so it uses the Rust `Future` trait, `Waker`, and `async/await`. This will be a relatively easy task for us now that we've pretty much covered the most complex aspects of asynchronous programming in Rust by building everything up ourselves. We have even gone into quite some detail on the design decisions that Rust had to make along the way.

The asynchronous programming model Rust has today is the result of an evolutionary process. Rust started in its early stages with green threads, but this was before it reached version 1.0. At the point of reaching version 1.0, Rust didn't have the notion of futures or asynchronous operations in its standard library at all. This space was explored on the side in the futures-rs crate (https://github.com/rust-lang/futures-rs), which still serves as a nursery for async abstractions today. However, it didn't take long before Rust settled around a version of the `Future` trait similar to what we have today, often referred to as *futures 0.1*. Supporting coroutines created by async/await was something that was in the works already at that point but it took a few years before the design reached its final stage and entered the stable version of the standard library.

So, many of the choices we had to make with our async implementation are real choices that Rust had to make along the way. However, it all brings us to this point, so let's get to it and start adapting our runtime so it works with Rust futures.

Before we get to the example, let's cover the things that are different from our current implementation:

- The `Future` trait Rust uses is slightly different from what we have now. The biggest difference is that it takes something called `Context` instead of `Waker`. The other difference is that it returns an enum called `Poll` instead of `PollState`.
- `Context` is a wrapper around Rust's `Waker` type. Its only purpose is to future-proof the API so it can hold additional data in the future without having to change anything related to `Waker`.
- The `Poll` enum returns one of two states, `Ready(T)` or `Pending`. This is slightly different from what we have now with our `PollState` enum, but the two states mean the same as `Ready(T)`/`NotReady` in our current implementation.
- `Waker`s in Rust is slightly more complex to create than what we're used to with our current `Waker`. We'll go through how and why later in the chapter.

Other than the differences outlined above, everything else can stay pretty much as is. For the most part, we're renaming and refactoring this time.

Now that we've got an idea of what we need to do, it's time to set everything up so we can get our new example up and running.

> **Note**
> Even though we create a runtime to run futures properly in Rust, we still try to keep this simple by avoiding error handling and not focusing on making our runtime more flexible. Improving our runtime is certainly possible, and while it can be a bit tricky at times to use the type system correctly and please the borrow checker, it has relatively little to do with *async* Rust and more to do with Rust being Rust.

Setting up our example

> **Tip**
> You'll find this example in the book's repository in the `ch10/a-rust-futures` folder.

We'll continue where we left off in the last chapter, so let's copy everything we had over to a new project:

1. Create a new folder called `a-rust-futures`.
2. Copy everything from the example in the previous chapter. If you followed the naming I suggested, it would be stored in the `e-coroutines-pin` folder.
3. You should now have a folder containing a copy of our previous example, so the last thing to do is to change the project name in `Cargo.toml` to `a-rust-futures`.

Okay, so let's start with the program we want to run. Open `main.rs`.

main.rs

We'll go back to the simplest version of our program and get it running before we try anything more complex. Open `main.rs` and replace all the code in that file with this:

ch10/a-rust-futures/src/main.rs

```rust
mod http;
mod runtime;
use crate::http::Http;
```

```
fn main() {
    let mut executor = runtime::init();
    executor.block_on(async_main());
}

async fn async_main() {
    println!("Program starting");
    let txt = Http::get("/600/HelloAsyncAwait").await;
    println!("{txt}");
    let txt = Http::get("/400/HelloAsyncAwait").await;
    println!("{txt}");
}
```

No need for `corofy` or anything special this time. The compiler will rewrite this for us.

> **Note**
>
> Notice that we've removed the declaration of the `future` module. That's because we simply don't need it anymore. The only exception is if you want to retain and use the `join_all` function we created to join multiple futures together. You can either try to rewrite that yourself or take a look in the repository and locate the `ch10/a-rust-futures-bonus/src/future.rs` file, where you'll find the same version of our example, only this version retains the future module with a `join_all` function that works with Rust futures.

future.rs

You can delete this file altogether as we don't need our own `Future` trait anymore.

Let's move right along to `http.rs` and see what we need to change there.

http.rs

The first thing we need to change is our dependencies. We'll no longer rely on our own `Future`, `Waker`, and `PollState`; instead, we'll depend on `Future`, `Context`, and `Poll` from the standard library. Our dependencies should look like this now:

ch10/a-rust-futures/src/http.rs

```
use crate::runtime::{self, reactor};
use mio::Interest;
use std::{
    future::Future,
    io::{ErrorKind, Read, Write},
```

```
    pin::Pin,
    task::{Context, Poll},
};
```

We have to do some minor refactoring in the `poll` implementation for `HttpGetFuture`.

First, we need to change the signature of the `poll` function so it complies with the new `Future` trait:

ch10/a-rust-futures/src/http.rs

```
fn poll(mut self: Pin<&mut Self>, cx: &mut Context) -> 
Poll<Self::Output>
```

Since we named the new argument `cx`, we have to change what we pass in to `set_waker` with the following:

ch10/a-rust-futures/src/http.rs

```
runtime::reactor().set_waker(cx, self.id);
```

Next, we need to change our future implementation so it returns `Poll` instead of `PollState`. To do that, locate the `poll` method and start by changing the signature so it matches the `Future` trait from the standard library:

ch10/a-rust-futures/src/http.rs

```
fn poll(mut self: Pin<&mut Self>, cx: &mut Context) -> 
Poll<Self::Output>
```

Next, we need to change our return types wherever we return from the function (I've only presented the relevant part of the function body here):

ch10/a-rust-futures/src/http.rs

```
loop {
            match self.stream.as_mut().unwrap().read(&mut buff) {
                Ok(0) => {
                    let s = String::from_utf8_lossy(&self.buffer).to_string();
                    runtime::reactor().deregister(self.stream.as_mut().unwrap(), id);
                    break Poll::Ready(s.to_string());
                }
                Ok(n) => {
                    self.buffer.extend(&buff[0..n]);
```

```
                    continue;
                }
                Err(e) if e.kind() == ErrorKind::WouldBlock => {
                    // always store the last given Waker
                    runtime::reactor().set_waker(cx, self.id);
                    break Poll::Pending;
                }

                Err(e) => panic!("{e:?}"),
            }
        }
    }
}
```

That's it for this file. Not bad, huh? Let's take a look at what we need to change in our executor and open `executor.rs`.

executor.rs

The first thing we need to change in `executor.rs` is our dependencies. This time, we only rely on types from the standard library, and our `dependencies` section should now look like this:

ch10/a-rust-futures/src/runtime/executor.rs

```
use std::{
    cell::{Cell, RefCell},
    collections::HashMap,
    future::Future,
    pin::Pin,
    sync::{Arc, Mutex},
    task::{Poll, Context, Wake, Waker},
    thread::{self, Thread},
};
```

Our coroutines will no longer be limited to only output String, so we can safely use a more sensible `Output` type for our top-level futures:

ch10/a-rust-futures/src/runtime/executor.rs

```
type Task = Pin<Box<dyn Future<Output = ()>>>;
```

The next thing we'll dive straight into is `Waker` since the changes we make here will result in several other changes to this file.

Creating a waker in Rust can be quite a complex task since Rust wants to give us maximum flexibility on how we choose to implement wakers. The reason for this is twofold:

- Wakers must work just as well on a server as it does on a microcontroller
- A waker must be a zero-cost abstraction

Realizing that most programmers never need to create their own wakers, the cost that the lack of ergonomics has was deemed acceptable.

Until quite recently, the only way to construct a waker in Rust was to create something very similar to a trait object without being a trait object. To do so, you had to go through quite a complex process of constructing a *v-table* (a set of function pointers), combining that with a pointer to the data that the waker stored, and creating `RawWaker`.

Fortunately, we don't actually have to go through this process anymore as Rust now has the `Wake` trait. The `Wake` trait works if the `Waker` type we create is placed in `Arc`.

Wrapping `Waker` in an `Arc` results in a heap allocation, but for most `Waker` implementations on the kind of systems we're talking about in this book, that's perfectly fine and what most production runtimes do. This simplifies things for us quite a bit.

> **Info**
> This is an example of Rust adopting what turns out to be best practices from the ecosystem. For a long time, a popular way to construct wakers was by implementing a trait called `ArcWake` provided by the `futures` crate (https://github.com/rust-lang/futures-rs). The `futures` crate is not a part of the language but it's in the rust-lang repository and can be viewed much like a toolbox and nursery for abstractions that might end up in the language at some point in the future.

To avoid confusion by having multiple things with the same name, let's rename our concrete `Waker` type to `MyWaker`:

ch10/a-rust-futures/src/runtime/executor.rs

```rust
#[derive(Clone)]
pub struct MyWaker {
    thread: Thread,
    id: usize,
    ready_queue: Arc<Mutex<Vec<usize>>>,
}
```

We can keep the implementation of wake pretty much the same, but we put it in the implementation of the Wake trait instead of just having a wake function on MyWaker:

ch10/a-rust-futures/src/runtime/executor.rs

```
impl Wake for MyWaker {
    fn wake(self: Arc<Self>) {
        self.ready_queue
            .lock()
            .map(|mut q| q.push(self.id))
            .unwrap();
        self.thread.unpark();
    }
}
```

You'll notice that the wake function takes a self: Arc<Self> argument, much like we saw when working with the Pin type. Writing the function signature this way means that wake is only callable on MyWaker instances that are wrapped in Arc.

Since our waker has changed slightly, there are a few places we need to make some minor corrections. The first is in the get_waker function:

ch10/a-rust-futures/src/runtime/executor.rs

```
fn get_waker(&self, id: usize) -> Arc<MyWaker> {
    Arc::new(MyWaker {
        id,
        thread: thread::current(),
        ready_queue: CURRENT_EXEC.with(|q| q.ready_queue.clone()),
    })
}
```

So, not a big change here. The only difference is that we heap-allocate the waker by placing it in Arc.

The next place we need to make a change is in the block_on function.

First, we need to change its signature so that it matches our new definition of a top-level future:

ch10/a-rust-futures/src/runtime/executor.rs

```
pub fn block_on<F>(&mut self, future: F)
where
    F: Future<Output = ()> + 'static,
{
```

The next step is to change how we create a waker and wrap it in a Context struct in the block_
on function:

ch10/a-rust-futures/src/runtime/executor.rs

```
...
                // guard against false wakeups
                  None => continue,
            };

            let waker: Waker = self.get_waker(id).into();
            let mut cx = Context::from_waker(&waker);

            match future.as_mut().poll(&mut cx) {
...
```

This change is a little bit complex, so we'll go through it step by step:

1. First, we get Arc<MyWaker> by calling the get_waker function just like we did before.
2. We convert MyWaker into a simple Waker by specifying the type we expect with let waker: Waker and calling into() on MyWaker. Since every instance of MyWaker is also a kind of Waker, this will convert it into the Waker type that's defined in the standard library, which is just what we need.
3. Since Future::poll expects Context and not Waker, we create a new Context struct with a reference to the waker we just created.

The last place we need to make changes is to the signature of our spawn function so that it takes the new definition of top-level futures as well:

ch10/a-rust-futures/src/runtime/executor.rs

```
pub fn spawn<F>(future: F)
where
    F: Future<Output = ()> + 'static,
```

That was the last thing we needed to change in our executor, and we're almost done. The last change we need to make to our runtime is in the reactor, so let's go ahead and open reactor.rs.

reactor.rs

The first thing we do is to make sure our dependencies are correct. We have to remove the dependency on our old Waker implementation and instead pull in these types from the standard library. The dependencies section should look like this:

ch10/a-rust-futures/src/runtime/reactor.rs

```rust
use mio::{net::TcpStream, Events, Interest, Poll, Registry, Token};
use std::{
    collections::HashMap,
    sync::{
        atomic::{AtomicUsize, Ordering},
        Arc, Mutex, OnceLock,
    },
    thread, task::{Context, Waker},
};
```

There are two minor changes we need to make. The first one is that our `set_waker` function now accepts `Context` from which it needs to get a `Waker` object:

ch10/a-rust-futures/src/runtime/reactor.rs

```rust
pub fn set_waker(&self, cx: &Context, id: usize) {
        let _ = self
            .wakers
            .lock()
            .map(|mut w| w.insert(id, cx.waker().clone()).is_none())
            .unwrap();
    }
```

The last change is that we need to call a slightly different method when calling wake in the event_loop function:

ch10/a-rust-futures/src/runtime/reactor.rs

```rust
if let Some(waker) = wakers.get(&id) {
    waker.wake_by_ref();
}
```

Since calling wake now consumes `self`, we call the version that takes `&self` instead since we want to hold on to that waker for later.

That's it. Our runtime can now run and take advantage of the full power of asynchronous Rust. Let's try it out by typing `cargo run` in the terminal.

We should get the same output as we've seen before:

```
Program starting
FIRST POLL - START OPERATION
main: 1 pending tasks. Sleep until notified.
HTTP/1.1 200 OK
content-length: 15
[==== ABBREVIATED ====]
HelloAsyncAwait
main: All tasks are finished
```

That's pretty neat, isn't it?

So, now we have created our own async runtime that uses Rust's Future, Waker, Context, and async/await.

Now that we can pride ourselves on being runtime implementors, it's time to do some experiments. I'll choose a few that will also teach us a few things about runtimes and futures in Rust. We're not done learning just yet.

Experimenting with our runtime

> **Note**
> You'll find this example in the book's repository in the ch10/b-rust-futures-experiments folder. The different experiments will be implemented as different versions of the async_main function numbered chronologically. I'll indicate which function corresponds with which function in the repository example in the heading of the code snippet.

Before we start experimenting, let's copy everything we have now to a new folder:

1. Create a new folder called b-rust-futures-experiments.
2. Copy everything from the a-rust-futures folder to the new folder.
3. Open Cargo.toml and change the name attribute to b-rust-futures-experiments.

The first experiment will be to exchange our very limited HTTP client with a proper one.

The easiest way to do that is to simply pick another production-quality HTTP client library that supports async Rust and use that instead.

So, when trying to find a suitable replacement for our HTTP client, we check the list of the most popular high-level HTTP client libraries and find reqwest at the top. That might work for our purposes, so let's try that first.

The first thing we do is add `reqwest` as a dependency in `Cargo.toml` by typing the following:

```
cargo add reqwest@0.11
```

Next, let's change our `async_main` function so we use `reqwest` instead of our own HTTP client:

ch10/b-rust-futures-examples/src/main.rs (async_main2)

```rust
async fn async_main() {
    println!("Program starting");
    let url = "http://127.0.0.1:8080/600/HelloAsyncAwait1";
    let res = reqwest::get(url).await.unwrap();
    let txt = res.text().await.unwrap();
    println!("{txt}");
    let url = "http://127.0.0.1:8080/400/HelloAsyncAwait2";
    let res = reqwest::get(url).await.unwrap();
    let txt = res.text().await.unwrap();
    println!("{txt}");
}
```

Besides using the `reqwest` API, I also changed the message we send. Most HTTP clients don't return the raw HTTP response to us and usually only provide a convenient way to get the *body* of the response, which up until now was similar for both our requests.

That should be all we need to change, so let's try to run our program by writing `cargo run`:

```
     Running `target\debug\a-rust-futures.exe`
Program starting
thread 'main' panicked at C:\Users\cf\.cargo\registry\src\index.
crates.io-6f17d22bba15001f\tokio-1.35.0\src\net\tcp\stream.rs:160:18:
there is no reactor running, must be called from the context of a
Tokio 1.x runtime
```

Okay, so the error tells us that there is no reactor running and that it must be called from the context of a Tokio 1.x runtime. Well, we know there is a reactor running, just not the one `reqwest` expects, so let's see how we can fix this.

We obviously need to add Tokio to our program, and since Tokio is heavily feature-gated (meaning that it has very few features enabled by default), we'll make it easy on ourselves and enable all of them:

```
cargo add tokio@1 --features full
```

According to the documentation, we need to start a Tokio runtime and explicitly enter it to enable the reactor. The `enter` function will return `EnterGuard` to us that we can hold on to it as long as we need the reactor up and running.

Adding this to the top of our `async_main` function should work:

ch10/b-rust-futures-examples/src/main.rs (async_main2)

```
use tokio::runtime::Runtime;
async fn async_main
    let rt = Runtime::new().unwrap();
    let _guard = rt.enter();
    println!("Program starting");
    let url = "http://127.0.0.1:8080/600/HelloAsyncAwait1";
    ...
```

> **Note**
>
> Calling `Runtime::new` creates a multithreaded Tokio runtime, but Tokio also has a single-threaded runtime that you can create by using the runtime builder like this: `Builder::new_current_thread().enable_all().build().unwrap()`. If you do that, you end up with a peculiar problem: a deadlock. The reason for that is interesting and one that you should know about.
>
> Tokio's single-threaded runtime uses only the thread it's called on for both the executor and the reactor. This is very similar to what we did in the first version of our runtime in *Chapter 8*. We used the `Poll` instance to park our executor directly. When both our reactor and executor execute on the same thread, they must have the same mechanism to park themselves and wait for new events, which means there will be a tight coupling between them.
>
> When handling an event, the reactor has to wake up first to call `Waker::wake`, but the executor is the last one to park the thread. If the executor parked itself by calling `thread::park` (like we do), the reactor is parked as well and will never wake up since they're running on the same thread. The only way for this to work is that the executor parks on something shared with the reactor (like we did with `Poll`). Since we're not tightly integrated with Tokio, all we get is a deadlock.

Now, if we try to run our program once more, we get the following output:

```
Program starting
main: 1 pending tasks. Sleep until notified.
main: 1 pending tasks. Sleep until notified.
main: 1 pending tasks. Sleep until notified.
HelloAsyncAwait1
main: 1 pending tasks. Sleep until notified.
main: 1 pending tasks. Sleep until notified.
main: 1 pending tasks. Sleep until notified.
HelloAsyncAwait2
main: All tasks are finished
```

Okay, so now everything works as expected. The only difference is that we get woken up a few extra times, but the program finishes and produces the expected result.

Before we discuss what we just witnessed, let's do one more experiment.

Isahc is an HTTP client library that promises to be *executor agnostic*, meaning that it doesn't rely on any specific executor. Let's put that to the test.

First, we add a dependency on `isahc` by typing the following:

```
cargo add isahc@1.7
```

Then, we rewrite our `main` function so it looks like this:

ch10/b-rust-futures-examples/src/main.rs (async_main3)

```rust
use isahc::prelude::*;
async fn async_main() {
    println!("Program starting");
    let url = "http://127.0.0.1:8080/600/HelloAsyncAwait1";
    let mut res = isahc::get_async(url).await.unwrap();
    let txt = res.text().await.unwrap();
    println!("{txt}");
    let url = "http://127.0.0.1:8080/400/HelloAsyncAwait2";
    let mut res = isahc::get_async(url).await.unwrap();
    let txt = res.text().await.unwrap();
    println!("{txt}");
}
```

Now, if we run our program by writing `cargo run`, we get the following output:

```
Program starting
main: 1 pending tasks. Sleep until notified.
main: 1 pending tasks. Sleep until notified.
main: 1 pending tasks. Sleep until notified.
HelloAsyncAwait1
main: 1 pending tasks. Sleep until notified.
main: 1 pending tasks. Sleep until notified.
main: 1 pending tasks. Sleep until notified.
HelloAsyncAwait2
main: All tasks are finished
```

So, we get the expected output without having to jump through any hoops.

Why does all this have to be so unintuitive?

The answer to that brings us to the topic of common challenges that we all face when programming with async Rust, so let's cover some of the most noticeable ones and explain the reason they exist so we can figure out how to best deal with them.

Challenges with asynchronous Rust

So, while we've seen with our own eyes that the executor and reactor could be loosely coupled, which in turn means that you could in theory mix and match reactors and executors, the question is why do we encounter so much friction when trying to do just that?

Most programmers that have used async Rust have experienced problems caused by incompatible async libraries, and we saw an example of the kind of error message you would get previously.

To understand this, we have to dive a little bit deeper into the existing async runtimes in Rust, specifically those we typically use for desktop and server applications.

Explicit versus implicit reactor instantiation

> **Info**
> The type of future we'll talk about going forward is leaf futures, the kind that actually represents an I/O operation (for example, `HttpGetFuture`).

When you create a runtime in Rust, you also need to create non-blocking primitives of the Rust standard library. Mutexes, channels, timers, TcpStreams, and so on are all things that need an async equivalent.

Most of these can be implemented as different kinds of reactors, but the question that then comes up is: how is that reactor started?

In both our own runtime and in Tokio, the reactor is started as part of the runtime initialization. We have a `runtime::init()` function that calls `reactor::start()`, and Tokio has a `Runtime::new()` and `Runtime::enter()` function.

If we try to create a leaf future (the only one we created ourselves is `HttpGetFuture`) without the reactor started, both our runtime and Tokio will panic. The reactor has to be instantiated *explicitly*.

Isahc, on the other hand, brings its own kind of reactor. Isahc is built on `libcurl`, a highly portable C library for **multiprotocol file transfer**. The thing that's relevant for us, however, is that `libcurl` accepts a callback that is called when an operation is ready. So, Isahc passes the waker it receives to this callback and makes sure that `Waker::wake` is called when the callback is executed. This is a bit oversimplified, but it's essentially what happens.

In practice, that means that Isahc brings its own reactor since it comes with the machinery to store wakers and call `wake` on them when an operation is ready. The reactor is started *implicitly*.

Incidentally, this is also one of the major differences between `async_std` and Tokio. Tokio requires *explicit* instantiation, and `async_std` relies on *implicit* instantiation.

I'm not going into so much detail on this just for fun; while this seems like a minor difference, it has a rather big impact on how intuitive asynchronous programming in Rust is.

This problem mostly arises when you start programming using a different runtime than Tokio and then have to use a library that internally relies on a Tokio reactor being present.

Since you can't have two Tokio instances running on the same thread, the library can't implicitly start a Tokio reactor. Instead, what often happens is that you try to use that library and get an error like we did in the preceding example.

Now, you have to solve this by starting a Tokio reactor yourself, use some kind of compatibility wrapper created by someone else, or seeing whether the runtime you use has a built-in mechanism for running futures that rely on a Tokio reactor being present.

For most people who don't know about reactors, executors, and different kinds of leaf futures, this can be quite unintuitive and cause quite a bit of frustration.

> **Note**
>
> The problem we describe here is quite common, and it's not helped by the fact that async libraries rarely explain this well or even try to be explicit about what kind of runtime they use. Some libraries might only mention that they're built on top of Tokio somewhere in the `README` file, and some might simply state that they're built on top of Hyper, for example, assuming that you know that Hyper is built on top of Tokio (at least by default).
>
> But now, you know that you should check this to avoid any surprises, and if you encounter this issue, you know exactly what the problem is.

Ergonomics versus efficiency and flexibility

Rust is good at being ergonomic *and* efficient, and that almost makes it difficult to remember that when Rust is faced with the choice between being efficient *or* ergonomic, it will choose to be efficient. Many of the most popular crates in the ecosystem echo these values, and that includes async runtimes.

Some tasks can be more efficient if they're tightly integrated with the executor, and therefore, if you use them in your library, you will be dependent on that specific runtime.

Let's take **timers** as an example, but task notifications where *Task A* notifies *Task B* that it can continue is another example with some of the same trade-offs.

> **Tasks**
>
> We've used the terms tasks and futures without making the difference explicitly clear, so let's clear that up here. We first covered tasks in *Chapter 1*, and they still retain the same general meaning, but when talking about runtimes in Rust, they have a more specific definition. A task is a *top-level future*, the one that we spawn onto our executor. The executor schedules between different tasks. Tasks in a runtime in many ways represent the same abstraction that threads do in an OS. Every task is a future in Rust, but every future is not a task by this definition.

You can think of thread::sleep as a timer, and we often need something like this in an asynchronous context, so our asynchronous runtime will therefore need to have a sleep equivalent that tells the executor to park this task for a specified duration.

We could implement this as a reactor and have separate OS-thread sleep for a specified duration and then wake the correct Waker. That would be simple and executor agnostic since the executor is oblivious to what happens and only concern itself with scheduling the task when Waker::wake is called. However, it's also not optimally efficient for all workloads (even if we used the same thread for all timers).

Another, and more common, way to solve this is to delegate this task to the executor. In our runtime, this could be done by having the executor store an ordered list of instants and a corresponding Waker, which is used to determine whether any timers have expired before it calls thread::park. If none have expired, we can calculate the duration until the next timer expires and use something such as thread::park_timeout to make sure that we at least wake up to handle that timer.

The algorithms used to store the timers can be heavily optimized and you avoid the need for one extra thread just for timers with the additional overhead of synchronization between these threads just to signal that a timer has expired. In a multithreaded runtime, there might even be contention when multiple executors frequently add timers to the same reactor.

Some timers are implemented reactor-style as separate libraries, and for many tasks, that will suffice. The important point here is that by using the defaults, you end up being tied to one specific runtime, and you have to make careful considerations if you want to avoid your library being tightly coupled to a specific runtime.

Common traits that everyone agrees about

The last topic that causes friction in async Rust is the lack of universally agreed-upon traits and interfaces for typical async operations.

I want to preface this segment by pointing out that this is one area that's improving day by day, and there is a nursery for the traits and abstractions for asynchronous Rust in the futures-rs crate (https://github.com/rust-lang/futures-rs). However, since it's still early days for async Rust, it's something worth mentioning in a book like this.

Let's take spawning as an example. When you write a high-level async library in Rust, such as a web server, you'll likely want to be able to spawn new tasks (top-level futures). For example, each connection to the server will most likely be a new task that you want to spawn onto the executor.

Now, spawning is specific to each executor, and Rust doesn't have a trait that defines how to spawn a task. There is a trait suggested for spawning in the `future-rs` crate, but creating a spawn trait that is both zero-cost and flexible enough to support all kinds of runtimes turns out to be very difficult.

There are ways around this. The popular HTTP library Hyper (`https://hyper.rs/`), for example, uses a trait to represent the executor and internally uses that to spawn new tasks. This makes it possible for users to implement this trait for a different executor and hand it back to Hyper. By implementing this trait for a different executor, Hyper will use a different spawner than its default option (which is the one in Tokio's executor). Here is an example of how this is used for `async_std` with Hyper: `https://github.com/async-rs/async-std-hyper`.

However, since there is no universal way of making this work, most libraries that rely on executor-specific functionality do one of two things:

1. Choose a runtime and stick with it.
2. Implement two versions of the library supporting different popular runtimes that users choose by enabling the correct features.

Async drop

Async drop, or async destructors, is an aspect of async Rust that's somewhat unresolved at the time of writing this book. Rust uses a pattern called RAII, which means that when a type is created, so are its resources, and when a type is dropped, the resources are freed as well. The compiler automatically inserts a call to drop on objects when they go out of scope.

If we take our runtime as an example, when resources are dropped, they do so in a blocking manner. This is normally not a big problem since a drop likely won't block the executor for too long, but it isn't always so.

If we have a drop implementation that takes a long time to finish (for example, if the drop needs to manage I/O, or makes a blocking call to the OS kernel, which is perfectly legal and sometimes even unavoidable in Rust), it can potentially block the executor. So, an async drop would somehow be able to yield to the scheduler in such cases, and this is not possible at the moment.

Now, this isn't a rough edge of async Rust you're likely to encounter as a user of async libraries, but it's worth knowing about since right now, the only way to make sure this doesn't cause issues is to be careful what you put in the drop implementation for types that are used in an async context.

So, while this is not an extensive list of everything that causes friction in async Rust, it's some of the points I find most noticeable and worth knowing about.

Before we round off this chapter, let's spend a little time talking about what we should expect in the future when it comes to asynchronous programming in Rust.

The future of asynchronous Rust

Some of the things that make async Rust different from other languages are unavoidable. Asynchronous Rust is very efficient, has low latency, and is backed by a very strong type system due to how the language is designed and its core values.

However, much of the perceived complexity today has more to do with the ecosystem and the kind of issues that result from a lot of programmers having to agree on the best way to solve different problems without any formal structure. The ecosystem gets fragmented for a while, and together with the fact that asynchronous programming is a topic that's difficult for a lot of programmers, it ends up adding to the cognitive load associated with asynchronous Rust.

All the issues and pain points I've mentioned in this chapter are constantly getting better. Some points that would have been on this list a few years ago are not even worth mentioning today.

More and more common traits and abstractions will end up in the standard library, making async Rust more ergonomic since everything that uses them will "just work."

As different experiments and designs gain more traction than others, they become the de facto standard, and even though you will still have a lot of choices when programming asynchronous Rust, there will be certain paths to choose that cause a minimal amount of friction for those that want something that "just works."

With enough knowledge about asynchronous Rust and asynchronous programming in general, the issues I've mentioned here are, after all, relatively minor, and since you know more about asynchronous Rust than most programmers, I have a hard time imagining that any of these issues will cause you a lot of trouble.

That doesn't mean it's not something worth knowing about since chances are your fellow programmers will struggle with some of these issues at some point.

Summary

So, in this chapter, we did two things. First, we made some rather minor changes to our runtime so it works as an actual runtime for Rust futures. We tested the runtime using two external HTTP client libraries to learn a thing or two about reactors, runtimes, and async libraries in Rust.

The next thing we did was to discuss some of the things that make asynchronous Rust difficult for many programmers coming from other languages. In the end, we also talked about what to expect going forward.

Depending on how you've followed along and how much you've experimented with the examples we created along the way, it's up to you what project to take on yourself if you want to learn more.

There is an important aspect of learning that only happens when you experiment on your own. Pick everything apart, see what breaks, and how to fix it. Improve the simple runtime we created to learn new stuff.

There are enough interesting projects to pick from, but here are some suggestions:

- Change out the parker implementation where we used `thread::park` with a proper parker. You can choose one from a library or create a parker yourself (I added a small bonus at the end of the `ch10` folder called `parker-bonus` where you get a simple parker implementation).
- Implement a simple `delayserver` using the runtime you've created yourself. To do this, you have to be able to write some raw HTTP responses and create a simple server. If you went through the free introductory book called *The Rust Programming Language,* you created a simple server in one of the last chapters (https://doc.rust-lang.org/book/ch20-02-multithreaded.html), which gives you the basics you need. You also need to create a timer as we discussed above or use an existing crate for async timers.
- You can create a "proper" multithreaded runtime and explore the possibilities that come with having a global task queue, or as an alternative, implement a work-stealing scheduler that can steal tasks from other executors' local queues when they're done with their own.

Only your imagination sets the limits on what you can do. The important thing to note is that there is a certain joy in doing something just because you can and just for fun, and I hope that you get some of the same enjoyment from this as I do.

I'll end this chapter with a few words on how to make your life as an asynchronous programmer as easy as possible.

The first thing is to realize that an async runtime is not just another library that you use. It's extremely invasive and impacts almost everything in your program. It's a layer that rewrites, schedules tasks, and reorders the program flow from what you're used to.

My clear recommendation if you're not specifically into learning about runtimes, or have very specific needs, is to pick one runtime and stick to it for a while. Learn everything about it – not necessarily *everything* from the start, but as you need more and more functionality from it, you will learn everything eventually. This is almost like getting comfortable with everything in Rust's standard library.

What runtime you start with depends a bit on what crates you're using the most. Smol and `async-std` share a lot of implementation details and will behave similarly. Their big selling point is that their API strives to stay as close as possible to the standard library. Combined with the fact that the reactors are instantiated implicitly, this can result in a slightly more intuitive experience and a more gentle learning curve. Both are production-quality runtimes and see a lot of use. Smol was originally created with the goal of having a code base that's easy for programmers to understand and learn from, which I think is true today as well.

With that said, the most popular alternative for users looking for a general-purpose runtime at the time of writing is **Tokio** (https://tokio.rs/). Tokio is one of the oldest async runtimes in Rust. It is actively developed and has a welcoming and active community. The documentation is excellent. Being one of the most popular runtimes also means there is a good chance that you'll find a library that does exactly what you need with support for Tokio out of the box. Personally, I tend to reach for Tokio for the reasons mentioned, but you can't really go wrong with either of these runtimes unless you have very specific requirements.

Finally, let's not forget to mention the `futures-rs` crate (https://github.com/rust-lang/futures-rs). I mentioned this crate earlier, but it's really useful to know about as it contains several traits, abstractions, and executors (https://docs.rs/futures/latest/futures/executor/index.html) for async Rust. It serves the purpose of an async toolbox that comes in handy in many situations.

Epilogue

So, you have reached the end. First of all, congratulations! You've come to the end of quite a journey!

We started by talking about concurrency and parallelism in *Chapter 1*. We even covered a bit about the history, CPUs and OSs, hardware, and interrupts. In *Chapter 2*, we discussed how programming languages modeled asynchronous program flow. We introduced coroutines and how stackful and stackless coroutines differ. We discussed OS threads, fibers/green threads, and callbacks and their pros and cons.

Then, in *Chapter 3*, we took a look at OS-backed event queues such as `epoll`, `kqueue`, and `IOCP`. We even took quite a deep dive into syscalls and cross-platform abstractions.

In *Chapter 4*, we hit some quite difficult terrain when implementing our own mio-like event queue using epoll. We even had to learn about the difference between edge-triggered and level-triggered events.

If *Chapter 4* was somewhat rough terrain, *Chapter 5* was more like climbing Mount Everest. No one expects you to remember everything covered there, but you read through it and have a working example you can use to experiment with. We implemented our own fibers/green threads, and while doing so, we learned a little bit about processor architectures, ISAs, ABIs, and calling conventions. We even learned quite a bit about inline assembly in Rust. If you ever felt insecure about the stack versus heap difference, you surely understand it now that you've created stacks that we made our CPU jump to ourselves.

In *Chapter 6*, we got a high-level introduction to asynchronous Rust, before we took a deep dive from *Chapter 7* and onward, starting with creating our own coroutines and our own `coroutine/wait` syntax. In *Chapter 8*, we created the first versions of our own runtime while discussing basic runtime design. We also deep-dived into reactors, executors, and wakers.

In *Chapter 9*, we improved our runtime and discovered the dangers of self-referential structs in Rust. We then took a thorough look at pinning in Rust and how that helped us solve the problems we got into.

Finally, in *Chapter 10*, we saw that by making some rather minor changes, our runtime became a fully functioning runtime for Rust futures. We rounded everything off by discussing some well-known challenges with asynchronous Rust and some expectations for the future.

The Rust community is very inclusive and welcoming, and we'd happily welcome you to engage and contribute if you find this topic interesting and want to learn more. One of the ways asynchronous Rust gets better is through contributions by people with all levels of experience. If you want to get involved, then the async work group (`https://rust-lang.github.io/wg-async/welcome.html`) is a good place to start. There is also a very active community centered around the Tokio project (`https://github.com/tokio-rs/tokio/blob/master/CONTRIBUTING.md`), and many, many more depending on what specific area you want to dive deeper into. Don't be afraid to join the different channels and ask questions.

Now that we're at the end I want to thank you for reading all the way to the end. I wanted this book to feel like a journey we took together, not like a lecture. I wanted you to be the focus, not me.

I hope I succeeded with that, and I genuinely hope that you learned something that you find useful and can take with you going forward. If you did, then I'm sincerely happy that my work was of value to you. I wish you the best of luck with your asynchronous programming going forward.

Until the next time!

Carl Fredrik

Index

Symbols

1:1 threading 29

A

address space 30
application binary interface (ABI) 97
arithmetic logic units (ALUs) 5
Assembly language 102
asymmetric coroutines 39, 40
async/await keywords 154, 155
asynchronous programming
   versus concurrency 13
asynchronous Rust
   challenges 265
   future 269
async runtime
   mental model 131-133
AT&T dialect 102
Await 39

B

base example
   current implementation, changing 177
   design 173-176
   http.rs, modifying 180-183
   improving 171, 173
   main.rs, modifying 177
   runtime.rs, modifying 177-179
b-async-await 156-160
bitflags 76, 78
bitmasks 75-78
Boost.Coroutine 112
BSD/macOS 51

C

callback based approaches 37
   advantages and drawbacks 37
callee saved 101
calling convention , 57
c-async-await 160-165
challenges, asynchronous Rust 267
   async drop 268
   ergonomics, versus efficiency
      and flexibility 266
   explicit, versus implicit reactor
      instantiation 265, 266
   traits 267
completion-based event queues 48, 49
completion port 49

Index

complex instruction set computers (CISC) 97
concurrency 9
  relation, to I/O 11
  right reference frame, selecting 12
  use cases 11
  versus asynchronous programming 12
  versus parallelism 7, 8, 9, 10
concurrent 8
continuation-passing style 39
cooperative multitasking 5, 26
corofy 155, 156
coroutine implementation 227-229
coroutine preprocessor 155, 156
coroutines 39
  advantages 40
  creating 147-153
  drawbacks 41
  implementation 149
  states 148
coroutine/wait syntax 155
CPU architecture 97
cross-platform abstractions 51
cross-platform event queues 50, 51
custom fibers
  implementing 112-115
  runtime, implementing 115-121

D

direct memory access controller (DMAC) 21
direct memory access (DMA) 21
DNS lookup 72
driver 21

E

edge-triggered event
  versus level-triggered event 78-81
Embassy 169
epoll 47, 49
  designing to 66-71
epoll/kqueue
  OS-backed event, queuing via 47
example project
  running 107, 108
  setting up 103-105
executor 170, 171
executor.rs 256-259

F

ffi module 73-76
  bitflags 76, 78
  bitmasks 76, 78
  level-triggered event, versus edge-triggered event 78-81
fibers and green threads 33
  context switching 35
  FFI functions 36
  scheduling 35
  task, setting up with stack of fixed size 34, 35
file descriptors 52
file I/O 72, 73
Firmware 22
foreign function interface (FFI) 36, 43, 51
  advantages and drawbacks 36
future 38, 39, 130
  definition, changing 191, 192
  poll phase 130
  wait phase 130
  wake phase 130

future.rs 254
futures 38, 39

G

generators
   versus, coroutines 139
Go 112
green threads 33
guard function 121-125

H

hand-written coroutines
   code, writing 153, 154
   example 139, 140
   futures module 141
   HTTP module 142-146
   lazy future 146, 147
hardware interrupts 6, 20, 22
highest level of abstraction 61
http.rs 254-256
hyper-threading 6
   performance 6

I

inline assembly 51
input/output completion port (ICOP) 48, 49
   OS-backed event, queuing via 47
instruction set architecture (ISA) 97
   ARM ISA 97
   x86 97
   x86-64 97
Intel Advanced Vector Extensions (AVX) 100
Intel dialect 102
interrupt descriptor table (IDT) 17, 20

interrupt handler 21
interrupt request line (IRQs) 20
interrupts 22
   hardware interrupts 22
   software interrupts 22
I/O intensive tasks
   versus CPU-intensive tasks 134
I/O operations
   blocking 72
   DNS lookup 72
   file I/O 72, 73
io_uring 44
Isahc 264

K

kernel thread 27
kqueue 47, 49

L

Last In First Out (LIFO) 197
leaf futures
   example 130
LEAN processes 9
level-triggered event
   versus edge-triggered event 78-81
libc 14
Linux 51
   examples, running 45
   OS-provided API, using in 56-58
   raw syscall on 52-54
lowest level, of abstraction 51
   raw syscall, on Linux 52-54
   raw syscall, on macOS 54, 55
   raw syscall, on Windows 55

M

M:1 threading 33
macOS
   OS-provided API, using in 56-58
   raw syscall on 54, 55
main.rs file 84-93, 253, 254
memory management unit (MMU) 17
mental model, of async runtime 131-133
M*N threading 28, 33
move 231, 232
multicore processors 6
multiprotocol file transfer 265
multitasking 4
   hyper-threading 5
   multicore processors 6
   non-preemptive multitasking 4
   preemptive multitasking 5
   synchronous code, writing 6
multithreaded programming 13

N

network call 19
   code 19
   events, registering with OS 20
network card 20
   data, reading and writing 21
next level of abstraction 55, 56
   OS-provided API, using in Linux and macOS 56-58
   Windows API, using 58-60
non-cooperative multitasking 26
non-leaf futures 130
   example 131
non-preemptive multitasking 4, 5

O

operating system
   and CPU 15-18
   communicating with 14
   concurrency 13
   role 13
   teaming up with 14
   threads 12
OS-backed event
   blocking I/O and non-blocking I/O 46
   queuing, need for 45
   queuing, via epoll/kqueue 47
   queuing, via IOCP 47
OS-provided API
   using, in Linux and macOS 56-58
OS threads 27-29
   asynchronous operations, decoupling 31
   drawbacks and complexities 29-31
   example 31, 32
out-of-order execution 7

P

parallel 8
parallelism 7
   versus concurrency 7-10
pinning 233, 234, 241
   executor.rs 246, 247
   future.rs 242
   http.rs 242, 243
   main.rs 244-246
   to heap 235, 236, 237
   to stack 237, 238, 239
   UnPin 234
pin_project
   reference link 241

pointers 231
polling 46
Poll module 81-84
preemptive multitasking 5
pre-empt running tasks 26
privilege level 18
process 30
promises 38, 39
proper Executor
   implementing 192-199
proper Reactor
   implementing 199-207
proper runtime
   creating 184-186

R

raw syscall
   on Linux 52-54
   on macOS 54, 55
reactor 170
reactor.rs 259, 260
readiness-based event queues 47, 48
real-time operating system (RTOS) 169
reduced instruction set
   computers (RISC) 97
references 222-227
repository
   using 96
resource 8
runtime design
   improvement, by adding Reactor
     and Walker 187, 188
runtimes 169
   example, using concurrency 208, 209
   experimenting with 208, 261-265

multiple futures, running concurrently
   and in parallel 209, 210
Rust
   language 133
   Pin<T> 234
   pinning 233, 234
   pinning, to heap 235-237
   pinning, to stack 237-239
   pin projections 234-41
   standard library 133
   structural pinning 235-241
   Unpin 234
Rust inline assembly macro 105, 106
   AT&T syntax 106
   Intel syntax 106
   options 107

S

scheduler 28
segmentation fault 17
self-referential structs 223
   discovering 229-231
   move 231, 232
single-threaded asynchronous system
   task scheduling 170
skip function 121-125
software interrupts 22
stack 109-111
   sizes 111
stack alignment 10
stackful tasks 27
stackless coroutines 138
stackless tasks 27
stack pointer 110
standard output (stdout) 51
static lifetimes 195
Streaming SIMD Extensions (SSE) 98

switch function 121-125
symmetric coroutines 39, 40
synchronous code
  writing 7
syscall ABI 51
system calls (syscalls) 14, 43, 51
System V ABI 98
  for x86-64 99-102

T

task 8, 27, 28
thread of execution 27
thread pool 72
threads 13, 27
  definition 28
  OS threads 27
  user-level threads 27
  versus concurrency 13
timers 266
Tokio 160

U

UNIX family 14
user-level threads 28

V

variables 214
  base examples, improving 217-222
  base examples, setting up 215-217

W

Waker 190
  creating 188-190
wepoll 44
Win64 98
WinAPI 14
Windows 51
  raw syscall on 55
Windows API
  using 58-60
Windows Subsystem for Linux (WSL) 45

⟨packt⟩

Packtpub.com

Subscribe to our online digital library for full access to over 7,000 books and videos, as well as industry leading tools to help you plan your personal development and advance your career. For more information, please visit our website.

Why subscribe?

- Spend less time learning and more time coding with practical eBooks and Videos from over 4,000 industry professionals
- Improve your learning with Skill Plans built especially for you
- Get a free eBook or video every month
- Fully searchable for easy access to vital information
- Copy and paste, print, and bookmark content

Did you know that Packt offers eBook versions of every book published, with PDF and ePub files available? You can upgrade to the eBook version at packtpub.com and as a print book customer, you are entitled to a discount on the eBook copy. Get in touch with us at customercare@packtpub.com for more details.

At www.packtpub.com, you can also read a collection of free technical articles, sign up for a range of free newsletters, and receive exclusive discounts and offers on Packt books and eBooks.

Other Books You May Enjoy

If you enjoyed this book, you may be interested in these other books by Packt:

Hands-On Concurrency with Rust

Brian L. Troutwine

ISBN: 9781788399975

- Probe your programs for performance and accuracy issues
- Create your own threading and multi-processing environment in Rust
- Use coarse locks from Rust's Standard library
- Solve common synchronization problems or avoid synchronization using atomic programming
- Build lock-free/wait-free structures in Rust and understand their implementations in the crates ecosystem
- Leverage Rust's memory model and type system to build safety properties into your parallel programs
- Understand the new features of the Rust programming language to ease the writing of parallel programs

Hands-On Microservices with Rust

Denis Kolodin

ISBN: 9781789342758

- Get acquainted with leveraging Rust web programming
- Get to grips with various Rust crates, such as hyper, Tokio, and Actix
- Explore RESTful microservices with Rust
- Understand how to pack Rust code to a container using Docker
- Familiarize yourself with Reactive microservices
- Deploy your microservices to modern cloud platforms such as AWS

Packt is searching for authors like you

If you're interested in becoming an author for Packt, please visit `authors.packtpub.com` and apply today. We have worked with thousands of developers and tech professionals, just like you, to help them share their insight with the global tech community. You can make a general application, apply for a specific hot topic that we are recruiting an author for, or submit your own idea.

Share your thoughts

Now you've finished *Asynchronous Programming in Rust*, we'd love to hear your thoughts! Scan the QR code below to go straight to the Amazon review page for this book and share your feedback or leave a review on the site that you purchased it from.

`https://packt.link/r/1805128132`

Your review is important to us and the tech community and will help us make sure we're delivering excellent quality content.

Download a free PDF copy of this book

Thanks for purchasing this book!

Do you like to read on the go but are unable to carry your print books everywhere?

Is your eBook purchase not compatible with the device of your choice?

Don't worry, now with every Packt book you get a DRM-free PDF version of that book at no cost.

Read anywhere, any place, on any device. Search, copy, and paste code from your favorite technical books directly into your application.

The perks don't stop there, you can get exclusive access to discounts, newsletters, and great free content in your inbox daily

Follow these simple steps to get the benefits:

1. Scan the QR code or visit the link below

   `https://packt.link/free-ebook/9781805128137`

2. Submit your proof of purchase
3. That's it! We'll send your free PDF and other benefits to your email directly

Printed in Great Britain
by Amazon